CareerView

EXPLORING THE WORLD OF WORK

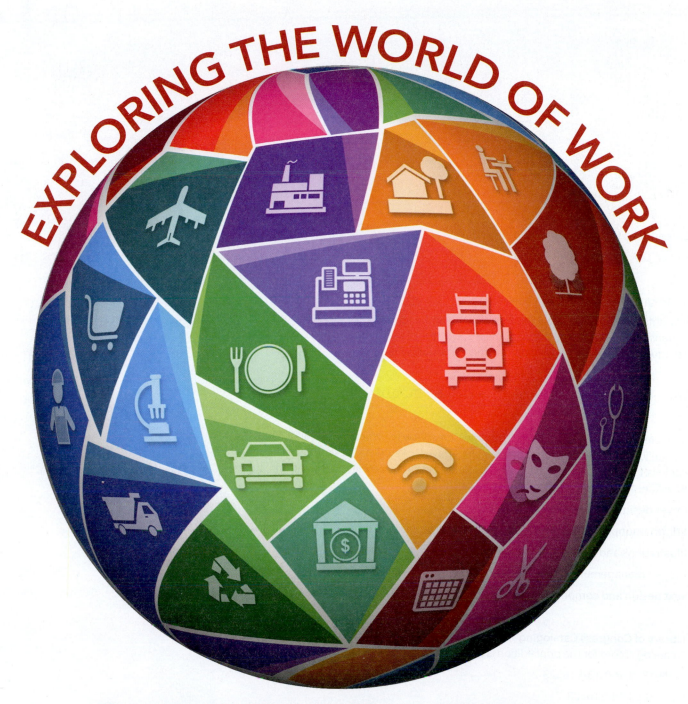

Steven J. Molinsky • Bill Bliss

Illustrated by

Richard E. Hill

CareerView: Exploring the World of Work

Steven J. Molinsky and Bill Bliss

Copyright © 2018 by Pearson Education, Inc.

Pearson Education, 221 River Street, Hoboken, NJ 07030 USA

Staff credits: The people who made up the *CareerView* team are Pietro Alongi, Elizabeth Barker, Jennifer Castro, Tracey Munz Cataldo, Dave Dickey, Gina DiLillo, Warren Fischbach, Pam Fishman, Nancy Flaggman, Lester Holmes, Gosia Jaros-White, Barry Katzen, Stuart Radcliffe, Alex Suarez, and Paula Van Ells.

Cover design: Wendy Wolf

Editorial support: Christine Cervoni, Camelot Editorial Services, LLC

Illustrations and research: Richard E. Hill

Project management: Jaime E. Lieber, JEL Collaborative, LLC

Text design and composition: Wendy Wolf

Library of Congress Cataloging-in-Publication Data
A catalog record for the print edition is available from the Library of Congress.

ISBN-13: 978-0-13-516523-2
ISBN-10: 0-13-516523-7

Printed in the United States of America

1 18

www.pearsoneltusa.com/careerview

CONTENTS

CONTENTS

Unit	Occupations	Workplace Communication*	On-the-Job Instructions
1 **Retail** Pages 2–15	• cashier • customer service manager • customer service representative • department manager • forklift operator • salesperson/sales associate • security person • stock clerk • store manager • trucker • warehouse manager • warehouse worker	• Answer a customer's question • Ask a co-worker for feedback • Ask a supervisor for feedback • Assign a task to an employee • Assist a customer • Give correction to an employee • Give feedback to a co-worker • Help a customer • Make a request of a co-worker • Process a transaction • Report a problem and offer to help • Respond to feedback	• How to bring a large item to customer pickup • How to check out a customer • How to process a return • How to unpack merchandise
2 **Culinary & Food Services** Pages 16–19	• baker • busperson • cafeteria attendant • cashier • chef • cook • dishwasher • food prep supervisor • food prep worker • food service manager • food service worker • grill cook • head cook • hospital dietician • host • hostess • kitchen manager • kitchen supervisor • line cook • pastry chef • restaurant manager • server • short-order cook • waiter • waitress	• Ask a co-worker for feedback • Ask a supervisor for feedback • Ask for assistance • Assign a task to an employee • Give correction to a new employee • Give feedback to a co-worker • Handle a customer complaint • Make a request • Offer assistance • Offer to do something • Take a customer's order	• How to chop an onion • How to operate a commercial dishwasher • How to prep a sandwich station • How to set a place setting
3 **Buildings & Grounds** Pages 30–43	• cleaning crew • cleaning supervisor • cleaning worker • custodian • grounds maintenance supervisor • grounds maintenance worker • head custodian • heating & air conditioning (HVAC) mechanic/technician • landscape supervisor • landscape worker • office cleaner/office cleaning worker • pesticide handler • security person • tree trimmer • window washer	• Ask a co-worker for feedback • Ask a supervisor for feedback • Give advice to a co-worker • Give correction to an employee • Give instructions • Make a request • Make a suggestion • Offer assistance • Point out a problem • Troubleshoot a problem • Warn a co-worker about a safety hazard	• How to buff floors • How to fertilize a lawn • How to lay sod • How to replace a furnace filter

* Workplace Communication competencies align with interpersonal skills and personal qualities objectives in the following:
  SCANS (Secretary's Commission on Achieving Necessary Skills), U.S. Department of Labor;
  Employability Skills Framework, U.S. Department of Education

Unit	Occupations	Workplace Communication	On-the-Job Instructions
4 ✂ **Cosmetology** Pages 44–57	• assistant/shampooist • colorist • esthetician • hair stylist • makeup artist • manicurist • masseur/masseuse/ massage therapist • receptionist • salon manager	• Ask a client for feedback • Ask a client's preference • Ask to borrow an item • Check on a co-worker's performance • Check on an assistant's progress • Correct an assistant's work • Discuss options with a client • Give instructions to a client • Report a supply shortage • Respond to a client's complaint	• How to apply acrylic nail tips • How to color hair • How to do pin curls • How to give a manicure
5 🏭 **Manufacturing** Pages 58–71	• assembler • bench assembler • distribution clerk • electronics assembler • fabricator • factory helper • factory line assembler • factory line supervisor • hand packer • packing clerk • paint robot operator • pinstripe artist • quality control inspector • quality control sampler • quality control tester • receiving clerk • shipping clerk • shop floor assistant • technical engineer • welder	• Ask a co-worker for feedback • Ask a co-worker for parts • Ask about quality control problems • Assign a worker to a workstation • Check on a worker's productivity • Coordinate a task with a co-worker • Correct someone's work • Give feedback to a worker • Orient a new employee • Point out a problem • Report an equipment malfunction	• How to assemble a motorcycle engine • How to do a quality control check • How to do PCB surface mount soldering • How to prepare a motorcycle for shipping
6 🏠 **Residential Construction** Pages 72–87	• blockmason • blockmason apprentice • brickmason • carpenter • carpenter's helper • carpet installer • construction laborer • drywall installer • drywall plasterer • drywall taper • electrician • electrician's assistant • finish carpenter • flooring installer • glazier • HVAC technician • insulation contractor • painter • paperhanger • plumber • roofer • skylight installer • tile installer	• Ask a co-worker for feedback • Ask a co-worker for instructions • Ask a co-worker for assistance • Check on job specifications • Coordinate tasks with a co-worker • Correct someone's work • Determine sufficient materials to complete a job • Notice a safety problem • Notice that a co-worker needs assistance • Offer to help a co-worker • Realize the need to confirm instructions	• How to frame a wall • How to install a toilet • How to install hanging cabinets • How to tape and mud drywall

Unit	Occupations	Workplace Communication	On-the-Job Instructions
7 **Commercial Construction** Pages 88–107	• automatic door installer • blockmason • brickmason • bulldozer operator • carpenter • ceiling tile installer • cement finisher • cement mason • cement truck operator • concrete finisher • concrete laborer • concrete pump truck operator • concrete worker • construction foreman • construction laborer • construction safety officer • construction supervisor • construction worker • crane truck operator • dump truck operator • electrician • equipment operator • excavator operator • flagger • flatbed truck driver • flatbed truck operator • formwork installer • glass processor apprentice • glazier • HVAC technician • insulation contractor • jobsite foreman • pipefitter • plasterer • plumber • project manager • roofer • solar panel installer • steelworker • stonemason • structural engineer • surveyor • tile setter • welder	• Ask a co-worker for feedback • Ask a co-worker for material • Ask a co-worker if a task has been completed • Ask a co-worker to do a task • Ask about the scope of a task • Communicate instructions using hand signals • Coordinate a task with a co-worker • Coordinate separate tasks with a co-worker • Correct a co-worker • Point out a problem to a worker • Warn a co-worker about a problem	• How to evacuate for a foundation • How to install modified bitumen roofing • How to lay a brick wall • How to pour a foundation
8 **Automotive Technology** Pages 108–121	• auto body repairperson • auto paint helper • auto painter • auto technician • auto upholsterer • automotive exhaust emissions technician • automotive suspension technician • brake specialist • collision repair technician • estimator • frame repairperson • lubrication/lube technician • service advisor • shop foreman • sunroof installer • tire specialist • tow truck driver • tune-up and electronics specialist • window tint specialist • windshield/auto glass technician	• Ask a co-worker for help • Ask a co-worker to check your work • Assess damage and determine a course of action • Call a co-worker's attention to a problem • Check on the status of a repair job • Coordinate tasks with a co-worker • Correct a co-worker • Deal with a customer's problem • Describe a problem to a co-worker • Diagnose a problem • Observe that a co-worker is having a problem	• How to change a spark plug • How to change engine oil • How to fix a dent • How to paint a repaired area

SCOPE AND SEQUENCE

Unit	Occupations	Workplace Communication	On-the-Job Instructions
9 **Medical Care** **Pages 122–135**	• anesthesiologist • certified nursing assistant (CNA) • dietetic technician/aide • doctor • emergency medical technician (EMT) • emergency room technician • home health aide • homemaker • licensed practical nurse (LPN) • medical equipment preparer/certified sterile processing and distribution (SPD) technician • orderly • patient transport attendant • physical therapist • physical therapist assistant • registered nurse (RN) • respiratory therapist • surgeon • surgical technician • visiting nurse	• Ask for feedback • Care for a client • Check on a patient • Coordinate tasks with a co-worker • Coordinate work schedules • Give correction • Give feedback to a co-worker • Give instructions • Prepare a client for bedtime • Reprimand a co-worker • Request assistance	• How to ambulate a patient with a gait belt • How to apply a clean dressing • How to measure a patient's output • How to take blood pressure
10 **Health Services** **Pages 136–149**	• administrative medical assistant • clinical medical assistant • dental assistant • dental hygienist • dental lab technician • dentist • doctor/physician • EKG technician • medical coder • medical lab technician • medical receptionist • medical transcriptionist • MRI technician • nuclear medicine technician • optical lab technician • optician • optometric assistant • optometrist • pharmacist • pharmacy assistant • pharmacy technician • phlebotomist • physician assistant • radiologist • radiology technician • X-ray technician	• Ask for feedback • Assist a dentist • Assist a doctor with a procedure • Do blood work on a patient • Give correction to a co-worker • Give feedback to a co-worker • Help a patient check in • Prepare a patient for an X-ray • Transcribe a doctor's notes • Update a patient's data • Verify a patient's readiness for an exam	• How to collect blood • How to do pre-examination procedures • How to take an EKG • How to take an X-ray

Unit	Occupations	Workplace Communication	On-the-Job Instructions
11 **Public Safety** Pages 150–163	• 911 operator • animal control officer • asset protection specialist • bailiff • corrections officer • detective • emergency medical technician (EMT) • emergency services dispatcher • engine chauffeur • fingerprint analyst • firefighter • forensic identification specialist • judge • K9 officer • law enforcement officer • paramedic • parking enforcement officer • parole agent • police officer • probation officer • public defender • public safety officer • school safety officer • security guard • security patrol officer • TSA agent • TSA officer • TSA screener • watchman	• Check in a visitor to a facility • Compliment a co-worker • Coordinate tasks at a crime scene • Correct a co-worker • Deal with a problem at a fire scene • Give feedback to a co-worker • Inquire about the analysis of evidence • Interview a witness • Meet with a parolee • Reprimand a worker • Screen carry-on baggage • Search an inmate's cell	• How to do a pat-down • How to frisk a suspect • How to put on firefighter turnout gear • How to search a prison cell
12 **Finance** Pages 164–177	• auto damage appraiser • auto loan officer • bank manager • bank security guard • call center supervisor • claims processing specialist • collection associate • collection specialist • customer service associate • drive-through teller • financial services rep • fraud detection associate • insurance adjuster • insurance agency manager • insurance agent • insurance appraiser • insurance examiner • insurance investigator • insurance sales agent • loan officer • member services representative • mortgage loan officer • new account associate • safe-deposit clerk • sales associate • small business loan officer • tax preparer • teller	• Ask a co-worker for feedback • Assist a credit card customer • Assist an applicant with an auto loan application • Express concern about an employee's job performance • Gather tax information from a client • Give feedback to a new employee • Greet a new customer • Help a customer cash a check • Help a customer with a mortgage application • Help a customer with an insurance claim • Inspect damage at a policyholder's home • Make a suggestion to an employee	• How to cash a customer's check • How to detect counterfeit currency • How to do an auto damage appraisal • How to write an automobile insurance policy

Unit	Occupations	Workplace Communication	On-the-Job Instructions
13 **Office Administration** Pages 178–191	• accounts payable clerk • accounts receivable clerk • administrative assistant • delivery person • executive • executive assistant • executive secretary • file clerk • general manager • human resource assistant • human resource director • mail clerk • marketing associate • marketing manager • office assistant • office clerk • office manager • payroll clerk • receptionist • repair technician • sales associate • sales manager • secretary	• Ask an assistant to place a call • Ask about a delivery • Ask for feedback • Correct a co-worker • Correct a new employee • Deal with an office problem • Do a task for a co-worker • Give instructions • Greet a visitor • Offer to help a co-worker • Prioritize tasks with a co-worker • Reprimand a co-worker	• How to fax a document • How to process an invoice • How to respond to an incoming call • How to write and send executive correspondence
14 **Home, Personal, & Community Services** Pages 192–205	• aerobics instructor • caregiver • carpet cleaner • child-care worker • clerk • courier/messenger • delivery person • dog walker • exterminator • fitness trainer • funeral attendant • funeral director • handyman • home appliance repair technician • home entertainment equipment installer • housekeeper • lawn care worker • lawyer • legal secretary • librarian • library assistant • locksmith • mail carrier • mail handler • nanny • paralegal/legal assistant • pet sitter • recreation program leader • recreation worker • senior citizen activities coordinator • teacher • teacher's aide • tow truck driver • tutor • veterinarian • veterinary technician	• Ask a customer to describe a problem • Ask about program attendance • Ask for feedback • Care for a client • Decide how to do an activity • Disagree about something • Explain a repair that is needed • Give instructions to an assistant • Learn from a customer that a procedure didn't work • Notice a problem with someone's work • Point out a problem to an assistant • Receive feedback	• How to change the drive belt on a washing machine • How to mount a flat-screen TV • How to shelve books in a library • How to train a client on the use of a treadmill

Unit	Occupations		Workplace Communication	On-the-Job Instructions
15 **Small Business, Franchise Ownership, & Entrepreneurship** **Pages 206–221**	• auto glass repairer • auto lube shop owner • auto lube shop technician • baker • barber • barista • bookstore owner • caterer • child-care worker • cobbler • coffee shop owner • convenience store owner • copy center manager • esthetician • floral designer • food cart vendor • food truck owner • hardware store manager • ice-cream shop owner • interior designer • jewelry designer • jobber/route distributor	• licensed day-care operator • limo driver/chauffeur • limo service owner • mailbox/packaging store manager • newsstand proprietor • personal trainer • pet food shop owner • pet groomer • pet shop owner • photographer • photography assistant • picture framer • sandwich shop owner • smoothie shop owner • sporting goods store manager • tailor • temp agency owner • temporary staffing specialist	• Ask a client for feedback • Ask a shop owner for feedback • Ask about missing delivery items • Check on the status of an order • Correct an employee • Discuss a work order • Give instructions to an employee • Order supplies • Report a supply shortage • Reprimand an employee • Sign up a new client • Tell a client about a job opportunity	• A day operating a small business • How to open a food truck business • How to open a franchise business • How to start a small business
16 **Travel & Hospitality** **Pages 222–235**	• auto rental agent • baggage handler • banquet manager • banquet server • bellhop • busperson • cabin serviceperson • concierge • curside check-in agent • doorman • event coordinator • event planner • first officer • flight attendant • food service worker • front desk clerk • gate agent • ground crew member • group tour guide • hotel maintenance worker	• housekeeper • housekeeping manager • houseperson • line service technician • pilot • room service attendant • service agent • shuttle driver • skycap • taxi driver/cab driver • ticket agent • tour bus driver • tour escort • travel agent • TSA screener • valet • wheelchair agent	• Ask for feedback • Assist a customer with a trip • Check in a hotel guest • Check in a passenger for a flight • Check on the status of work completed • Coordinate completion of a task • Coordinate tasks with a co-worker • Give positive feedback • Point out a problem • Reassure a passenger • Report a problem	• How to check in an airline passenger • How to prepare the cabin for takeoff • How to register a hotel guest • How to set up for a banquet event

Unit	Occupations		Workplace Communication	On-the-Job Instructions
17 Communication & the Arts **Pages 236–257**	• abstract artist • actor • actress • architect • architectural model maker • art director • assignment editor • assistant art director • assistant buyer • assistant camera operator • assistant casting director • assistant choreographer • assistant copy editor • assistant director • assistant fashion designer • assistant film editor • assistant producer • assistant prop master • assistant recording engineer • assistant set designer • assistant stage manager • author/writer • board operator • boom operator • broadcast technician • buyer • CAD operator • camera operator • casting director • ceramicist • choreographer • clapper • columnist • conductor • copywriter • creative director • dancer • desktop publisher • digital editor • digital press operator • digital staff writer • director • draftsperson • ENG operator • fashion designer • fashion model • fashion photographer • field camera operator • field reporter • film editor • finisher • floor manager	• Foley artist • gaffer • glassblower • graphic designer • grip • illustrator • intern • lighting technician • meteorologist/weather reporter • musician • newscast producer • newscaster • on-set dresser • online content producer • pattern maker • photography assistant • photojournalist • portrait painter • prepress technician • press operator • producer • program director • prop manager • prop master • publication assistant • radio announcer • radio broadcast technician • radio broadcaster • recording engineer • recording mixer • reporter • researcher/archivist • scenic artist • screenwriter • sculptor • set carpenter • set designer • set dresser • set painter • set production assistant • singer • sound assistant • sound engineer • sound technician • staffer • stage manager • story analyst/script reader • technical writer • web designer • web developer • writer assistant	• Apologize for making a mistake • Ask a co-worker for a part to a piece of equipment • Ask for feedback • Brainstorm ideas with a co-worker • Check on a co-worker's progress • Check on the status of a job • Coordinate tasks with a co-worker • Discuss with a colleague how to do a task • Give timing cues to a performer • Make a suggestion • Point out a possible error in someone's work • Point out a problem • Prepare someone to read for an audition • Prepare to do a live remote broadcast • Prepare to go out on an assignment • Reprimand a worker • Troubleshoot and resolve a problem • Work with a colleague to solve a problem	• How to bring a new clothing design to market • How to design and prepare a publication using desktop publishing software • How to engineer a recording session • How to operate a boom microphone

Unit	Occupations	Workplace Communication	On-the-Job Instructions
18 Telecommunications Pages 258–271	• 611 customer service assistant • 711 communication assistant • 711 relay operator • cable (company) installer • cell tower climber • central office technician • customer service assistant • fiber optic cable installer • line installer • PBX installer • phone company installer • satellite TV installer • security/fire alarm installer • telecommunications installer • telecommunications lineperson • telecommunications sales associate • telecommunications technician • TTY/TDD 711 relay operator/711 communication assistant • voice communication analyst	• Assist a caller • Check on a colleague's work • Compliment a sales associate • Coordinate tasks with a co-worker • Deal with a customer complaint • Get information needed to do a job • Help a customer with a problem • Reprimand a worker on a job safety issue • Troubleshoot a problem • Work on an installation with a co-worker	• How to dig a trench and lay cable • How to install a satellite dish • How to install a security system • How to relay a 711 call from a hearing-impaired person
19 Information Technology Pages 272–287	• computer installer • computer programmer • computer repair technician • computer service technician • computer/network administrator • computer support specialist • data entry keyer • data recovery specialist • game designer • game developer • game producer • game tester • help desk technician • information processing worker • information systems security specialist • mobile app designer • mobile app developer • network engineer • systems analyst • technical support specialist • UI (user interface) artist • video game music composer	• Ask a co-worker for feedback • Check on the completion of a task • Check on the progress of an installation • Check on the progress of someone's work • Check on the status of a project • Correct a co-worker • Give positive feedback • Help a customer with a problem • Offer to help a co-worker • Work with a colleague on an installation	• How to develop a video game • How to punch a patch panel • How to replace an internal hard drive • How to set up a computer workstation

Welcome to *CareerView: Exploring the World of Work*!

The mission of this course is to help students develop career and academic readiness skills while they explore their work interests, the array of career opportunities across many employment sectors, and the pathways for achieving short-term and long-term goals. Together with its companion *Career & Academic Readiness Workbook*, the **CareerView** course helps prepare high-intermediate and advanced English language learners for a successful transition to continuing education, vocational training, and employment. The integrated curriculum promotes the employability and academic readiness goals of the new English Language Proficiency Standards (ELPS), the College and Career Readiness Skills (CCRS), and the Workforce Improvement & Opportunity Act (WIOA). Technology tasks throughout the course promote learners' development of digital information skills to find, evaluate, organize, create, and present information to prepare for the world of work as well as continuing education.

CareerView can serve as the capstone level of a traditional basal English series, as a stand-alone or supplemental high-intermediate or transition/bridge/advanced English course, and as an introductory career exploration resource for students entering continuing education, occupational training settings, and high school career and technical education programs. School employment counselors, career navigators, and other guidance professionals can also use the core text with student advisees to help them explore career pathways.

The four key course objectives are:

- Career exploration
- Effective communication skills for employability and success in the workforce
- Academic readiness for continuing education
- Development of learners' digital information skills and use of technology

The Curriculum

CareerView combines a general soft-skills approach to employment preparation with contextualized instruction that is organized by the career pathways established by the U.S. government for career and technical education. There are sixteen pathways, but there are twenty units in the course, as the construction and health care employment sectors require two units each for adequate coverage, and the small business/

entrepreneurship and green job sectors warrant their own units rather than being folded into multiple pathways. (For instructional purposes, units focus on particular work settings rather than attempting to feature all types of occupations and workplaces in each pathway.)

The core text focuses on vocabulary development and communication skills for employability through contextualized instruction tied to the employment sectors and designed to help students answer these seven key questions about possible career pathways:

- What kinds of occupations are there?
- What occupations might interest me?
- Where would I work?
- Who would I work with?
- What would I do in this occupation?
- What tools, equipment, and technology would I use?
- How would I learn things on the job?

For each employment sector, unit content includes key occupational vocabulary (names of occupations; worksite locations; job responsibilities; and equipment, tools, and objects) and key forms of workplace communication (discourse with supervisors, co-workers, and customers; giving and receiving on-the-job instructions; and discussing job performance). While each unit contains vocabulary specific to its employment sector, the workplace communication skills are universal and portable *soft skills*—functional skills that apply across the full range of employment. Examples include giving and following instructions, offering and asking for assistance, giving and responding to feedback and correction, coordinating tasks with co-workers, identifying and reporting problems, making recommendations, and helping customers.

At the end of each unit, an inventory provides a useful overview of all the employment sector vocabulary, and a multi-page Skills Check provides comprehensive review practice.

Units may be used in any sequence, and completion of all 20 units isn't necessary for students to benefit from the course. Programs may wish to emphasize units that align with local and regional employment opportunities or career training options within their institutions or other nearby programs. Teachers may also wish to allow their students to vote on the units they would like to study by using the reproducible interest survey ballot provided in the Teacher's Resources. Another mode of selecting units is to focus on employment sectors that are of general interest, such as food, health, finance, retail, and community services.

Structure of a Unit

Each unit begins with three lessons that focus on employment sector vocabulary presented in a picture dictionary format, followed by three lessons that offer communication practice in the sector's workplace contexts, a unit inventory section with lists of key vocabulary and expressions, and a final skills check section with review activities.

Lesson 1: Occupations and worksite locations
Lesson 2: Job responsibilities
Lesson 3: Equipment, tools, and objects
Lesson 4: Workplace communication
Lesson 5: On-the-job instructions
Lesson 6: Job performance
Section 7: Unit inventory
Section 8: Skills check

At the bottom of pages in Lessons 1–3, there are vocabulary practice instructions and questions for students to discuss in class and, if desired, to respond to in writing. These questions encourage students to relate the workplace context to their own lives and experiences, to share opinions, and to engage in critical thinking.

In Lessons 4 and 6, each workplace communication and job performance conversation has an accompanying activity at the bottom of the page. These are designed to promote general communication skills for employability through contextualized practice with common situations that occur in the employment sector.

- Role-play scenarios prompt students to work with a partner to create and present new interactions based on the functional communication skills featured in the lesson conversations. These scenarios include communication between co-workers, between employees and supervisors, and between workers and customers.

- Questions about workplace values and expectations get students talking about important employability concepts such as taking initiative, giving and responding to feedback, coping with difficult situations, and other aspects of work attitudes and behavior.

- Brainstorming activities encourage students to use lesson conversations as springboards to think of other situations that may occur at the workplace.

- Personalization questions invite students to share about their own experiences with situations depicted in the conversations.

- Critical thinking "What would you do . . .?" questions prompt students to think about problem situations that are posed in some conversations and to share their solutions.

The Career & Academic Readiness Workbook

The **CareerView** Career & Academic Readiness Workbook reinforces the core text curriculum while focusing on personal career exploration, information about each employment sector, academic readiness, and the development of digital information skills.

An initial career exploration section helps students identify and describe their interests, personal characteristics, work styles, and other self-evaluation dimensions as they relate to employment options. Students also learn how to use the federal O*Net Career Exploration Tools at the mynextmove.org website to learn about jobs that may interest them.

The main section of the workbook provides supplemental activities, readings, and academic lessons to support each of the 20 units in the core text. A career vocabulary cloze activity synthesizes the unit's occupation names; worksite locations; job responsibilities; and equipment, tools, and objects. A career research lesson prompts students to use the O*Net Career Exploration Tools to find information about a unit's occupation that might interest them and to prepare and present this information to the class. An on-the-job instructions activity offers practice reading workplace notices, safety procedures, and other instructions. A civics connection profile in some units features an interview that focuses on the relationship between the employment sector and community life. An academic lesson gives students experience with lengthy subject-matter material on a unit-related STEAM topic (Science and Sustainability; Technology; Engineering; Arts and Architecture; or Math). A Listening activity offers practice with employment communication contexts and prepares students for the types of listening items that appear in standardized tests.

A final workbook section helps learners synthesize their self-evaluations and career explorations, offers information about different education and training options, provides graphic organizers and forms students can use to record their short-term and long-term goals and a personal pathway to accomplish them, and templates for resumes and cover letters.

Tech Tasks

The **CareerView** technology goal views students not as *consumers* of digitally-delivered workbook-style practice, but rather as *users* of technology and *producers* of digital content in the spirit of the WIOA workforce education guidelines––to find, evaluate, organize, create, and share information in a manner that prepares students for the world of work and continuing education. This is accomplished through Tech Tasks for each unit, which create a seminar environment in the classroom as students research, prepare, and present information to each other. The Tech Tasks are described in the Appendix on pages 312–313, and some Tech Tasks are supported by activities in the workbook. While it is preferable for students to complete the tasks using computers, they should be able to accomplish most of them using smartphones.

TECH TASK 1:

After students have learned the basic vocabulary of an employment sector in a unit's first three lessons, they are tasked with researching and organizing information about an occupation in the unit in order to answer these questions:

- Where does a person with this job work?
- What does this person do?
- What tools and equipment does this person use?
- What technology does this person use?
- What skills and abilities are important to do this job well?
- What education is required?
- What is the salary and the job outlook?

The workbook has a lesson page devoted to this activity, with an information chart showing the job zone education and skill requirements of each occupation in the unit. Students can use the O*Net Career Exploration Tools as their information source and record their information in the workbook. Then they prepare and give a short presentation to the class about the occupation. If classroom resources permit, it is strongly recommended that students use

presentation software to create a slide show for the class. The website resources often include short videos about jobs produced by One-Stop Career Centers. These can be useful and motivating for students to include in their presentations. Alternatively, students can write a report about the occupation and give an oral presentation to the class.

TECH TASK 2:

The fifth lesson in each unit features four sets of multistep activities that are common in the employment sector, such as instructions for operating equipment, procedures for doing a customer transaction, and safety instructions. After students have completed the lesson, they are tasked to use YouTube, WikiHow, or another online source to search for a demonstration of how to do a procedure related to the unit's employment sector. (The workbook activity page related to the lesson includes suggested search terms students can use to find interesting procedures.) Students write out the instructions and, if resources permit, they prepare a slide show presentation for the class. Alternatively, they can do a demonstration that models the steps of the procedure. Students are encouraged to use their smartphones or computers to make screenshots of steps in the procedures and include them in their presentations.

TECH TASK 3:

If workplace locations in your area are willing to participate, you can assign students an interview task to visit a workplace related to a unit's employment sector, talk with a worker about the person's job, and report back to the class. If students have permission from the workplace and the worker, they can use smartphones to record some or all of their interviews and share excerpts with the class.

If students record interviews, encourage them to stand close to the interviewee for better video and audio quality, hold the smartphone horizontally instead of vertically in order to fill the screen, and hold it steady to avoid shaking or distortion. They should also record the video so that they can keep it or transfer it to a computer, rather than using one of the Stories apps in which videos disappear after 24 hours. Some students may have video-editing skills through their use of social media. Encourage them to use their skills and the simple video-editing apps available for smartphones or computers to create their presentations, and to help other students as well.

TECH TASK 4:

As students are completing the unit's Skills Check, have them do an online search to find a sector-related news story, prepare a summary, and present it to the class. Motivating topics can include an unusual occupation or workplace, a current safety issue, working conditions, employee rights, and occupational outlooks.

TECH TASK 5:

As part of a final workbook lesson on the importance of managing social media reputations, students carefully prepare and deploy their own LinkedIn profiles.

The Audio Program App

The *CareerView* core text audio program offers listening practice with all vocabulary and dialogs. The workbook audio program provides the complete workbook listening activities. For students' personal listening practice, these audio programs are delivered via the Pearson Go mobile app (iOS and Android), which students can access on smartphones and computers. The app enables students to easily navigate through the audio program, follow a transcript as they listen, practice at their own pace, and use the speed control function to adjust playback without losing sound quality. For listening practice in the classroom, language lab, or other setting, audio mp3 files are also available for purchase separately.

The *CareerView* ToolSite

The *CareerView* *ToolSite*, at pearsoneltusa.com/careerview, provides downloadable resources to help with lesson planning and instruction. Reproducible materials include an interest survey ballot (for students to vote on employment sectors they would like to explore), teaching instructions for each type of lesson, unit glossaries, additional employment sector information, and activity masters that provide additional lesson practice, job application forms, resume and cover letter templates, and other resources. To access the *ToolSite* go to pearsoneltusa.com/careerview and select ToolSite Resources from the menu.

Teaching Strategies

We encourage you to use the *CareerView* course in a manner that best meets the needs and goals of your students and enables you to employ instructional strategies you find most effective for developing learners' vocabulary and communication skills and encouraging their active participation. You may find it helpful to incorporate some of the following strategies in your lesson planning and instruction.

LESSON 1:
OCCUPATIONS AND WORKSITE LOCATIONS

The first lesson in each unit features one or more workplace scenes that depict a variety of occupations and worksite locations. Some lessons also include worksite equipment. In the scenes and the word lists below them, the occupations are numbered, and the locations and equipment are indicated by letters.

1. **Activate prior knowledge:** Have students cover the word lists and just look at the scenes. Ask them what words they already know. You may want to write the words on the board or display them on screen if you use a projection device.

2. **Explore the vocabulary:** Have students look at the scenes and word lists and describe what they see.

3. **Present the vocabulary:** Say each word and have the class repeat it chorally. (You can also play the word list on the Audio Program.)

4. **Practice the vocabulary:** Have students practice the vocabulary as a class, in pairs, or in small groups, using one or both of the following activities:

   a. Have students just look at the scenes (not the word lists). Say a word and have students tell the correct number or letter. Or, give a number or letter and have students say the word.

   b. Have students look at the scenes and word lists and create descriptive sentences about the occupations, worksite locations, and equipment. For example, sentences related to the department store scene on pages 2–3 might include:

   > There's a stock clerk in the warehouse area.
   > Cashiers are in the checkout area.
   > There's a lot of merchandise on the shelves.

5. **Topics for discussion and writing:** Use the questions in the blue-shaded section at the bottom of the page to encourage students to relate the workplace context to their own lives and experiences and to stimulate class discussion. You may want to have students write responses to the questions at home, share their written work with other students, and then discuss in class.

6. **Skills Check:** After completing Lesson 1, students can do the *Occupations* and *Workplace Locations* activities at the end of the unit. Or, since these activities include vocabulary related to job responsibilities, they may prefer to wait until they complete Lesson 2.

LESSON 2:
JOB RESPONSIBILITIES

The second lesson in each unit provides numbered illustrations that depict tasks people do in their jobs.

1. **Activate prior knowledge:** Have students cover the lists and just look at the illustrations. Ask them what job tasks they already know how to describe. You may want to write the tasks on the board or display them on screen if you use a projection device.

2. **Present the vocabulary:** Say each task as it appears in the list, and have the class repeat it chorally. (You can also play the list on the Audio Program.) Or, say each task as a full sentence that describes what is happening in the illustration. For example, sentences related to the first three tasks on page 4 could be as follows:

    She's stocking shelves.
    He's arranging merchandise.
    She's assisting a customer.

3. **Practice the vocabulary:** Have students practice the vocabulary as a class, in pairs, or in small groups. Have students just look at the illustrations (not the lists). Say a sentence about a task (e.g., She's stocking shelves.) and have students tell the correct number. Or, give a number and have students say a sentence about the task.

4. **Apply the vocabulary:** Have students do the activity suggested in the blue-shaded section at the bottom of the page. They should look at the scenes in Lesson 1 and describe what the people are doing, using full sentences that contain the tasks listed in Lesson 2. You may want to have students write a description of what people are doing in the scenes as preparation for discussing this in class.

5. **Skills Check:** If students haven't already done the *Occupations* and *Workplace Locations* activities at the end of the unit, a good time to do them is after they have completed Lesson 2.

LESSON 3:
EQUIPMENT, TOOLS, AND OBJECTS

The third lesson displays equipment, tools, and objects that are common at worksites depicted in the unit.

1. **Activate prior knowledge:** Have students cover the lists and just look at the illustrations. Ask them what words they already know. You may want to write the words on the board or display them on screen if you use a projection device.

2. **Present the vocabulary:** Say each item and have the class repeat it chorally. (You can also play the list on the Audio Program.)

3. **Practice the vocabulary:** Have students practice the items as a class, in pairs, or in small groups. They should just look at the illustrations (not the lists). Say an item and have students tell the correct number. Or, give a number and have students say the item.

4. **Apply the vocabulary:** Have students do the activity suggested in the blue-shaded section at the bottom of the page. They should look at the scenes in Lesson 1 and the tasks illustrated in Lesson 2 and describe the equipment, tools, and objects they see. For example, sentences about how the items on page 6 appear on pages 2–5 could include the following:

    There's merchandise in a display case in the electronics department.

    There are clothing racks in the clothing department.

You should also encourage students to create lengthier descriptions that combine vocabulary from Lessons 1, 2, and 3, including the verbs describing job responsibilities. For example:

    A forklift operator is operating a forklift in the warehouse area.

    A stock clerk is stocking the shelves with items that are on an inventory cart.

You may want to have students write a descriptive paragraph about the scene, using as much vocabulary as they can, and then share their written work with other students.

5. **Skills Check:** After completing Lesson 3, students can do the *Equipment, Tools, & Objects* activity at the end of the unit.

▶ **Tech Task 1:** After completing Lessons 1–3, students are ready to do Tech Task 1. (See page 312.)

LESSON 4:
WORKPLACE COMMUNICATION

The fourth lesson in each unit focuses on workplace communication *soft skills*—functional employability skills that help students use language proficiently for successful interpersonal communication in the workplace. The dialogs in the lesson are in the situational contexts of the unit's employment sector, but the *soft skills* they include are universal and portable—they apply across the full range of work settings. Here are some suggestions for communication practice with each dialog.

1. **Set the scene and context:** Have students look at the dialog title, illustration, and caption. Have them discuss who the speakers are and where the conversation is taking place. You can exploit the illustration details for additional preparatory practice. For example, on page 8, dialog 1, you might ask students what kind of merchandise is sold in that department, what information is provided on the shelf display, or even hypothetical questions, such as how long students think the sales associate has worked at the store.

2. **Model the conversation:** Present each line of the conversation, have two students perform it, or play the Audio Program.

3. **Practice the conversation:** Have students practice each line of the conversation chorally, in small groups, or in pairs.

4. **Practice new conversations:** Have students work in pairs and practice new conversations based on the original but with some changes in the situation or context. For example, here are some changes students might apply to the conversations on page 8.

   Dialog 1: The item isn't on sale now, but it will be going on sale in two weeks.

   Dialog 2: The customer wants to buy a different item that's in the display case.

   Dialog 3: The customer isn't going to use a credit card at the checkout counter.

   Dialog 4: The customer has coupons for different products with different expiration dates.

5. **More conversation practice and topics for discussion and writing:** Each dialog in the lesson has an accompanying activity in the blue-shaded section at the bottom of the page. It might be an instruction to create a role-play with a specific context, a brainstorming activity that encourages students to think of situations that might occur at work, a question that encourages students to share experiences or opinions, or a critical thinking "What would you do . . . ?" question that prompts students to think about problems and solutions. Some of the most important questions stimulate discussions about workplace values and expectations. Their purpose is to get students talking about concepts that are important for employability and promotion on the job, including taking initiative, being helpful, coping with difficult situations, and other aspects of work attitudes and behavior. *(Please don't skip these activities! They may not occupy much space on the page, but they are central to the mission of the course. The class time you devote to these activities will be an important factor in learners' success achieving the employability goals.)*

LESSON 5:
ON-THE-JOB INSTRUCTIONS

The fifth lesson in each unit features four sets of multistep activities that are common in the employment sector, such as instructions for following a procedure, operating equipment, or handling a customer transaction. The steps are numbered, depicted in a series of illustrations, and written as a list of imperative statements. Through this practice, students will become familiar with the way workers might learn such instructions through demonstration by a co-worker or supervisor, via instructional videos, or through computer-based training. Here are some suggestions for practice with each set of instructions.

1. **Set the scene and context:** Have students look at the title and the illustrations. Have them describe who they see in the illustration, what the person's occupation is, what the person is doing, and where the activity is taking place. Students will be able to discuss this based on what they have learned in the previous lessons. For example, on page 10, On-the-Job Instructions part A, students will be able to express that a stock clerk is opening a box and unpacking merchandise in a warehouse area. You can also exploit the illustration for additional lesson review by asking about equipment, tools, and objects that are shown, such as:

   What tool is the stock clerk using in picture 2? (A handheld inventory unit)

   What object do you see in pictures 5 and 7? (A rack)

2. **Model the instructions:** Say each instruction and have the class repeat it chorally. (You can also play the instructions on the Audio Program.)

3. **Practice the instructions:** Have students practice the instructions in small groups or in pairs.

4. **Model communication strategies:** Create (or have a pair of students create) a dialog in which one worker gives instructions to another to offer training on the procedure. The dialog should use the communication strategies that occur when people give and receive instructions, such as asking for repetition, clarifying an instruction, repeating something to verify understanding, asking for more information, and saying you understand or don't understand. For example, a dialog based on page 10, On-the-Job Instructions part A, might be as follows:

   A. Since this is your first day on the job, let me show you how to unpack merchandise.
   B. Okay.
   A. First, open the box. Then scan the packing sheet.
   B. The packing sheet?
   A. Yes. This is the packing sheet. After you scan the packing sheet, remove the packing material, and remove the items from the box.
   B. I see.
   A. Hang the items on a rolling rack. Then take the plastic or other protective covering off the items.
   B. Did you say take the protective covering off the items?
   A. Yes. That's right. Then take the items to the staging area.
   B. I'm sorry. Where's the staging area?
   A. Over there. Then cut up the box, and take the cardboard and packing materials to the compactor.
   B. Could you repeat the last instruction?
   A. Yes. Cut up the box, and take the cardboard and packing materials to the compactor. Have you got all that?
   B. Yes. I've got it. Thanks.

5. **Practice conversations:** Have students work in pairs and practice conversations based on the lesson's multistep instructions, including communication strategies, and present their conversations to the class.

6. **Play with the instructions:** For motivating practice, you might consider doing one or both of the following activities using sentence strips, each containing one of the instructions:

   a. Give some students the sentence strips. Have them circulate around the room, say the instructions on their sentence strips, and put themselves in the correct sequence in front of the class.

   b. Give some students the sentence strips. Have them pantomime their actions as other students guess what they are doing and then tell them where to stand to be in the correct sequence in front of the class.

7. **Skills Check:** After completing Lesson 5, students can do the *Workplace Actions* activity at the end of the unit.

▶ **Tech Task 2:** After completing Lesson 5, students are ready to do Tech Task 2. (See pages 312–313.)

LESSON 6:
JOB PERFORMANCE

Similar to Lesson 4, the sixth lesson in each unit provides workplace communication practice to develop students' *soft skills*. However, the dialogs in Lesson 6 have a special focus on job performance—the ways that people give, receive, and react to feedback on the job. You can use the Lesson 4 suggestions for communication practice with each dialog.

1. **Set the scene and context.**

2. **Model the conversation.**

3. **Practice the conversation.**

4. **Practice new conversations.**

5. **More conversation practice and topics for discussion and writing**

6. **Skills Check:** After completing Lesson 6, students can do the *Workplace Communication* activity at the end of the unit.

▶ **Tech Tasks 3–5:** Please see page 313 for descriptions of additional Tech Tasks for each unit and suggestions on when to include them in your lesson planning.

It can be an exciting, challenging, and hopeful time as students prepare to enter the world of work and continue their education. We hope that *CareerView* helps them explore their work interests and options, develop their skills, and prepare for a successful journey on whatever pathway they choose to follow to achieve their goals.

Bill Bliss
Steven J. Molinsky

1 customer	**4** warehouse worker	**a** aisle	**f** electronics department	**j** ladder
2 stock clerk	**5** trucker	**b** merchandise	**g** display case	**k** truck
3 salesperson/ sales associate	**6** warehouse manager	**c** shelf	**h** warehouse area	**l** pallet
	7 forklift operator	**d** hand truck	**i** warehouse shelves	**m** forklift
		e carton		**n** rack

What occupations do you see in this department store?

What workplace objects and equipment do you see?

8 cashier
9 security person
10 customer service
   representative
11 customer service
   manager
12 store manager
13 department
   manager

o shopping cart
p checkout area
q scanner
r cash register
s register lane

t bagging area
u shopping bag
v customer
  service
  counter

w clothing
  department
x electronic tablet
y display table
z sale sign

In addition to the electronics and men's clothing departments, what other departments do you think this store has?

Is there a store like this in your community? What's the name of the store? Where is it? Do you shop there?

1 stock shelves
2 arrange merchandise
3 assist a customer
4 give information to a customer

5 sign for a delivery
6 unload a truck
7 operate a forklift
8 move pallets

9 unpack items from a shipping carton
10 scan merchandise into store inventory
11 stock items onto warehouse shelves
12 use a ladder safely

13 lift heavy items correctly
14 bring out a large item to a customer
15 operate a hand truck
16 recycle packing materials

Look at pages 2 and 3. What are the store employees doing? Describe their actions.

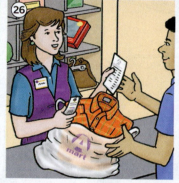
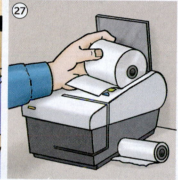

17 scan an item

18 process a customer's transaction

19 take a customer's cash

20 make change

21 swipe a customer's credit card

22 check a customer's ID*

23 redeem a customer's coupon

24 confirm sale items in a store flyer

25 bag items

26 process a return

27 change a cash register receipt tape

28 provide a raincheck for an out-of-stock item

29 make an announcement over the PA* system

30 take inventory

31 set up a display

32 straighten up a display table

* ID = identification
  PA = public address

1 merchandise	5 clothing rack	9 shipping carton	12 delivery truck
2 shelf	6 forklift	10 ladder	13 inventory cart
3 warehouse shelves	7 pallet	11 safety back brace support	14 packing materials
4 display case	8 hand truck		

Look at pages 2–5. What equipment, tools, and objects do you see?

15 cash register
16 cashier screen/monitor
17 cashier keyboard
18 cash drawer
19 till

20 sale sign
21 display table
22 shopping cart
23 handheld inventory unit
24 scanner
25 UPC* price tag

26 receipt tape
27 card reader
28 credit card
29 PA system
30 folding table

31 shopping bag
32 raincheck
33 receipt
34 coupon
35 store flyer

* UPC = Universal Product Code

Do you sometimes "clip coupons" for products? What do you buy with them?

Do you usually pay by credit card, cash, or check when you shop in a store?

1 **A Sales Associate and a Customer**

A sales associate is answering a customer's question.

A. May I help you?

B. Yes, please. Is this on sale?

A. Yes. It's 25% off until the end of the week.

B. Thanks.

2 **A Customer and a Sales Associate**

A sales associate is assisting a customer.

A. Excuse me. Can you help me?

B. Yes. What can I do for you?

A. I'd like to buy that camera.

B. Okay. Let me get the key and I'll open up the display case.

3 **A Cashier and a Customer**

A cashier is processing a transaction.

A. Will that be cash or credit?

B. I'll use my credit card.

A. All right. Please swipe your card through the card reader.

B. Okay.

4 **A Customer and a Cashier**

A cashier is helping a customer.

A. I have a couple of coupons.

B. Okay. Let's see . . . You can use the coupon for the towels. The coupon for the flashlight has expired.

A. Oh. I see.

1 What other questions do customers ask sales associates in a department store?

2 What items are usually locked in a store display case?

3 What do you think is better to use—cash, a check, or a credit or debit card? Why?

4 How much do you think shoppers save by using coupons?

5 A Department Manager and a Sales Associate

A supervisor is assigning a task to an employee.

A. Are you almost finished setting up this display?
B. Yes. I'll be done in about five minutes.
A. Good. When you finish, could you please help Stan change the sale signs?
B. Sure. I'd be happy to.

6 A Sales Associate and a Department Manager

A sales associate reports a problem and offers to help.

A. I'm free right now. Should I straighten up the dressing rooms? They're a mess!
B. Good idea!
A. Do you want me to restock the items?
B. Yes. Thanks.

7 A Customer and a Customer Service Representative

A customer service representative is processing a return.

A. I'd like to return this toaster oven.
B. Do you have the receipt?
A. Yes. Here you are.
B. Okay. Please sign here. The amount will be credited back to your account.

8 Two Co-Workers

A co-worker is making a request.

A. Could you do something for me?
B. Sure. What is it?
A. Could you restock these items?
B. No problem. I'll be happy to.

5 What are some typical tasks supervisors ask employees to do in a retail store?
6 The sales associate is "taking initiative" by offering to do something. Why is this a good idea?
7 What is the "return policy" in a store where you shop?
8 What are different ways co-workers can be helpful to each other in a retail store?

A HOW TO UNPACK MERCHANDISE

1. Open the box.
2. Scan the packing sheet.
3. Remove the packing material.
4. Remove the items from the box.
5. Hang the items on a rolling rack.
6. Take the plastic or other protective covering off the items.
7. Take the items to the staging area.
8. Cut up the box.
9. Take the cardboard and packing materials to the compactor.

B HOW TO BRING A LARGE ITEM TO CUSTOMER PICKUP

1. Get the merchandise pickup ticket.
2. Scan the ticket for the item's bin location in the warehouse.
3. Put on your safety back brace.
4. Locate the item.
5. Lift the item properly onto a hand truck.
6. Scan the item.
7. Bring the item to the customer pickup area.
8. Match the merchandise pickup ticket and the customer's receipt.
9. Put the item into the customer's vehicle.

C HOW TO CHECK OUT A CUSTOMER

1 Greet the customer in a friendly manner.
2 Scan the customer's items.
3 Deactivate security sensors on merchandise.

4 Redeem any customer coupons.
5 Total the transaction.
6 Take the customer's payment.

7 Give the customer the receipt.
8 Remove any security devices on merchandise.
9 Bag the items.

D HOW TO PROCESS A RETURN

1 Greet the customer.
2 Take the item the customer is returning.
3 Ask for the receipt.
4 Match the receipt with the item.

5 Scan the barcode on the receipt.
6 Scan the barcode on the item.

7a Credit the refund amount to the customer's credit card. (or)
7b Give the customer a cash refund.
8 Give the customer the original receipt and the return receipt.

1 A Supervisor and an Employee

A supervisor is giving correction to an employee.

A. You aren't setting up the display correctly.
B. What should I be doing differently?
A. You should arrange the pants by size, not by color.
B. Oh, okay. Thanks for letting me know.

2 An Employee and a Supervisor

An employee is asking a supervisor for feedback.

A. Am I stacking the boxes correctly?
B. No, you aren't. You're supposed to stack them with the barcodes facing out.
A. Oh, I see. I'll restack them now.

3 An Employee and a Co-Worker

An employee is giving helpful feedback to a co-worker.

A. Dave? I just noticed . . . You're forgetting to remove the security devices before you bag the customer's clothing items.
B. Oh, you're right! Thanks for pointing that out.
A. No problem.

4 A New Employee and a Co-Worker

A new employee is asking a co-worker for feedback.

A. Excuse me. I'm new on the job. I'm not sure I'm stocking this shelf the right way.
B. It looks fine to me.
A. Should I be putting all the oversized items on the top shelf?
B. Yes. You're doing it correctly.

1 What are some other things that employees in a retail store might do incorrectly?

2-4 Imagine some feedback conversations between employees, supervisors, and co-workers.

OCCUPATIONS

cashier	security person
customer service manager	stock clerk
customer service representative	store manager
department manager	trucker
forklift operator	warehouse manager
salesperson/sales associate	warehouse worker

WORKPLACE LOCATIONS

aisle	customer service counter
bagging area	dressing room
bin location	electronics department
checkout area	register lane
clothing department	staging area
customer pickup area	warehouse area

EQUIPMENT, TOOLS, & OBJECTS

barcode	display	oversized item	sale item
box	display case	PA system	sale sign
card reader	display table	packing materials	scanner
cardboard	electronic tablet	packing sheet	security device
carton	folding table	pallet	security sensor
cash drawer	forklift	payment	shelf
cash refund	hand truck	pickup ticket	shipping carton
cash register	handheld inventory unit	protective covering	shopping bag
cashier keyboard	inventory	rack	shopping cart
cashier screen/monitor	inventory cart	raincheck	store flyer
clothing rack	item	receipt	till
compactor	ladder	receipt tape	transaction
coupon	merchandise	return receipt	truck
credit card	original receipt	rolling rack	UPC price tag
delivery truck	out-of-stock item	safety back brace (support)	warehouse shelves

WORKPLACE ACTIONS

arrange merchandise	lift heavy items correctly	recycle packing materials	straighten up a display table
assist a customer	make an announcement over the PA system	redeem a customer's coupon	swipe a customer's credit card
bag items	make change	scan an item	take a customer's cash
bring out a large item to a customer	move pallets	scan merchandise into store inventory	take inventory
change a cash register receipt tape	operate a forklift	set up a display	unload a truck
check a customer's ID	operate a hand truck	sign for a delivery	unpack items from a shipping carton
confirm sale items in a store flyer	process a customer's transaction	stock items onto warehouse shelves	use a ladder safely
give information to a customer	process a return	stock shelves	
	provide a raincheck for an out-of-stock item		

WORKPLACE COMMUNICATION

answer a customer's question	assist a customer	make a request of a co-worker
ask a co-worker for feedback	give correction to an employee	process a transaction
ask a supervisor for feedback	give feedback to a co-worker	report a problem and offer to help
assign a task to an employee	help a customer	respond to feedback

OCCUPATIONS

A WHAT ARE THEIR JOBS?

cashier	sales associate	stock clerk	trucker
customer service	security person	store manager	warehouse manager

1. I collect the payments for customers' purchases. I'm a _____cashier_____.

2. Shirley is a _____. She delivers merchandise to stores.

3. I'm the _____. I'm in charge of the store.

4. Timothy is a _____. He puts merchandise on the store shelves.

5. The _____ is responsible for safety in our store.

6. I'm the _____. I'm in charge of the warehouse.

7. Robert is a _____. He sells merchandise at the SuperMax Discount Store.

8. Our _____ representative helps customers who have questions or problems.

WORKPLACE LOCATIONS

B WHAT'S THE LOCATION?

__e__ 1. Marta sells suits and ties. She works in the ____.

____ 2. Merchandise is stored in the ____.

____ 3. You can try on that dress in the ____.

____ 4. You'll find cameras in the ____.

____ 5. If you want to return a product, you need to go to the ____.

____ 6. When you check out, you need to go through a ____.

____ 7. My car is parked in the ____.

____ 8. In which ____ can I find toys?

a. customer service counter

b. aisle

c. customer pickup area

d. register lane

e. clothing department

f. electronics department

g. dressing room

h. warehouse

EQUIPMENT, TOOLS, & OBJECTS

C WHAT'S THE ITEM?

__c__ 1. card

____ 2. cash

____ 3. credit

____ 4. inventory

____ 5. protective

____ 6. electronic

____ 7. delivery

____ 8. store

____ 9. warehouse

____ 10. PA

a. flyer

b. truck

c. reader

d. system

e. shelves

f. register

g. cart

h. card

i. covering

j. tablet

____ 11. clothing

____ 12. shopping

____ 13. cash

____ 14. security

____ 15. pickup

____ 16. price

____ 17. sale

____ 18. packing

____ 19. receipt

____ 20. display

k. bag

l. case

m. tape

n. materials

o. drawer

p. ticket

q. rack

r. sign

s. tag

t. sensor

WORKPLACE ACTIONS

D WHAT'S THE ACTION?

arrange	change	confirm	lift	operate	redeem	swipe	unpack
assist	check	give	make	recycle	sign	take	use

1. You need to _____ **swipe** _____ the customer's credit card.

2. Please _____ those items from the shipping cartons that just arrived.

3. You need to _____ the cash register receipt tape.

4. Do you know how to _____ a forklift?

5. It's important to know how to _____ a ladder safely.

6. Make sure you always _____ a customer's ID.

7. Do you know how to _____ a customer's coupon?

8. Please _____ for this delivery.

9. It's important to _____ the merchandise on the shelves neatly.

10. Charlie, these customers need some help. Can you please _____ them?

11. We make sure that all of our employees know how to _____ heavy items correctly.

12. Can you please _____ these sale items in our store flyer?

13. I need you to come in this Sunday. That's the day we're going to _____ inventory.

14. Please _____ this announcement over the PA system.

15. This company is concerned about the environment. We _____ all of our packing materials.

16. Make sure you always _____ accurate information to customers.

WORKPLACE COMMUNICATION

E WHAT ARE THEY SAYING?

_g_ 1. answer a customer's question

___ 2. assist a customer

___ 3. process a transaction

___ 4. help a customer use coupons

___ 5. assign a task to an employee

___ 6. report a problem and offer to help

___ 7. process a return

___ 8. make a request

___ 9. give correction

___ 10. ask for feedback

___ 11. respond to feedback

a. "You can use the coupon for the towels."

b. "Should I straighten up the dressing room? It's a mess!"

c. "Oh, you're right. Thanks for pointing that out."

d. "What can I do for you?"

e. "Am I stacking the boxes correctly?"

f. "Could you do something for me?"

g. "Yes. It's 25% off until the end of the week."

h. "Please help Stan change the sale signs."

i. "Do you have the receipt?"

j. "Will that be cash or credit?"

k. "You aren't setting up the display correctly."

Hospital Kitchen

1 kitchen manager
2 hospital dietician
3 chef
4 food prep worker
5 food prep supervisor
6 cook

7 head cook
8 dishwasher
9 food service worker
10 kitchen supervisor
11 pastry chef
12 baker

a receiving area
b produce
c chef's office
d dishwasher
e salad prep area

f cooking area
g stove
h broiler
i oven

j roasting oven
k cart
l baking area
m baking rack
n baking oven

What occupations do you see in this hospital kitchen, restaurant, and cafeteria?

What workplace objects and equipment do you see?

Restaurant

13 head cook
14 line cook
15 busperson
16 food service worker
17 hostess/host
18 waiter/server
19 waitress/server
20 restaurant manager

Cafeteria

21 grill cook
22 short-order cook
23 food service manager
24 food service worker
25 cashier
26 cafeteria attendant

o food prep area
p grill
q exhaust hood
r heat lamps
s salad bar
t host stand

u sandwich prep area
v storage closet
w dessert case
x steam table
y steam table pan
z pass-through

Describe a restaurant or cafeteria you are familiar with.

What are some differences between restaurants with table service and cafeterias?

1 chop vegetables
2 broil fish
3 boil pasta
4 prepare salad

5 roast chicken
6 make soup
7 bake rolls
8 decorate cakes

9 weigh food portions
10 load a dishwasher
11 clean counters
12 plan a menu

13 taste food
14 supervise food preparation
15 supervise food service workers
16 check/verify a food delivery

Look at pages 16 and 17. What are the food service workers doing? Describe their actions.

17 cook vegetables
18 fry chicken
19 grill steak
20 make sandwiches

21 grill hot dogs and hamburgers
22 replenish a salad bar
23 greet customers
24 take a food order

25 call out orders
26 serve meals
27 bus a table
28 dish out food

29 check out customers
30 check food supplies
31 take reservations
32 resolve customer complaints

1 mixing bowls
2 glass rack
3 dish rack
4 dishwashing gloves
5 portion scale
6 wooden spoon

7 pot
8 pot cover
9 ladle
10 slotted spoon
11 boning knife
12 cutting board

13 cleaver
14 chef's knife
15 sharpening steel
16 cake pan
17 baking pan

18 rubber spatula
19 icing knife
20 icing bag
21 icing tips
22 rolling pin

23 dough scraper/
   bench knife
24 pastry brush
25 oven mitt
26 pot holder

Look at pages 16–19. What equipment, tools, and objects do you see?

27 tongs
28 saucepan
29 saute pan
30 fry pan
31 deep fryer basket

32 condiment tray
33 measuring cup
34 measuring spoons
35 order ticket
36 menu

37 serving tray
38 tray stand
39 hairnet
40 bus box
41 seating chart

42 reservation sheet
43 spatula
44 serrated knife
45 paring knife

46 serving fork
47 serving spoon
48 serving scoop

1 A Kitchen Supervisor & a Food Service Worker

A supervisor is assigning a task to an employee.

A. Ramon?
B. Yes?
A. When you finish wiping the counters, please mop the floor near the dishwasher.
B. Certainly. I'll be happy to.

2 A Food Prep Supervisor & a Food Prep Worker

A supervisor is making a request.

A. When will you be taking your break?
B. In about fifteen minutes.
A. Then before your break, would you please help Victor cut up vegetables for the soup?
B. I'll be glad to.

3 Two Co-Workers

A co-worker is asking for assistance.

A. Could you give me a hand?
B. Sure.
A. Could you help me unload this cart?
B. Okay.
A. Thanks.

4 A Cook & a Head Cook

A cook is asking a head cook for feedback.

A. Ms. Wagner?
B. Yes?
A. Could I ask you to check my tomato sauce?
B. Sure. Give me a moment and I'll come over and taste it.

1–2 You're a supervisor in an institutional kitchen. Assign tasks to employees and make some requests.
3 Ask a kitchen co-worker for assistance.
4 Ask a kitchen co-worker for feedback.

5 A Busperson & a Food Service Manager

A busperson is offering to do something.

A. Should I get some more napkins from the supply room?
B. Yes. And get some more straws and plastic utensils, too.
A. All right.

6 A Waitress & a Food Service Worker

A co-worker is offering assistance.

A. I see you're really busy. Would you like me to replenish the salad bar for you?
B. Yes. We're out of tomatoes and cucumbers.
A. And I see we're running low on Italian dressing. I'll take care of it.
B. Thanks very much.

7 A Server & a Customer

A server is taking a customer's order.

A. May I take your order?
B. Yes. I'll have the broiled chicken with a baked potato and peas.
A. Would you like a side salad with that?
B. No, thanks.

8 A Restaurant Manager & a Customer

A restaurant manager is handling a customer complaint.

A. What seems to be the problem?
B. This soup is too salty. I can't eat it!
A. I apologize. Would you care for a salad instead?
B. Yes. That would be fine.

5–6 Why is it a good idea to "take initiative" by offering to do things and offering assistance at work?

7 You're a server in a restaurant. Take a customer's order.

8 You're the manager! Handle a customer complaint

A HOW TO CHOP AN ONION

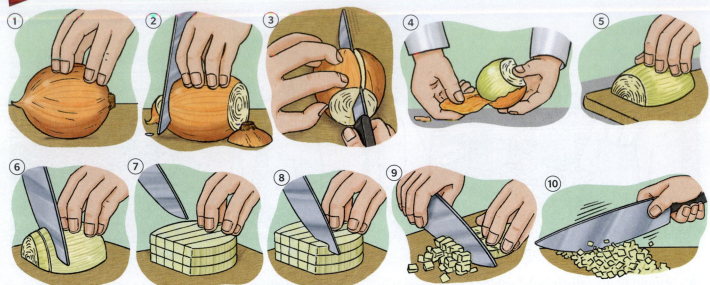

1 Grip the onion properly.
2 Trim the ends off the onion.
3 Cut the onion in half lengthwise.
4 Peel the skin.
5 Position the flat side of the onion on a cutting board.
6 Slice the onion into sections.
7 Turn the sections sideways.
8 Cut downward along the straight edge.
9 Slice toward the outer ring.
10 Finish with a quick chop.

B HOW TO OPERATE A COMMERCIAL DISHWASHER

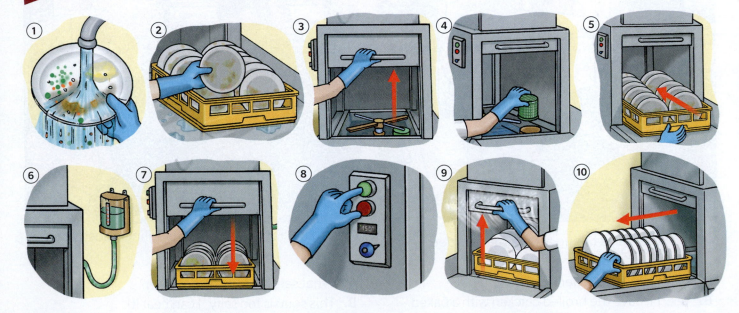

1 Rinse excess food from the dishes.
2 Stack the dishes in the rack.
3 Open the chamber.
4 Make sure the filter is clean.
5 Put the rack in the chamber.
6 Check the detergent level.
7 Close the chamber.
8 Start the cleaning cycle.
9 At the end of the cycle, open the chamber.
10 Take out the clean rack of dishes.

C HOW TO SET A PLACE SETTING

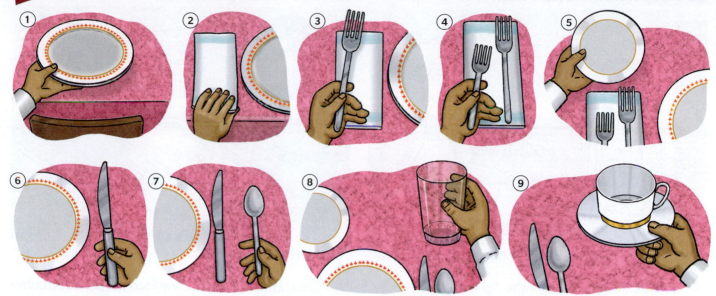

1 Place a dinner plate directly in front of the seat.

2 Put a napkin to the left of the dinner plate.

3 Place a dinner fork on the napkin.

4 Place a salad fork to the left of the dinner fork.

5 Put a salad plate to the left above the forks.

6 Put a knife, with the sharp edge facing inward, to the right of the plate.

7 Put a spoon to the right of the knife.

8 Place a water glass on the right above the knife.

9 Place a cup and saucer to the right of the knife and spoon.

D HOW TO PREP A SANDWICH STATION

1 Slice the meats and cheese.

2 Weigh and portion the meats and cheese.

3 Fill the meat and cheese containers.

4 Cut and sort the vegetables and toppings.

5 Fill the condiment containers with the vegetables and toppings.

6 Fill the squeeze bottles with condiments and dressings.

7 Stock and fill the bread supply.

8 Stock and fill the plates.

9 Put out the prep utensils.

1 A Supervisor & a New Employee

A supervisor is giving correction to a new employee.

A. You aren't icing the cake the right way.
B. What am I doing wrong?
A. You're using too much frosting.
B. Oh, I see. Thank you for letting me know.

2 A New Employee & a Co-Worker

A new employee is asking a co-worker for feedback.

A. Clara, am I dishing out the food portions correctly?
B. Yes. You're serving exactly the right amount.
A. Thanks. I just wanted to make sure since it's my first day.
B. You're doing fine.

3 Two Co-Workers

An employee is giving helpful feedback to a co-worker.

A. Sam? I think you're putting too many dishes in the bus box.
B. I am?
A. Yes. It's going to be too heavy to carry into the kitchen.
B. You're right. Thanks for pointing that out.

4 A New Employee & a Supervisor

A new employee is asking a supervisor for feedback.

A. Excuse me, Ms. Garcia. I'm not sure I'm putting the chickens in the roaster the right way.
B. You aren't. They all need to face in the same direction.
A. Oh. I had the feeling I was doing something wrong. Sorry.
B. It's okay. You're new here. It's always best to ask if you aren't sure how to do something.

1 How do you feel when someone gives you correction?
2 What is difficult about the first day on a new job?
3–4 You work in an institutional kitchen. Give feedback to a co-worker.

OCCUPATIONS

baker	food service manager	kitchen supervisor
busperson	food service worker	line cook
cafeteria attendant	grill cook	pastry chef
cashier	head cook	restaurant manager
chef	hospital dietician	server
cook	host	short-order cook
dishwasher	hostess	waiter
food prep supervisor	kitchen manager	waitress
food prep worker		

WORKPLACE LOCATIONS

baking area	restaurant
cafeteria	salad bar
chef's office	salad prep area
cooking area	salad station
food prep area	sandwich prep area
hospital kitchen	storage closet
host stand	
pass-through	
receiving area	

EQUIPMENT, TOOLS, & OBJECTS

baking oven	cutting board	fry pan	paring knife	serrated knife
baking pan	deep fryer basket	glass rack	pastry brush	serving fork
baking rack	dessert case	grill	place setting	serving scoop
bench knife	detergent	hairnet	plate	serving spoon
boning knife	dinner fork	heat lamps	portion scale	serving tray
bread supply	dinner plate	icing bag	pot	sharpening steel
broiler	dish rack	icing knife	pot cover	slotted spoon
bus box	dishwasher	icing tips	pot holder	spatula
cake pan	dishwasher chamber	knife	produce	spoon
cart	dishwashing gloves	ladle	rack	squeeze bottle
cheese container	dough scraper	measuring cup	reservation sheet	steam table
chef's knife	dressing	measuring spoons	roasting oven/roaster	steam table pan
cleaning cycle	exhaust hood	meat container	rolling pin	stove
cleaver	filter	menu	rubber spatula	tongs
condiment container	food delivery	mixing bowls	salad fork	toppings
condiment tray	food order	napkin	salad plate	tray stand
condiments	food portion	order ticket	saucepan	utensils
counter	food supplies	oven	saute pan	water glass
cup and saucer	frosting	oven mitt	seating chart	wooden spoon

WORKPLACE ACTIONS

bake rolls	chop vegetables	grill steak	roast chicken
boil pasta	clean counters	load a dishwasher	serve meals
broil fish	cook vegetables	make sandwiches	supervise food preparation
bus a table	decorate cakes	make soup	supervise food service workers
call out orders	dish out food	plan a menu	take a food order
check food supplies	fry chicken	prepare salad	take reservations
check out customers	greet customers	replenish a salad bar	taste food
check/verify a food delivery	grill hot dogs and hamburgers	resolve customer complaints	weigh food portions

WORKPLACE COMMUNICATION

ask a co-worker for feedback	give correction to a new employee	offer assistance
ask a supervisor for feedback	give feedback to a co-worker	offer to do something
ask for assistance	handle a customer complaint	take a customer's order
assign a task to an employee	make a request	

OCCUPATIONS

A WHAT ARE THEIR JOBS?

| busperson | cashier | dishwasher | hospital dietician | kitchen manager | server |
| cafeteria attendant | chef | food prep supervisor | hostess | pastry chef | short-order cook |

1. A _____server_____ takes people's orders in a restaurant.
2. A _____ sets and clears tables in a restaurant.
3. A _____ is in charge of the workers, food, and menus in a restaurant.
4. A _____ hires and trains food service workers.
5. A _____ prepares fast, simple food very quickly.
6. A _____ takes people's money and gives them change and a receipt.
7. A _____ is trained to prepare desserts, breads, and other baked goods.
8. A _____ greets customers when they arrive and takes them to their tables.
9. A _____ brings trays to the pass-through after customers leave.
10. A _____ oversees all food service operations and nutrition services in a hospital.
11. A _____ makes sure the dishes and glasses in a restaurant are clean.
12. A _____ is responsible for the operation of a restaurant kitchen.

B WHICH ONE DOESN'T BELONG?

1. short-order   line   (cafeteria)   grill
2. cooking   baking   receiving   sandwich prep
3. waiter   waitress   server   dietician
4. busperson   cook   food prep worker   chef
5. host   kitchen manager   cashier   hostess

WORKPLACE LOCATIONS

C WHAT'S THE LOCATION?

_d_ 1. Cooks prepare food in the _____.
____ 2. A pastry chef works in the _____.
____ 3. Food service workers cut vegetables in the _____.
____ 4. Restaurant customers are greeted at the _____.
____ 5. The restaurant's food supplies are in the _____.
____ 6. All new deliveries arrive at the _____.
____ 7. In some restaurants customers get their salads at the _____.

a. salad prep area
b. receiving area
c. host stand
d. cooking area
e. salad bar
f. storage room
g. baking area

EQUIPMENT, TOOLS, & OBJECTS

D WHAT'S THE ITEM?

_d_ 1. baking   a. spoon
____ 2. slotted   b. mitt
____ 3. measuring   c. scraper
____ 4. dough   d. pan
____ 5. oven   e. cup

____ 6. condiment   f. hood
____ 7. exhaust   g. tips
____ 8. deep fryer   h. board
____ 9. cutting   i. tray
____ 10. icing   j. basket

WORKPLACE ACTIONS

E WHAT'S THE ACTION?

| boil | broil | check | decorate | greet | load | replenish | resolve | supervise | weigh |

1. Remember to always smile when you _____ **greet** _____ the customers.

2. Be careful with the glasses when you _____ the dishwasher.

3. Alan, I think it's time to _____ the salad bar.

4. Here at the Plaza Café, we carefully _____ all the food preparation in our restaurant.

5. It's time to _____ the pasta and _____ the fish.

6. You need to carefully _____ all the food portions.

7. Please _____ the food supplies in the storage room.

8. Florence, how long do you think it will take to _____ all these cakes?

9. It's important to quickly _____ all customer complaints.

WORKPLACE COMMUNICATION

F WHAT ARE THEY SAYING?

_f_ 1. assign a task to an employee
____ 2. request that an employee help a co-worker
____ 3. ask for assistance
____ 4. offer to do something
____ 5. take a customer's order
____ 6. handle a customer's complaint
____ 7. give correction
____ 8. ask for feedback
____ 9. respond to feedback

a. "What seems to be the problem?"

b. "I see we're running low on Italian dressing. I'll take care of it."

c. "You aren't icing the cake the right way."

d. "Would you please help Victor cut up the vegetables?"

e. "Am I dishing out the food portions correctly?"

f. "Please mop the floor near the dishwasher."

g. "You're right. Thanks for pointing that out."

h. "May I take your order?"

i. "Could you give me a hand?"

1 tree trimmer
2 pesticide handler
3 landscape worker
4 window washer
5 heating & air conditioning (HVAC) mechanic/technician

6 grounds maintenance supervisor
7 grounds maintenance worker
8 landscape supervisor

a HVAC equipment
b walkway
c lawn
d landscaped bed
e trash receptacle
f hedges

g window washing scaffolding/ hanging scaffold
h power washer
i ride-on lawnmower

j cherry picker/ aerial platform
k utility vehicle
l roller
m sod
n office park

What occupations do you see in this office park?
What workplace objects and equipment do you see?

What are key differences between office parks like this and office buildings in the centers of cities?

9 office cleaner/office cleaning worker
10 custodian
11 security person
12 head custodian
13 cleaning supervisor

a office building
b carpet extractor
c carpeted floor
d tiled floor
e floor buffer/floor polishing machine

f employee lounge
g workstation
h office
i desk
j step ladder

k storage room
l boiler room
m platform utility cart
n dumpster

In your opinion, what are some pros and cons of working during the day and working at night?

1 prune trees and shrubs
2 fertilize
3 trim hedges
4 plant shrubbery
5 wash/clean windows
6 spray pesticides
7 clean walkways
8 maintain HVAC equipment
9 mow the lawn
10 trim edges (of lawns)
11 lay sod
12 supervise landscape workers
13 pick up litter
14 supervise grounds maintenance workers
15 remove debris
16 change light bulbs

Look at pages 30 and 31. What are the workers doing? Describe their actions.

17 sweep the floor
18 wet mop the floor
19 dry mop the floor
20 polish/buff the floor

21 vacuum
22 shampoo carpets
23 wipe down walls
24 dust

25 remove trash
26 empty trash
27 change fluorescent ceiling lights
28 change filters

29 do repairs
30 move furniture
31 maintain building security
32 supervise cleaning workers

1 broadcast spreader
2 pole pruner
3 pruning saw
4 safety glasses
5 spray respirator/ mask

6 landscape/work gloves
7 hedge trimmer
8 pump sprayer
9 wheelbarrow
10 safety harness

11 litter stick
12 draw hoe
13 square point shovel
14 round point shovel
15 power edger

16 squeegee
17 window washer mop
18 clamp meter

Look at pages 30–33. What equipment, tools, and objects do you see?

19 upright vacuum
20 fluorescent light/tube
21 floor hazard sign/
   floor safety sign
22 mop bucket and wringer

23 wet mop
24 dry mop/dust mop
25 duster
26 push broom
27 sponge

28 cleaning bucket
29 cleaning supplies
30 cleaning gloves
31 furnace filter
32 wastebasket

33 trash cart
34 trash bag
35 tool box
36 tools

1 A Supervisor & a Landscape Worker

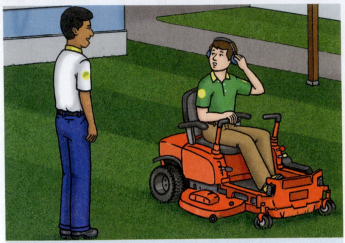

A supervisor is making a request.

A. Did you mow around Building Five yet?
B. No. Not yet.
A. Please make sure you do it before your shift ends.
B. I will.

2 A Grounds Maintenance Worker & a Supervisor

A worker is making a suggestion.

A. I think we need an additional trash receptacle in this area.
B. That's a good suggestion. Where do you think we should put it?
A. I'd put it between Building One and Building Two.

3 Two HVAC Technicians

Two HVAC technicians are troubleshooting a problem.

A. I think I figured out the problem with the AC unit.
B. What's wrong with it?
A. The compressor has burned out.
B. Okay. We'll need to order a new one.

4 A Landscape Worker & an Office Worker

A landscape worker is warning someone about a trip hazard.

A. Excuse me. Please watch your step! I don't want you to trip.
B. Thanks.
A. You're welcome.

1 You're a grounds maintenance supervisor. Ask a landscape worker to do something.
2 You're a grounds maintenance worker. Suggest something to your supervisor.
3 Are you good at troubleshooting? Tell about a problem you could or couldn't figure out.
4 What are some hazards in different kinds of workplaces?

5 Two Co-Workers

A co-worker is offering assistance.

A. Can I help you with those boxes?
B. Sure. That would be great. I have to recycle them.
A. Let me give you a hand.
B. Thanks. I appreciate that.

6 Two Co-Workers

A co-worker is pointing out a repair problem.

A. I think you need to check the women's restroom on the third floor.
B. Oh? What's the problem?
A. One of the toilets is leaking.
B. Okay. I'll take care of it. Thanks for letting me know.

7 A Cleaning Worker & an Office Worker

A cleaning worker is asking if it's okay to work in an area.

A. Excuse me. Will it disturb you if I vacuum here now?
B. Actually, could you do this area later? I'm working late tonight to finish a report.
A. Sure. I'll come back in about an hour.

8 A Cleaning Supervisor & a Cleaning Crew

A cleaning supervisor is describing tasks to employees at the beginning of a shift.

A. Okay. Tonight we're shampooing the carpeting on the second floor, and we're polishing the floors in all the employee lounges. Any questions?
B. Yes. Where's Rosa?
A. She called in sick.

---

5 What materials do you recycle at home and at work?

6 Tell about repair problems that happened where you live or where you work.

7 You're the cleaning worker in this situation, but you can't come back later. Imagine a conversation.

8 Rosa called in sick. What are some other good reasons to have to miss work?

A   HOW TO FERTILIZE A LAWN

1 Place soil samples in a bag.
2 Send the samples to a testing lab.
3 Evaluate the test results.
4 Select the proper grade of fertilizer.

5 Wait for a day with no wind or heavy rain.
6 Make sure the soil is moist.
7 Put fertilizer in the broadcast spreader.

8 Begin spreading around the perimeter of the area.
9 Then spread over the area going north and south.
10 Finally, spread over the area going east and west.

B   HOW TO LAY SOD

1 Remove all weeds and stones from the area.
2 Apply a starter fertilizer.
3 Rake the soil bed so it's smooth and level.
4 Unroll a strip of sod gently and lay out the first row in a straight line.
5 Lay out a second strip of sod so its end tightly abuts the first strip.

6 Lay out additional rows so that end seams in one row are in the center of strips in the previous row.
7 Fill in any gaps with loose soil.
8 Go over the sod with a roller.
9 Water the lawn every day for the first three weeks and then every other day for the next three weeks.

C HOW TO BUFF FLOORS

1 Place floor hazard signs near the area to be buffed.
2 Dry mop the area before buffing.
3 Spray the buff spray in the area that you will buff.

4 Place the buffer pad under the floor polishing machine.
5 Start buffing along the baseboards that are at the farthest corner of the area.
6 Buff the floor with a side-to-side motion in strokes of about ten feet.

7 As you keep buffing, move backward and overlap the strokes.
8 After you finish buffing, use a dry mop to pick up any dust that is left behind.
9 Clean your equipment.

D HOW TO REPLACE A FURNACE FILTER

1 Shut off the furnace using the emergency shut-off switch.
2 Vacuum the area around the furnace.
3 Open the furnace filter compartment.

4 Slide out the filter from its holding chamber.
5 Hold up the filter to a light to determine if it's dirty or clogged and needs to be replaced.
6 Vacuum out the filter channel to remove any dirt.

7 Locate the arrows on the new filter.
8 Insert the new filter in the direction of the air flow.
9 Replace the compartment cover.
10 Turn the furnace back on.

1 Two Co-Workers

An employee is giving helpful advice to a co-worker.

A. I think these bushes are a little too close together.
B. Hmm. Do you think I should plant them farther apart?
A. Yes. That would look better.

2 An Employee & a Supervisor

An employee is asking a supervisor for feedback.

A. Am I laying out this sod okay?
B. Actually, you're leaving gaps between the strips. Try to lay them out tighter.
A. Okay.

3 A Supervisor & an Employee

A supervisor is giving correction to an employee.

A. You missed a spot!
B. Oh? Where?
A. There. Next to the vending machine.
B. Thanks for telling me.

4 A New Employee & a Co-Worker

A new employee is asking a co-worker for feedback.

A. Do you think I put too much soap in the water?
B. Definitely! The soap is really concentrated. You don't have to use a lot.
A. That's what I thought.

---

1 You're a grounds maintenance worker. Give some helpful advice to a co-worker.

2 You're a grounds maintenance supervisor. Tell one of your employees to do something better.

3 You're a cleaning supervisor. Give correction to an employee.

4 You're a new office cleaning worker. Ask a co-worker for feedback.

OCCUPATIONS

cleaning crew
cleaning supervisor
cleaning worker
custodian
grounds maintenance supervisor

grounds maintenance worker
head custodian
heating & air conditioning (HVAC) mechanic/ technician
landscape supervisor
landscape worker

office cleaner/ office cleaning worker
pesticide handler
security person
tree trimmer
window washer

WORKPLACE LOCATIONS

boiler room
employee lounge
landscaped bed
lawn
office
office building

office park
storage room
testing lab
walkway
workstation

EQUIPMENT, TOOLS, & OBJECTS

air conditioning unit/ AC unit
broadcast spreader
buff spray
buffer pad
carpet extractor
carpeted floor
cherry picker/aerial platform
clamp meter
cleaning bucket
cleaning gloves
cleaning supplies
compartment cover
compressor
debris
draw hoe
dry mop
dumpster

duster
emergency shut-off switch
fertilizer
filter
filter channel
floor buffer/floor polishing machine
floor hazard sign/ floor safety sign
fluorescent ceiling light
fluorescent light/ tube
furnace
furnace filter
furnace filter compartment
hedges

hedge trimmer
holding chamber
HVAC equipment
landscape/work gloves
light bulb
litter
litter stick
mop
mop bucket and wringer
pesticide
platform utility cart
pole pruner
power edger
power washer
pruning saw
pump sprayer
push broom

ride-on lawnmower
roller
round point shovel
safety glasses
safety harness
shrubs/shrubbery
sod
soil bed
soil sample
sponge
spray respirator/ mask
square point shovel
squeegee
starter fertilizer
step ladder
tiled floor
tool box

tools
trash
trash bag
trash cart
trash receptacle
upright vacuum
utility vehicle
wastebasket
weeds
wet mop
wheelbarrow
window washer mop
window washing scaffolding/ hanging scaffolding

WORKPLACE ACTIONS

change filters
change fluorescent ceiling lights
change lightbulbs
clean walkways
do repairs
dry mop a floor
dust
empty trash

fertilize
lay sod
maintain building security
maintain HVAC equipment
move furniture
mow a lawn
pick up litter
plant shrubbery
polish/buff a floor

prune trees and shrubs
remove debris
remove trash
shampoo carpets
spray pesticides
supervise cleaning workers
supervise grounds maintenance workers

supervise landscape workers
sweep a floor
trim edges (of lawns)
trim hedges
vacuum
wash/clean windows
wet mop a floor
wipe down walls

WORKPLACE COMMUNICATION

ask a co-worker for feedback
ask a supervisor for feedback
give advice to a co-worker
give correction to an employee

give instructions
make a request
make a suggestion
offer assistance

point out a problem
troubleshoot a problem
warn a co-worker about a safety hazard

OCCUPATIONS

A WHAT ARE THEIR JOBS?

cleaning supervisor	grounds maintenance worker	landscape supervisor	security person	window washer
custodian	HVAC mechanic	pesticide handler	tree trimmer	

1. A _____landscape supervisor_____ is in charge of all the landscape workers.

2. A _____ cuts and trims trees.

3. A _____ cleans buildings and does minor repairs.

4. A _____ takes care of lawns, trees, flowers, and shrubs.

5. A _____ takes care of insects and other pests.

6. A _____ washes and cleans windows.

7. A _____ guards buildings.

8. An _____ installs and repairs heating and air conditioning systems.

9. A _____ is in charge of office cleaning workers.

WORKPLACE LOCATIONS

B WHAT'S THE LOCATION?

___e___ 1. The furnace is in the _____.   **a.** employee lounge

_____ 2. Workers take their breaks in the _____.   **b.** landscape bed

_____ 3. We're going to plant more flowers in each _____.   **c.** testing lab

_____ 4. We keep supplies in the _____.   **d.** lawn

_____ 5. Landscape workers take care of the _____.   **e.** boiler room

_____ 6. We need to send these soil samples to the _____.   **f.** storage room

EQUIPMENT, TOOLS, & OBJECTS

C WHAT'S THE ITEM?

___f___ 1. push   **a.** pruner   _____ 10. cleaning   **j.** sprayer

_____ 2. broadcast   **b.** fertilizer   _____ 11. floor hazard   **k.** washer

_____ 3. wet   **c.** spreader   _____ 12. upright   **l.** bucket

_____ 4. pole   **d.** harness   _____ 13. pump   **m.** ladder

_____ 5. hedge   **e.** receptacle   _____ 14. ride-on   **n.** pad

_____ 6. trash   **f.** broom   _____ 15. step   **o.** vacuum

_____ 7. safety   **g.** trimmer   _____ 16. power   **p.** filter

_____ 8. floor   **h.** mop   _____ 17. furnace   **q.** sign

_____ 9. starter   **i.** buffer   _____ 18. buffer   **r.** lawnmower

WORKPLACE ACTIONS

D WHAT'S THE ACTION?

_f_ 1. spray   **a.** the lawn

____ 2. remove   **b.** the floor

____ 3. lay   **c.** debris

____ 4. mow   **d.** shrubbery

____ 5. plant   **e.** walls

____ 6. polish   **f.** pesticides

____ 7. empty   **g.** sod

____ 8. wipe down   **h.** trash

____ 9. change   **i.** the carpet

____ 10. prune   **j.** workers

____ 11. shampoo   **k.** lightbulbs

____ 12. maintain   **l.** furniture

____ 13. dry mop   **m.** litter

____ 14. supervise   **n.** shrubs

____ 15. pick up   **o.** security

____ 16. move   **p.** the floor

E WHICH ACTION DOESN'T BELONG?

1. fertilize   mow   (change)   trim

2. empty trash   do repairs   remove debris   pick up litter

3. dry mop   mow   sweep   polish

4. fertilize   clean walkways   shampoo carpets   wash windows

5. prune trees   trim hedges   maintain HVAC equipment   trim edges

6. lay sod   clean walkways   prune shrubs   shampoo carpets

7. buff the floor   change ceiling lights   plant shrubbery   move furniture

8. spray pesticides   pick up litter   wet mop the floor   shampoo carpets

WORKPLACE COMMUNICATION

F WHAT ARE THEY SAYING?

_l_ 1. make a request   **a.** "I think I figured out the problem with the AC unit."

____ 2. make a suggestion   **b.** "Will it disturb you if I vacuum here now?"

____ 3. troubleshoot a problem   **c.** "Can I help you with those boxes?"

____ 4. warn someone   **d.** "Thanks for telling me."

____ 5. offer assistance   **e.** "Am I laying out this sod okay?"

____ 6. point out a problem   **f.** "I think we need an additional trash receptacle in this area."

____ 7. ask if it's okay to do something   **g.** "Do you think I should plant these bushes farther apart?"

____ 8. describe a task   **h.** "Please watch your step!"

____ 9. ask for advice   **i.** "You missed a spot!"

____ 10. ask for feedback   **j.** "Tonight we're shampooing the carpeting on the second floor."

____ 11. give correction   **k.** "One of the toilets is leaking."

____ 12. respond to feedback   **l.** "Please make sure you mow around Building Five before your shift ends."

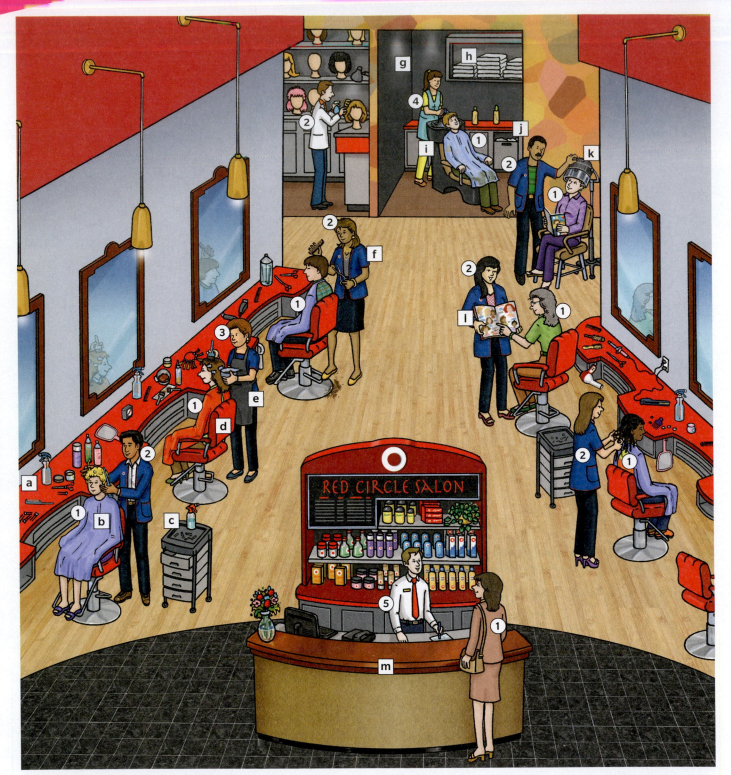

RED CIRCLE SALON

1 client/customer	**a** stylist station	**f** smock	**j** towel bin
2 hair stylist	**b** cape	**g** shampooing area	**k** standing hair dryer
3 colorist	**c** hair trolley	**h** towels	**l** sample book
4 assistant/shampooist	**d** salon chair	**i** shampoo bowl and chair	**m** check-in counter/ reception area
5 salon manager	**e** colorist apron		

What occupations do you see in this hair salon, nail salon, and spa? What workplace objects and equipment do you see?

Are there businesses like this in your community?

6 manicurist	**n** manicurist station	**s** wax heater	**x** makeup chair
7 esthetician	**o** manicure lamp	**t** spa area	**y** pedicurist stool
8 masseur/masseuse/ massage therapist	**p** arm rest	**u** makeup mirror	**z** pedicure spa chair
9 makeup artist	**q** nail UV* lamp dryer	**v** makeup bib	
10 pedicurist	**r** massage table	**w** brush and tool apron	
11 receptionist			

* UV = ultraviolet

1 consult with a client
2 show different hairstyles
3 shampoo hair
4 rinse hair

5 do pin curls
6 cut hair
7 trim hair
8 disinfect implements

9 comb hair
10 blow dry hair
11 brush out hair
12 select a color

13 mix a color
14 apply color
15 braid hair
16 style a hairpiece/wig

Look at pages 44 and 45. What are the workers doing? Describe their actions.

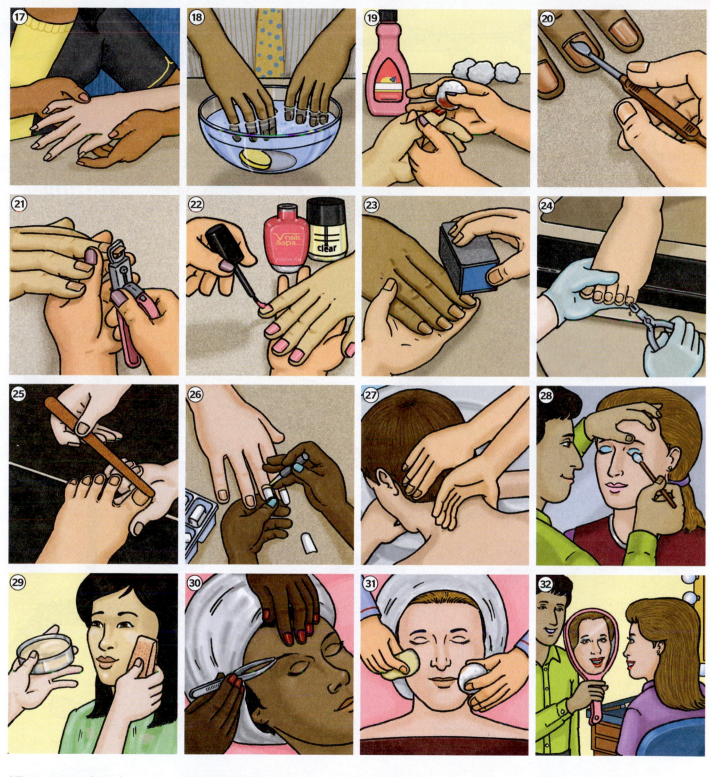

17 massage hands
18 soak fingers
19 remove nail polish
20 push back cuticles

21 trim nails
22 apply a base coat
23 buff nails
24 clip toenails

25 file nails
26 glue on artificial nails
27 massage neck
28 apply eye shadow

29 blend makeup
30 pluck eyebrows
31 cleanse skin
32 show finished makeup

1 shears/scissors
2 thinning shears
3 rat tail comb
4 styling comb
5 electric clipper
6 comb attachment

7 hair dryer
8 disinfectant jar
9 wig
10 wig stand
11 wig comb
12 hair pik
13 curling iron

14 straightening iron
15 standing hair dryer
16 sculpting brush
17 radial brush
18 mixing brush
19 mixing bowl
20 handheld mirror

21 salon timer
22 spray bottle
23 bobby pin
24 pin-curl clip
25 perm rod

Look at pages 44–47. What equipment, tools, and objects do you see?

26 nail clipper	**31** manicure scissors	**38** acetone	**45** eyelash and eyebrow comb
27 acrylic nail clipper	**32** orange stick	**39** nail polish	**46** blending brush
28 cuticle pusher	**33** foot file	**40** lipstick	**47** foundation brush
29 tweezers	**34** buffing block	**41** eyeliner	**48** mascara
30 nippers	**35** pumice rock	**42** electric nail drill	**49** wax heater
	36 callus shaver	**43** foundation sponge	**50** massage stone warmer
	37 toe spacers	**44** fan brush	**51** massage stones

1 **A Hair Stylist & a Client**

A hair stylist is asking a client how she wants her hair done.

A. How would you like your hair done today?
B. I'm not sure. I think I'd like it a little shorter than usual.
A. Okay. I can also curl your hair to add some body to it.
B. That sounds good.

2 **A Hair Stylist & an Assistant**

A hair stylist is checking on an assistant's progress.

A. Are you almost finished?
B. Yes. I'll be done in a minute or two.
A. Great. When you're through, can you bring him over to my station?
B. Sure.

3 **A Hair Stylist & a Client**

A hair stylist is asking a client for feedback.

A. How do you like the highlights?
B. I like them a lot. What do *you* think?
A. They're the perfect color for your complexion.
B. How long should I wait to wash my hair?
A. You shouldn't shampoo for at least 24 hours.

4 **A Hair Stylist & a Co-Worker**

A hair stylist is asking to borrow an item.

A. Have you seen my 5-inch styling shears?
B. No, I haven't.
A. Hmm. I can't seem to find them. Can I borrow yours?
B. Sure. Here you are!

1 You're a hair stylist. Ask what your client would like and make a suggestion.
2 This hair salon has both male and female clients. Where do women and men have their hair done where you live?
3 You're a hair stylist. Ask your client for feedback.
4 You're a hair stylist. You can't find an item you need. Ask to borrow a co-worker's.

5 A Manicurist & a Client

A manicurist is giving instructions to a client.

A. Just soak your fingers for a few minutes.
B. A few minutes?
A. Yes. Then I'll be able to push back and trim your cuticles.
B. Okay.

6 A Makeup Artist & a Client

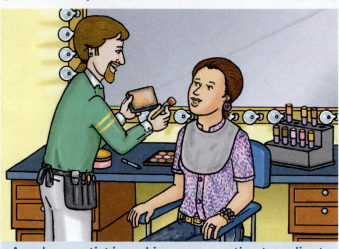

A makeup artist is making a suggestion to a client.

A. I'm going to highlight your cheekbones. Okay?
B. Yes. Will you also darken my eyes?
A. Honestly, I think a midtone may look better on you.
B. Okay. I trust your advice.

7 A Manicurist & the Salon Manager

An employee is reporting a supply shortage.

A. It looks like we're running low on acetone.
B. Did you check the supply closet?
A. Yes. There's only one container left.
B. I'll call our supplier and order some more.

8 A Manicurist & a Client

A manicurist is asking a client for feedback.

A. How do you like this shade of red?
B. It's awesome! What's it called?
A. "Mystery Red." It's one of my favorites.
B. I love it!

---

5 You're a manicurist. Give instructions to a client.

6 You're a makeup artist. Make a suggestion to a client.

7 Acetone and other salon chemicals are hazardous to breathe. How can salon workers protect themselves?

8 Brainstorm names for some nail polish colors. Be creative!

A HOW TO DO PIN CURLS

1 Apply mousse to hair.
2 Comb out hair.
3 Section hair into one-inch sections using a rat tail comb.
4 Twist each hair section from the end to the root.

5 Wind the twisted hair around your finger.
6 Place the curl close to the head.
7 Secure the curl with a pin-curl clip.

8 Do more pin curls and let them set.
9 Remove the pin-curl clips.
10 Brush out hair for an all-over wavy effect.

B HOW TO COLOR HAIR

1 Help the client choose a hair color.
2 Mix the hair color and developer.
3 Apply a base protectant around the hairline.

4 Section hair into four sections.
5 Apply color with a brush.
6 Apply color to roots.
7 Blend color at the color line.

8 Shampoo, condition, and rinse hair.
9 Dry hair with a towel.

C HOW TO GIVE A MANICURE

1 Remove the old nail polish.
2 Shape the nails.
3 Soak the nails to soften the cuticles.

4 Push back the cuticles.
5 Trim the cuticles.
6 Buff the nails.

7 Apply a base coat.
8 Apply two coats of nail polish.
9 Apply a top coat.

D HOW TO APPLY ACRYLIC NAIL TIPS

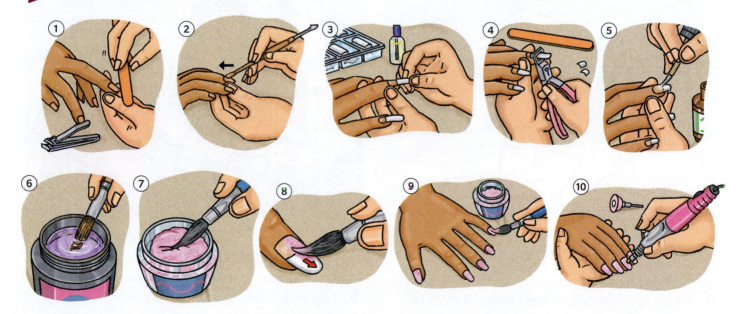

1 Trim and file the nails.
2 Push back the cuticles.
3 Choose and apply acrylic nail tips.
4 Clip and file the tips to the desired length.

5 Apply primer to the natural nail.
6 Dip a brush into monomer.
7 Shape the brush and draw it through acrylic powder.

8 Brush from the center of a nail to the tip.
9 Repeat this procedure on all nails.
10 File down and buff the acrylics before painting.

1 A Hair Stylist & a Client

A hair stylist is asking a client for feedback.

A. How do you like the length in the back?
B. Actually, I think it could be a little shorter.
A. A little shorter? Okay.
B. Thanks.

2 A Hair Stylist & an Assistant

A hair stylist is correcting an assistant's work.

A. I don't think you're rinsing sufficiently.
B. Oh, really?
A. Yes. There still seems to be some shampoo left over.
B. Oh. I'm sorry. I'll be sure to rinse more thoroughly from now on. Thanks for letting me know.

3 A Client & a Massage Therapist

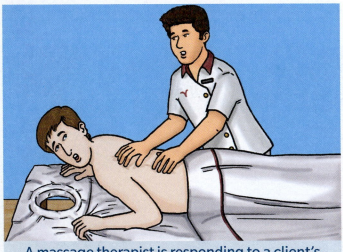

A massage therapist is responding to a client's complaint.

A. Ouch! That hurts!
B. Sorry. You're very tight right here. I'll try to be more gentle.
A. Thanks. I'd appreciate that.

4 A Salon Manager & a Hair Colorist

A salon manager is checking on a colorist's work.

A. That's a very unusual combination of colors!
B. I agree, but this is what she requested.
A. Okay. I just wanted to make sure.

1 You're a hair stylist. Your client isn't satisfied. Imagine a conversation.
2 The assistant apologizes for a mistake, makes a promise, and says "thank you." Why is this important?
3 What are the health benefits of a massage?
4 What is the most unusual hairstyle or color you have ever seen?

OCCUPATIONS

assistant/shampooist
colorist
esthetician
hair stylist
makeup artist

manicurist
masseur/masseuse/massage therapist
receptionist
salon manager

WORKPLACE LOCATIONS

check-in counter/reception area
manicurist station
shampooing area
spa area
stylist station
supply closet

EQUIPMENT, TOOLS, & OBJECTS

acetone
acrylic nail clipper
acrylic nail tips
acrylic powder
arm rest
artificial nails
base coat
blending brush
bobby pin
brush and tool apron
buffing block
cape
colorist apron
comb attachment
corn cutter
curling iron
cuticle
cuticle pusher

disinfectant jar
dust away brush
electric clipper
electric nail drill
eye shadow
eyelash comb
eyeliner
foot file
foundation brush
foundation sponge
hair dryer
hair pik
hair straightener
hair trolley
hairpiece/wig
handheld mirror
lipstick
makeup

makeup bib
makeup chair
makeup mirror
manicure lamp
manicure scissors
mascara
massage stone warmer
massage stones
massage table
midtone
mixing bowl
mixing brush
monomer
mousse
nail clipper
nail polish
nail UV lamp dryer

nippers
orange stick
pedicure spa chair
pedicurist stool
perm rod
pin-curl clip
primer
pumice rock
radial brush
rat tail comb
salon chair
salon timer
sample book
sculpting brush
shampoo bowl and chair
shears/scissors

smock
spray bottle
standing hair dryer
styling comb
styling shears
thinning shears
toe spacers
top coat
towel bin
towels
tweezers
wax heater
wig
wig comb
wig stand

WORKPLACE ACTIONS

apply a base coat
apply color
apply eye shadow
blend makeup
blow dry hair
braid hair
brush out hair
buff nails

cleanse skin
clip toenails
comb hair
consult with a client
cut hair
disinfect implements
do pin curls
file nails

glue on artificial nails
massage hands
massage neck
mix a color
pluck eyebrows
push cuticles back
remove nail polish
rinse hair

select a color
shampoo hair
show different hairstyles
show finished makeup
soak fingers
style a hairpiece/wig
trim hair
trim nails

WORKPLACE COMMUNICATION

ask a client for feedback
ask a client's preference
ask to borrow an item
check on a co-worker's performance

check on an assistant's progress
correct an assistant's work
discuss options with a client

give instructions to a client
report a supply shortage
respond to a client's complaint

OCCUPATIONS

A WHAT ARE THEIR JOBS?

colorist	hair stylist	manicurist	receptionist	shampooist
esthetician	makeup artist	massage therapist	salon manager	

1. An _____ **esthetician** _____ treats people's faces.
2. A _____ is in charge of a salon.
3. A _____ cuts people's hair.
4. A _____ washes people's hair.
5. A _____ greets clients and books appointments.
6. A _____ cuts, paints, and polishes people's nails.
7. A _____ dyes people's hair.
8. A _____ applies cosmetics to people's faces.
9. A _____ works on people's muscles.

WORKPLACE LOCATIONS

B WHAT'S THE LOCATION?

_c_ 1. When you arrive at the salon, go to the _____.   a. spa area

____ 2. Marc will wash your hair in the _____.   b. stylist station

____ 3. Nikki cuts people's nails. She works at a _____.   c. check-in counter

____ 4. If you're here for a massage, you need to go to the _____. d. supply closet

____ 5. Marissa cuts people's hair. She works at a _____.   e. shampooing area

____ 6. We keep all of our beauty supplies in the _____.   f. manicurist station

EQUIPMENT, TOOLS, & OBJECTS

C WHAT'S THE CATEGORY?

1. nippers   thinning shears   nail clipper   These are all used for _____ **cutting** _____.
2. sculpting   radial   mixing   These are types of _____.
3. rat tail   styling   wig   These are types of _____.
4. hair dryer   curling iron   electric clipper   You need to _____ these items.
5. foot file   callus shaver   toe spacers   These are all used on people's _____.
6. perm rod   bobby pin   pin-curl clip   These are all used on people's _____.
7. foundation sponge   foundation brush   blending brush   These are _____ implements.

WORKPLACE ACTIONS

D COSMETOLOGY *IN ACTION!*

1. I'm going to apply _____.
a. your neck
b. a base coat
c. a mirror
d. your hair

2. Can you _____ my hair?
a. blow dry
b. mix
c. consult with
d. buff

3. I need to _____ your makeup.
a. glue on
b. push back
c. trim
d. blend

4. I'd like to braid your _____.
a. neck
b. nails
c. hair
d. nail polish

5. I'm going to _____ your nails.
a. consult with
b. buff
c. style
d. remove

6. I need to _____ your skin.
a. cleanse
b. glue on
c. apply
d. comb

7. I'm going to _____ your toenails.
a. blow dry
b. clip
c. brush out
d. mix

8. Please _____ these implements.
a. disinfect
b. trim
c. cut
d. style

9. Can you _____ pin curls?
a. show
b. rinse
c. do
d. select

10. I'm going to file your _____.
a. nails
b. neck
c. toes
d. hair

11. Please _____ my neck.
a. brush
b. massage
c. mix
d. remove

12. I need to _____ your nails.
a. pluck
b. shampoo
c. trim
d. comb

13. Can you _____ my eyebrows?
a. pluck
b. select
c. push
d. buff

14. I'm going to glue on _____.
a. your head
b. artificial nails
c. nail polish
d. mascara

15. I need to _____ your fingers.
a. cut
b. file
c. soak
d. trim

WORKPLACE COMMUNICATION

E WHAT ARE THEY SAYING?

_f_ **1.** ask a client's preference

____ **2.** check on a co-worker's progress

____ **3.** ask to borrow an item

____ **4.** give instructions to a client

____ **5.** make a suggestion

____ **6.** report a supply shortage

____ **7.** ask a client for feedback

____ **8.** respond to a client's complaint

____ **9.** give correction

a. "How do you like this shade of red?"

b. "Honestly, I think a midtone may look better on you."

c. "Just soak your fingers for a few minutes."

d. "Are you almost finished?"

e. "I don't think you're rinsing sufficiently."

f. "How would you like your hair done today?"

g. "Sorry. I'll try to be more gentle."

h. "Can I borrow your styling shears?"

i. "It looks like we're running low on acetone."

1 receiving clerk
2 distribution clerk
3 bench assembler
4 welder
5 fabricator
6 paint robot operator
7 pinstripe artist

8 shop floor assistant
9 factory line assembler
10 quality control inspector
11 factory line supervisor
12 quality control tester
13 packing clerk
14 shipping clerk

a shipping crate
b parts rack
c engine
d workbench
e jig
f paint booth
g articulated paint robot

h paint robot controller
i suspended conveyor rack
j C-hook
k parts cart
l hydraulic assist machine

m mobile production bench
n dynamometer
o hoist
p shipping box
q rolling conveyor

What departments do you see in this motorcycle factory? What occupations do you see in each department? What workplace objects do you see?

15 technical engineer
16 distribution clerk
17 electronics assembler
18 assembler

19 quality control sampler
20 hand packer
21 factory helper

r technical drawings/specs
s utility cart
t clean room
u airlock
v production line

w assembly line conveyor belt
x quality control checkpoint
y packing area
z shipping box

What occupations do you see in this electronics assembly plant? What workplace objects do you see?

What are some similarities and differences between these two manufacturing settings?

1 unload a crate from a truck
2 move materials/parts
3 grind an engine part
4 seal a gasket
5 bend tubing
6 weld frame pieces
7 paint a gas tank
8 pinstripe a gas tank
9 move a rear assembly, using an assist machine
10 attach a front wheel
11 bring finished parts to the production floor
12 tighten handlebars
13 organize fasteners
14 attach an exhaust
15 point out a safety issue
16 feel for imperfections

Look at pages 58 and 59. What are the workers doing? Describe their actions.

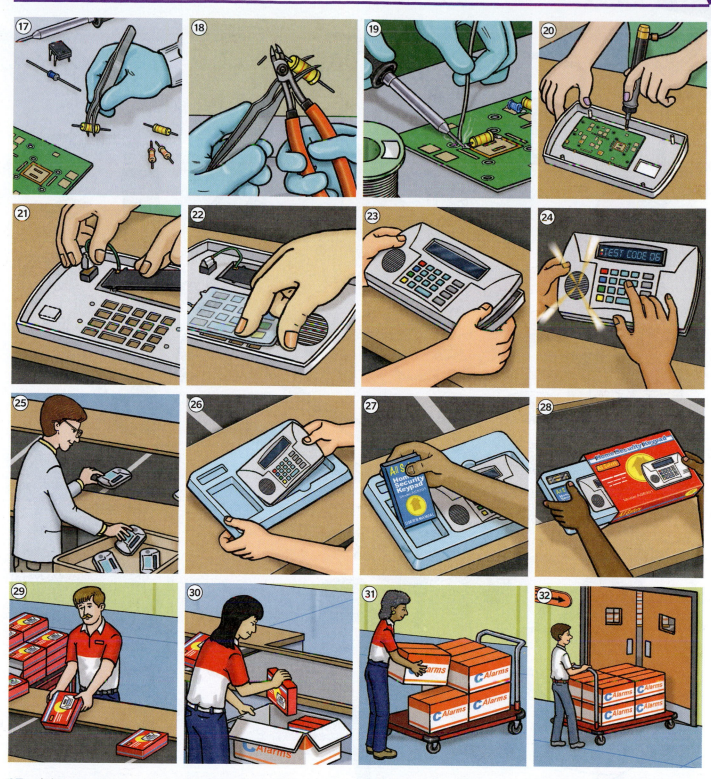

17 pick up a component
18 trim wires on a component
19 solder a component to a PCB*
20 screw a PCB into a casing bottom

21 attach an LCD* to a casing top
22 attach a keypad to a casing top
23 snap a cover onto the bottom of a casing
24 test a unit

25 put a defective unit in a bin
26 place a unit in a plastic packing tray
27 put an owner's manual into a tray
28 slide a tray into a product box

29 put a product box on the conveyor belt
30 put a product box into a shipping carton
31 put a shipping carton onto a cart
32 bring shipping cartons to the shipping department

* PCB = printed circuit board
  LCD = liquid crystal display

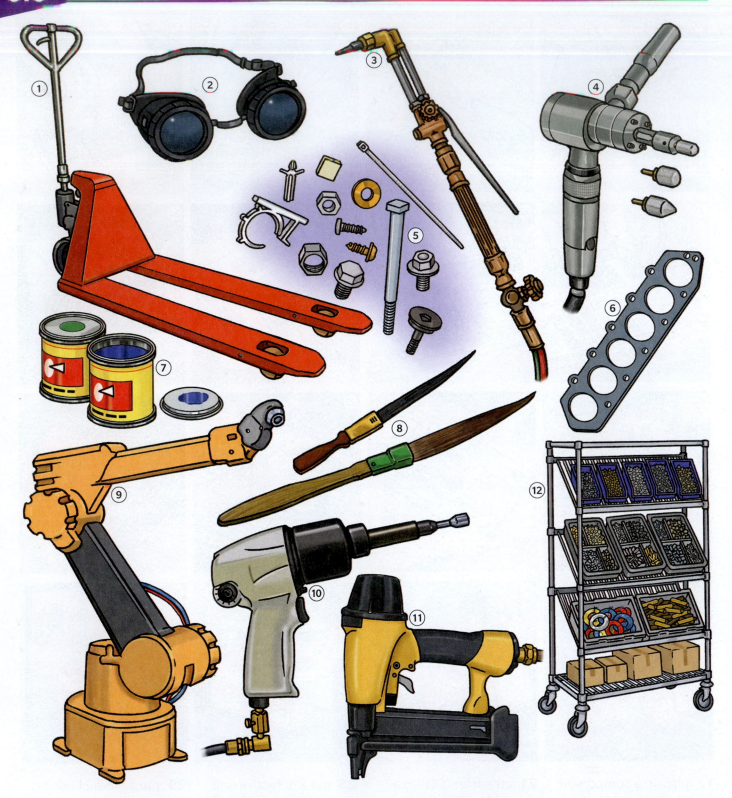

1 hydraulic pallet truck
2 welding goggles
3 acetylene torch

4 pneumatic hand grinder
5 fasteners
6 gasket
7 enamel paint

8 pinstripe brushes
9 articulated paint robot

10 pneumatic wrench
11 air stapler
12 parts dispensing cart

Look at pages 58–61. What equipment, tools, and objects do you see?

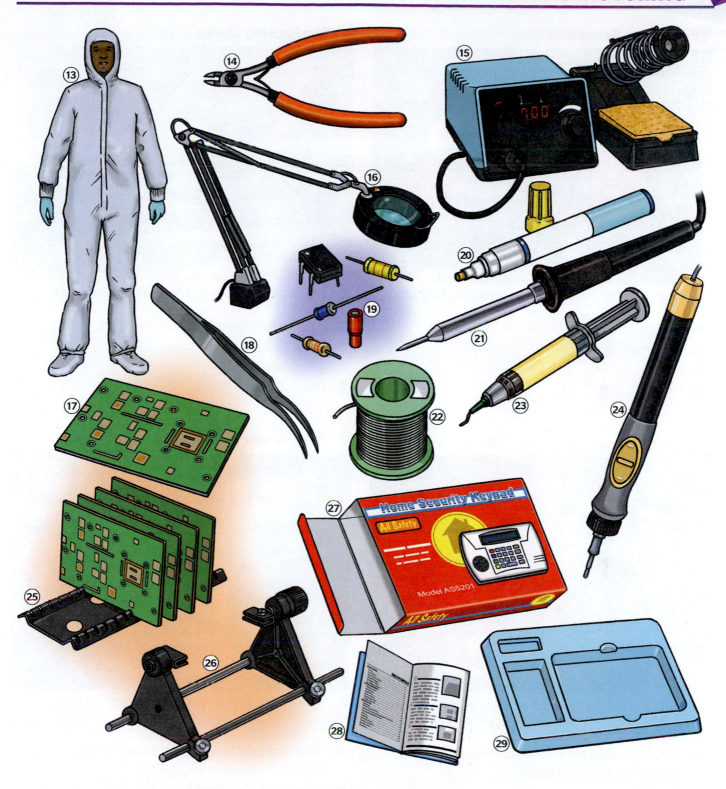

13 clean room suit
14 precision wire cutters
15 soldering station
16 inspection magnifier workbench lamp

17 PCB
18 precision tweezers
19 PCB components
20 liquid flux pen
21 soldering iron

22 solder lead
23 solder paste applicator
24 micro screwdriver
25 PCB rack
26 PCB holder

27 product box
28 user's manual
29 vacuum formed product tray

1 Two Line Assemblers

A line assembler is asking a co-worker for parts.

A. I'm out of one-inch bolts.
B. How many do you need?
A. I could use six.
B. Here you are!

2 Two Packing Clerks

Two packing clerks are working together.

A. Just move the bike a little to the right.
B. Is that okay?
A. Yes. Now lower it.
B. Okay. I'm lowering it.

3 A Supervisor & an Assembler

A supervisor is assigning an assembler to a different workstation.

A. Lorenzo called in sick today. Have you been trained on the paint robot?
B. Yes, I have.
A. Good. I'm going to reassign you to operate that system today.
B. Okay. No problem.

4 A Fabricator & a Supervisor

A fabricator is reporting an equipment malfunction.

A. There's a problem with the tube-bending machine. It's jamming.
B. Did you shut it down?
A. Yes. Right away.
B. Good. I'll write up a repair order.

---

1 You're a line assembler. You need some parts. Ask a co-worker.

2 You're a packing clerk. You and a co-worker are working together on a task. Give some instructions to your co-worker.

3 You're a supervisor. An employee is out sick. Reassign the person's work to somebody else.

4 You're a worker in this factory. Report an equipment problem.

5 A Supervisor & a New Employee

A supervisor is orienting a new employee.

A. Here's where you'll be working.
B. Is this the clean room?
A. Yes. Be sure to keep this door to the airlock entrance closed tightly.
B. I understand.

6 A Supervisor & an Electronics Assembler

A supervisor is checking on a worker's productivity.

A. When did you start your shift?
B. At three o'clock.
A. How many circuit boards have you finished?
B. I've completed twelve.

7 An Electronics Assembler & a Co-Worker

Two assemblers are noticing a problem.

A. Are you having trouble snapping in the circuit boards?
B. Yes, I am. They don't seem to fit correctly.
A. I'm having the same problem. We'd better let the supervisor know right away.

8 A Supervisor & a Quality Control Sampler

A supervisor is asking about quality control problems.

A. How many defective units have you found today?
B. Two.
A. What was wrong with them?
B. Some components weren't soldered correctly.

5 You're a supervisor. Give instructions to a new employee.

6 You're a supervisor. Check on a worker's punctuality and productivity.

7 You and a co-worker are noticing a problem. Discuss it.

8 You're a supervisor. Ask a worker about a quality control problem.

A HOW TO ASSEMBLE A MOTORCYCLE ENGINE

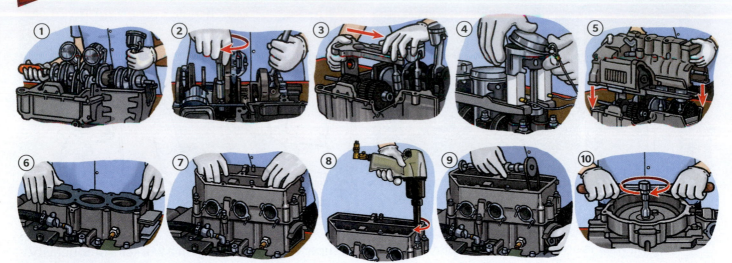

1 Fit the crankshaft and pistons into the engine block.
2 Tighten the bearings and caps.
3 Slide in the fork.
4 Compress the piston rings.

5 Install the other half of the engine block.
6 Place a gasket on top of the block.
7 Install the cylinder head.

8 Tighten the bolts to attach the cylinder head to the block assembly.
9 Install the camshaft in the cylinder head unit.
10 Rotate the crankshaft to fine-tune its action.

B HOW TO PREPARE A MOTORCYCLE FOR SHIPPING

1 Hook up the bike to the overhead hoist.
2 Raise the bike.
3 Remove the front wheel.
4 Move the bike to the packing area.

5 Lower the bike and secure it into the shipping base.
6 Put the front wheel into the shipping base.
7 Put the box supports in place.

8 Tie down the straps.
9 Cover the bike with an insulation blanket.
10 Put on the shipping box and attach the shipping labels.

C HOW TO DO PCB SURFACE MOUNT SOLDERING

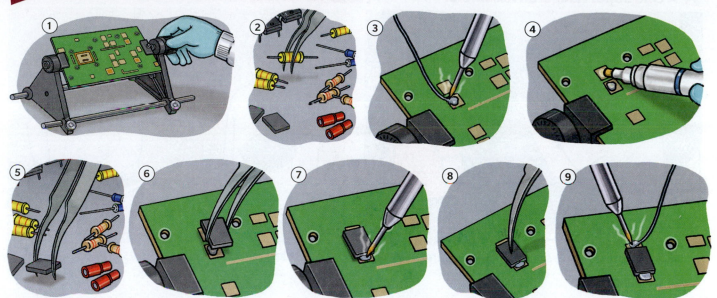

1 Place and adjust the PCB in the holder.
2 Sort the components to be used.
3 Apply a small bead of solder to a pad on the PCB.
4 Apply liquid flux to the solder bead and to the other pad for that component.
5 Start with the smallest and flattest component.
6 Place the component over the appropriate pad.
7 Heat the solder bead.
8 Position the component flush against the pad.
9 Solder the other end of the component.

D HOW TO DO A QUALITY CONTROL CHECK

1 Take the product off the conveyor belt.
2 Look for visual defects.
3 Feel the product to make sure there are no defects.
4 Open and close the front panel.
5 Test and listen for correct alert tones.
6 Check the lighted keypad.
7 Check the LCD display.
8 If okay, put it back on the conveyor belt for packaging.
9 If defective, put it in the proper bin.

1 A Line Supervisor & an Assembler

A line supervisor is correcting an assembler's work.

A. This fastener isn't attached correctly.
B. It isn't?
A. No, it isn't. Make sure to check them all.
B. Okay, I will.

2 An Electronics Assembler & a Co-Worker

A new electronics assembler is asking a co-worker for feedback.

A. Am I using the right amount of solder paste?
B. Yes. That looks good.
A. Thanks. I just wanted to make sure.
B. You're doing fine.

3 A Line Supervisor & a Pinstripe Artist

A line supervisor is giving feedback to a worker.

A. How are you doing with the new pinstriping brushes?
B. Okay, I think. How do these pinstripes look to you?
A. They look fine. You're doing a good job.
B. Thanks.

4 A New Assembler & a Co-Worker

A new assembler is asking a co-worker for feedback.

A. This keypad doesn't look right. Am I doing something wrong?
B. You didn't attach it correctly.
A. I can't. It won't fit in the casing.
B. That happens sometimes. Just put that part aside and report it.

1 You're a line supervisor. Give correction to an employee.
2 You're a new electronics assembler. Ask a co-worker for feedback.
3 You're a line supervisor. Check on an employee's work and give positive feedback.
4 You're a new assembler. Ask a co-worker for feedback.

OCCUPATIONS

assembler
bench assembler
distribution clerk
electronics
  assembler
fabricator
factory helper
factory line
  assembler

factory line
  supervisor
hand packer
packing clerk
paint robot
  operator
pinstripe artist
quality control
  inspector

quality control
  sampler
quality control
  tester
receiving clerk
shipping clerk
shop floor assistant
technical engineer
welder

WORKPLACE LOCATIONS

airlock
airlock entrance
bike assembly area
clean room
crating area
engine assembly
  area
fabrication area
packing area

paint booth
paint shop
production floor
production line
quality control
quality control
  checkpoint
receiving
shipping department

EQUIPMENT, TOOLS, & OBJECTS

acetylene torch
air stapler
alert tone
articulated paint
  robot
assembly line
  conveyor belt
assist machine
bearings
bin
bolt
C-hook
camshaft
caps
cart
casing
casing bottom
casing top
circuit board
clean room suit
component

cover
crankshaft
crate
cylinder head
cylinder head unit
defect
dynamometer
enamel paint
engine
engine block
engine part
exhaust
fasteners
finished parts
frame
front panel
front wheel
gas tank
gasket
handlebars
hoist

hydraulic assist
  machine
hydraulic pallet truck
inspection magnifier
  workbench lamp
insulation blanket
jig
keypad
LCD display
liquid flux pen
micro screwdriver
mobile production
  bench
overhead hoist
owner's manual
paint robot controller
parts cart
parts dispensing cart
parts rack
PCB (printed circuit
  board)

PCB components
PCB holder
PCB pad
PCB rack
pinstripe brushes
piston
piston ring
plastic packing
  tray
pneumatic hand
  grinder
pneumatic
  wrench
precision
  tweezers
precision wire
  cutters
product box
rear assembly
repair order
rolling conveyor

shipping box
shipping carton
shipping crate
shipping label
solder
solder bead
solder lead
solder paste
solder paste applicator
soldering iron
soldering station
suspended conveyor rack
technical drawings/specs
tray
tube-bending machine
tubing
user's manual
vacuum formed product tray
welding goggles
workbench

WORKPLACE ACTIONS

attach a front wheel
attach a keypad to a casing top
attach an exhaust
attach an LCD to a casing top
bend tubing
bring finished parts to a
  production floor
bring shipping cartons to a
  shipping department
feel for imperfections
grind an engine part

move a rear assembly,
  using an assist machine
move materials/parts
organize fasteners
paint a gas tank
pick up a component
pinstripe a gas tank
place a unit in a plastic
  packing tray
point out a safety issue
put a defective unit in a bin

put a product box
  into a shipping
  carton
put a product box
  on a conveyor belt
put a shipping
  carton onto a cart
put an owner's
  manual into a tray
screw a PCB into a
  casing bottom

seal a gasket
slide a tray into a product
  box
snap a cover onto the
  bottom of a casing
solder a component to a PCB
test a unit
tighten handlebars
trim wires on a component
unload a crate from a truck
weld frame pieces

WORKPLACE COMMUNICATION

ask a co-worker for feedback
ask a co-worker for parts
ask about quality control problems
assign a worker to a workstation

check on a worker's productivity
coordinate a task with a co-worker
correct someone's work
give feedback to a worker

orient a new employee
point out a problem
report an equipment malfunction

OCCUPATIONS

A WHAT ARE THEIR JOBS?

assembler	factory helper	packing clerk	quality control tester	technical engineer
distribution clerk	factory line supervisor	paint robot operator	receiving clerk	welder
fabricator	hand packer	pinstripe artist	shipping clerk	

1. A _____welder_____ welds pieces of metal together.
2. A _____ attaches metal parts that have been welded together.
3. A _____ packs and unpacks items in a factory.
4. A _____ supervises the manufacturing of products.
5. An _____ puts together parts of a product.
6. A _____ draws thin decorative lines.
7. A _____ operates a mechanical arm that paints items on an assembly line.
8. A _____ checks and unloads incoming shipments.
9. A _____ does a variety of non-skilled tasks on a production line.
10. A _____ keeps records of all items that are shipped from a factory.
11. A _____ checks to make sure a product has been made correctly.
12. A _____ brings incoming parts and materials to the appropriate workers in a factory.
13. A _____ puts different pieces of a product into its package before it's shipped.
14. A _____ handles technical issues related to the production of a product.

WORKPLACE LOCATIONS

B WHAT'S THE LOCATION?

_e_ 1. There is no dust or dirt in the factory's ____.
____ 2. Before you enter the clean room, you must go through the ____.
____ 3. The packing clerks work in the ____.
____ 4. Welders work in the ____.
____ 5. Assemblers work on the ____.
____ 6. Parts are put together in the ____.
____ 7. Pinstripe artists work in the ____.
____ 8. Parts are delivered to ____.
____ 9. Inspectors and testers work in ____.

a. shipping department
b. production line
c. quality control
d. paint booth
e. clean room
f. receiving
g. airlock
h. assembly area
i. fabrication area

EQUIPMENT, TOOLS, & OBJECTS

C WHAT'S THE ITEM?

_d_ 1. acetylene	a. bead	___ 6. casing	f. hoist	___ 11. shipping	k. screwdriver
___ 2. paint	b. ring	___ 7. overhead	g. wrench	___ 12. micro	l. goggles
___ 3. engine	c. robot	___ 8. PCB	h. bottom	___ 13. circuit	m. display
___ 4. piston	d. torch	___ 9. solder	i. pad	___ 14. LCD	n. board
___ 5. solder	e. block	___ 10. pneumatic	j. bead	___ 15. welding	o. crate

WORKPLACE ACTIONS

D MANUFACTURING IN ACTION!

attach   bend   put   seal   snap   solder   tighten   unload   weld

1. You need to _____ seal _____ this gasket.
2. Can you help me _____ this crate?
3. We need to _____ the handlebars.
4. I'm trying to _____ this front wheel to the car.
5. Next I'm going to _____ this component to a PCB.
6. You need to _____ this cover into a casing bottom.
7. Can you _____ these frame pieces?
8. You need to _____ this tubing.
9. This unit is defective. Be sure to _____ it into a bin.

WORKPLACE COMMUNICATION

E WHAT ARE THEY SAYING?

_e_ 1. ask a co-worker for parts
___ 2. coordinate a task with a co-worker
___ 3. assign a worker to a different workstation
___ 4. report an equipment malfunction
___ 5. orient a new employee
___ 6. check on a worker's productivity
___ 7. notice a parts assembly problem
___ 8. ask about quality control problems
___ 9. correct someone's work
___ 10. ask for feedback
___ 11. give feedback

a. "There's a problem with the tube-bending machine."
b. "Lorenzo called in sick. I'm going to reassign you."
c. "How many circuit boards have you finished?"
d. "How many defective units have you found today?"
e. "I'm out of one-inch bolts. I could use six."
f. "They don't seem to fit correctly."
g. "This fastener isn't attached correctly."
h. "Am I using the right amount of solder paste?"
i. "Here's where you'll be working."
j. "The pinstripes look fine. You're doing a good job."
k. "Just move the bike a little to the right. Now lower it."

1 roofer
2 skylight installer
3 brickmason
4 HVAC technician
5 construction laborer

6 carpenter
7 carpenter's helper
8 blockmason
9 blockmason apprentice
10 glazier

a plywood
b tar paper
c bricks
d fascia board
e ductwork

f shingles
g OSB*
h extension ladder
i sawhorse

j framed wall/ wall studs
k concrete slab
l concrete block
m wheelbarrow

* OSB = oriented strand board

What occupations do you see at this construction site?
What workplace objects do you see?

Is there any new home construction in your community? Where?

11 plumber	**15** drywall installer	**n** skylight	**r** insulation	**w** clapboard
12 insulation contractor	**16** electrician	**o** chimney	**s** sheet of drywall	**x** HVAC unit
13 drywall plasterer	**17** electrician's assistant	**p** fireplace	**t** electrical panel	**y** house wrap
14 drywall taper		**q** water meter	**u** water heater	
			v radial arm saw	

1 tile installer	**6** flooring installer	**a** tile	**e** pasting table	**j** countertop
2 plumber	**7** finish carpenter	**b** carpet	**f** wallpaper roll	**k** water spigot
3 carpet installer	**8** electrician	**c** sliding door	**g** drop cloth	**l** step ladder
4 paperhanger	**9** carpenter	**d** double-hung window	**h** wood flooring	**m** interior door
5 painter			**i** cabinets	**n** garage door

What occupations and objects do you see? | The scenes on pages 72–74 show different stages of home building. In your opinion, which stage of the work is the most interesting? the most difficult? Why?

1 mix mortar
2 cut a cement block
3 butter a brick
4 set a brick

5 staple tar paper
6 attach shingles
7 secure a ladder
8 mark dimensions

9 measure a wall
10 check a level
11 drill a hole
12 shim a door frame

13 install a window
14 cut a skylight opening
15 caulk a skylight
16 run ductwork

Look at page 72. What are the workers doing? Describe their actions.

17 cut a pipe
18 solder a fitting
19 apply PVC* cement
20 tighten a connection

21 position a water heater
22 install insulation
23 score drywall
24 screw in drywall

25 tape a seam
26 plaster/skim coat a wall
27 saw a piece of clapboard
28 nail clapboard to the sheathing

29 staple house wrap
30 wire an electrical panel
31 test voltage
32 charge the AC* unit

* PVC = polyvinyl chloride
  AC = air conditioning

Look at page 73. What are the workers doing? Describe their actions.

33 paint an interior wall
34 paint the trim
35 spray paint an exterior wall
36 brush on wallpaper paste

37 hang wallpaper
38 install a floor
39 lay carpet
40 trim carpet

41 install a cabinet door
42 insert a faucet
43 wrap the threaded end of a pipe with tape
44 set a toilet bowl

45 grout tile
46 twist on wire nuts
47 tighten a ground wire
48 stack garage door panels

Look at page 74. What are the workers doing? Describe their actions.

1 caulking gun
2 reciprocating saw
3 staple hammer
4 trowel
5 claw hammer
6 roofing nail gun

7 tape measure
8 level
9 carpenter's square
10 circular saw
11 mason hammer
12 mason chisel

13 propane torch
14 plumbing solder
15 PVC cement
16 PVC pipe elbow
17 plasterer's trowel
18 plasterer's hawk

19 utility knife
20 drywall tape
21 drywall screwdriver
22 drywall screw

Look at pages 72–77. What equipment, tools, and objects do you see?

23 tube cutter	**29** notched trowel	**35** paint roller	**39** electrical wire
24 voltage tester	**30** carpet knee kicker	**36** paint brush	**40** wire nuts
25 staple gun	**31** carpet cutter	**37** pneumatic floor nailer	**41** spray gun
26 circuit breaker	**32** paperhanger's brush		**42** water spigot
27 hacksaw	**33** seam roller	**38** wall receptacle	**43** plumber's teflon tape
28 HVAC manifold	**34** paint		

1 A Carpenter's Helper & a Carpenter

A carpenter's helper is asking a carpenter for instructions.

A. What should I do next?
B. Can you measure the spacing for the studs?
A. Sure. How far apart should they be?
B. Make them every 16 inches on center.

2 A Mason's Apprentice & a Mason

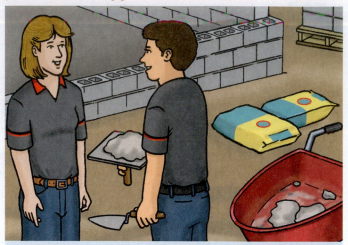

Two masons are determining if they have sufficient material to complete the job.

A. Do we have enough mortar to finish?
B. I don't think so. I think we're going to run out.
A. I'll mix some more.
B. Great! Thanks.

3 Two HVAC Technicians

One HVAC technician is offering to help another.

A. Do you need a hand?
B. Yes. Can you run this section of flexible duct?
A. Sure. Where?
B. To the rear bedroom vent.

4 An Electrician's Assistant & an Electrician

An electrician's assistant is checking on job specifications.

A. Mark?
B. Yes?
A. Just checking to make sure: What size circuit breakers are you using for the bedrooms?
B. 15 AMP breakers for those rooms.
A. And how about for the kitchen?
B. 20 AMP breakers for the kitchen.

1 You're a carpenter's helper. Ask for instructions.

2 You're a mason. Ask a co-worker if there is sufficient material to complete a task.

3 You're an HVAC technician. Offer to help a co-worker.

4 You're an electrician's assistant. Check on some job specifications.

5 Two Plumbers

A plumber is asking another plumber for assistance.

A. I just finished roughing out the plumbing for the water heater.

B. Is it ready to hook up?

A. Yes. Can you help me move it into place?

B. Sure. No problem.

6 A Plumber & a Carpenter

A plumber and a carpenter are coordinating their tasks.

A. How much longer will you be installing the cabinets?

B. I should be finished in about an hour.

A. Okay. Then I'll be able to hook up the sink.

B. All right. See you in an hour.

7 Two Carpet Installers

A carpet installer is noticing that a co-worker needs assistance.

A. You seem to be having trouble.

B. I am. I'm having a problem cutting this carpet.

A. Let me see that carpet trimmer. Here, look! It needs a new blade.

B. You're right. I'll get one from the truck.

8 Two Painters

Two painters are realizing they need to confirm instructions.

A. Which color paint goes where?

B. I think the cream is for the wall and the blue is for the trim.

A. Are you sure? I thought it was the other way—blue for the wall and cream for the trim.

B. We'd better ask!

5 You're a plumber. Ask another plumber for assistance.

6 You're a carpenter. Coordinate a task with a plumber.

7 You're a carpet installer. Notice a problem a co-worker is having and suggest a solution.

8 You're a painter. You aren't sure about some instructions. Discuss with a co-worker.

A HOW TO INSTALL HANGING CABINETS

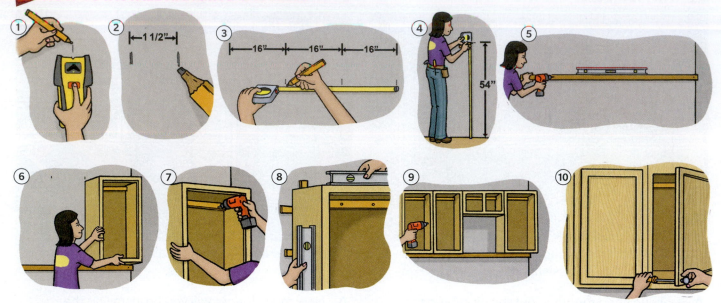

1. Use a stud finder to find a stud and mark its middle.
2. Mark both edges of the stud.
3. Measure 16 inches on center to locate the rest of the studs.
4. Measure 54 inches up from the floor at both ends of the wall.
5. Using a level, install the ledger board.
6. Start with a corner cabinet and place it on the ledger board.
7. Attach the cabinet by screwing through its support strip into a stud.
8. Level the cabinet using a level and shims.
9. Install, level, and connect the other cabinets.
10. Remove the ledger board and install the cabinet doors and hardware.

B HOW TO FRAME A WALL

1. Lay down a top plate and a bottom plate.
2. For an 8-foot high wall, measure studs to 7 feet 9 inches and mark them.
3. Cut studs on the mark.
4. Place the first stud at the end.
5. Measure and mark the top and bottom plates at 16 inches on center.
6. Place the remaining studs at the marks.
7. Hammer nails through the plate into the end of each stud.
8. Repeat until all the studs are nailed to plates.
9. Lift the framed wall into position.

C HOW TO TAPE AND MUD DRYWALL

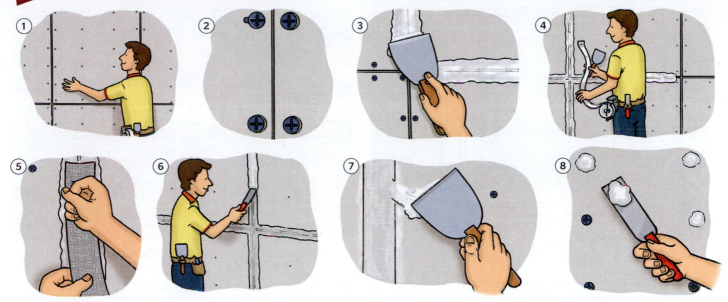

1 Check to see that the drywall is correctly attached to the studs.
2 Make sure that all drywall screws are countersunk.
3 Apply mud into each seam.
4 Roll out and cut a piece of drywall tape.
5 Press the tape into the mud.
6 Press and pull the drywall knife along the seam.
7 Smooth out and remove the extra mud.
8 Fill and smooth any screw holes.

D HOW TO INSTALL A TOILET

1 Cut a hole in the sub floor the size of the closet flange.
2 Use PVC cement to connect the flange to the soil pipe.
3 Twist and press the flange so the collar is seated to the floor.
4 Screw the collar to the sub floor.
5 Solder the stop valve.
6 Insert the closet bolts with washers.
7 Press the wax ring over the flange.
8 Lower and press the toilet bowl onto the wax ring.
9 Bolt down the toilet bowl.
10 Install the tank and hardware.
11 Install the supply line and the seat assembly.

1 A Carpenter & a Carpenter's Helper

A carpenter is correcting a carpenter's helper's work.

A. This window doesn't look level.
B. Hmm. Oh, you're right.
A. Use this level, then shim it square.
B. Okay. Sorry for the mistake.

2 A Roofer & a Construction Laborer

A roofer is noticing a safety problem.

A. Are you the one who secured this ladder?
B. Yes. Is there a problem?
A. Yes. You didn't completely tie off the ladder top.
B. Oh. Sorry. I'll do that right now.

3 A Painter & a Painter's Helper

A painter is correcting a painter's helper's work.

A. Alex? You need to spray more evenly. Use a steady back-and-forth motion.
B. A steady back-and-forth motion? Got it.
A. And where's your painting mask?
B. My painting mask? Oh, yeah. I'll get it.

4 Two Paperhangers

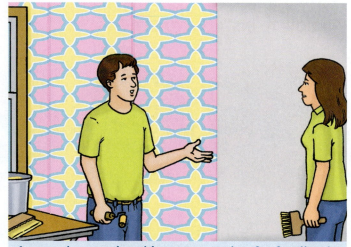

A paperhanger is asking a co-worker for feedback.

A. How does this wallpaper look to you?
B. I hate to say it, but the pattern doesn't line up.
A. You're right. I can fix it. The paste hasn't set yet.
B. That's good. I'm glad we caught it early.

1 You're a carpenter. Give correction to your helper.
2 You're a roofer. Point out a safety problem.
3 You're a painter. Give correction to your helper.
4 You're a paperhanger. Ask a co-worker for feedback.

OCCUPATIONS

blockmason	carpet installer	electrician	glazier	paperhanger
blockmason apprentice	construction laborer	electrician's assistant	HVAC technician	plumber
brickmason	drywall installer	finish carpenter	insulation contractor	roofer
carpenter	drywall plasterer	flooring installer	painter	skylight installer
carpenter's helper	drywall taper			tile installer

EQUIPMENT, TOOLS, & OBJECTS

AC (air conditioning) unit	connection	flexible duct	OSB	seam roller	threaded end
AMP (amp)	countertop	framed wall/ wall studs	paint	sheet of drywall	tile
blade	dimensions	garage door	paint brush	shims	toilet bowl
bolt	door frame	garage door panel	paint roller	shingle	trim
brick	double-hung window	ground wire	painting mask	skylight	trowel
cabinet	drop cloth	hacksaw	paperhanger's brush	sliding door	tube cutter
cabinet door	drywall	hardware	pasting table	soil pipe	utility knife
carpenter's square	drywall knife	house wrap	pipe	spray gun	vent
carpet	drywall screw	HVAC manifold	plasterer's hawk	staple gun	voltage
carpet cutter	drywall screwdriver	HVAC unit	plasterer's trowel	staple	voltage tester
carpet knee kicker	drywall tape	insulation	plumber's teflon tape	staple hammer	wall receptacle
carpet trimmer	ductwork	interior door	plumbing solder	step ladder	wallpaper paste
caulking gun	electrical panel	interior wall	plywood	stop valve	wallpaper roll
cement block	electrical wire	ladder	pneumatic floor nailer	stud	washer
chimney	extension ladder	ledger board	propane torch	sub floor	water heater
circuit breaker	exterior wall	level	PVC cement	supply line	water meter
circular saw	fascia board	mason chisel	PVC pipe elbow	support strip	water spigot
clapboard	faucet	mason hammer	radial arm saw	tank	wax ring
claw hammer	fireplace	mortar	reciprocating saw	tape	wheelbarrow
collar	fitting	mud	roofing nail gun	tape measure	wire nuts
concrete block	flange	notched trowel	sawhorse	tar paper	wood flooring
concrete slab			screw hole		
			seam		

WORKPLACE ACTIONS

apply PVC cement	install a cabinet door	plaster/skim coat a wall	stack garage door panels
attach shingles	insert a faucet	position a water heater	staple house wrap
brush on wallpaper paste	install a floor	run ductwork	staple tar paper
butter a brick	install a window	saw a piece of clapboard	tape a seam
caulk a skylight	install insulation	score drywall	test voltage
charge an AC unit	lay carpet	screw in drywall	tighten a connection
check a level	mark dimensions	secure a ladder	tighten a ground wire
cut a cement block	measure a wall	set a brick	trim carpet
cut a pipe	mix mortar	set a toilet bowl	twist on wire nuts
cut a skylight opening	nail clapboard to sheathing	shim a door frame	wire an electrical panel
drill a hole	paint an interior wall	solder a fitting	wrap the threaded end of a pipe with tape
grout tile	paint trim	spray paint an exterior wall	
hang wallpaper			

WORKPLACE COMMUNICATION

ask a co-worker for feedback	coordinate tasks with a co-worker	notice a safety problem
ask a co-worker for instructions	correct someone's work	notice that a co-worker needs assistance
ask a co-worker for assistance	determine sufficient materials to complete a job	offer to help a co-worker
check on job specifications		realize the need to confirm instructions

OCCUPATIONS

A WHAT'S THE OCCUPATION?

blockmason apprentice	carpet installer	electrician's assistant	insulation contractor	roofer
brickmason	drywall installer	flooring installer	paperhanger	skylight installer
carpenter	drywall taper	glazier	plumber	tile installer
carpenter's helper	electrician	HVAC tech		

1. A. This person lays bricks.
   B. What is a ___brickmason___?

2. A. This person lays carpet.
   B. What is a _____?

3. A. This person installs electrical systems.
   B. What is an _____?

4. A. This person hangs wallpaper.
   B. What is a _____?

5. A. This person builds things out of wood.
   B. What is a _____?

6. A. This person installs drywall.
   B. What is a _____?

7. A. This person installs glass.
   B. What is a _____?

8. A. This person installs piping systems.
   B. What is a _____?

9. A. This person installs roofs.
   B. What is a _____?

10. A. This person assists a carpenter.
    B. What is a _____?

11. A. This person installs insulation.
    B. What is an _____?

12. A. This person helps a block mason.
    B. What is a _____?

13. A. This person tapes drywall.
    B. What is a _____?

14. A. This person helps an electrician.
    B. What is an _____?

15. A. This person installs floors.
    B. What is an _____?

16. A. This person puts in skylights.
    B. What is a _____?

17. A. This person lays tiles.
    B. What is a _____?

18. A. This person installs heating and air conditioning.
    B. What is an _____?

EQUIPMENT, TOOLS, & OBJECTS

B WHAT'S THE ASSOCIATION?

_d_ 1. knife   screw   screwdriver
___ 2. cutter   knee kicker   trimmer
___ 3. faucet   toilet bowl   flange
___ 4. brush   roller   mask
___ 5. chisel   mortar   brick
___ 6. circuit breaker   voltage tester   AMP
___ 7. claw hammer   level   reciprocating saw

a. carpet installer
b. mason
c. painter
d. drywall installer
e. carpenter
f. plumber
g. electrician

WORKPLACE ACTIONS

C WHAT DO CONSTRUCTION WORKERS DO?

1. apply _____
   a. a wall
   b. PVC cement ⓑ
   c. a carpet
   d. ductwork

2. tighten _____
   a. a connection
   b. tar paper
   c. a shingle
   d. a block

3. skim coat _____
   a. a brick
   b. a carpet
   c. a wall
   d. a bolt

4. staple _____
   a. a window
   b. house wrap
   c. cement
   d. a block

5. install _____
   a. paint
   b. wallpaper paste
   c. a window
   d. a ladder

6. grout _____
   a. tile
   b. a pipe
   c. plywood
   d. cement

7. test _____
   a. mud
   b. voltage
   c. hardware
   d. a wheelbarrow

8. caulk _____
   a. a ladder
   b. a carpet
   c. a level
   d. a skylight

9. set _____
   a. carpet
   b. a brick
   c. ductwork
   d. a chisel

10. lay _____
    a. mud
    b. an electrical panel
    c. carpet
    d. a hole

11. hang _____
    a. insulation
    b. wire nuts
    c. a wall
    d. wallpaper

12. shim _____
    a. a door frame
    b. shingles
    c. clapboard
    d. a water heater

13. cut _____
    a. cement
    b. a toilet
    c. a pipe
    d. a faucet

14. nail _____
    a. paint
    b. clapboard
    c. mortar
    d. tile

15. run _____
    a. wallpaper
    b. a window
    c. voltage
    d. ductwork

16. solder _____
    a. a fitting
    b. an AC unit
    c. cement
    d. house wrap

WORKPLACE COMMUNICATION

D WHAT ARE THEY SAYING?

_g_ 1. ask for instructions

___ 2. determine if material is sufficient

___ 3. offer to help

___ 4. check on job specifications

___ 5. ask for assistance

___ 6. coordinate tasks with a co-worker

___ 7. notice that a co-worker needs assistance

___ 8. realize the need to confirm instructions

___ 9. correct someone's work

___ 10. notice a safety problem

___ 11. ask for feedback

___ 12. respond to feedback

a. "What size circuit breakers are we using for the bedrooms?"

b. "After you install the cabinets, I'll be able to work on the sink."

c. "You didn't completely tie off the ladder."

d. "Do we have enough mortar to finish?"

e. "This window doesn't look level."

f. "Do you need a hand?"

g. "What should I do next?"

h. "How does this wallpaper look to you?"

i. "We'd better ask."

j. "Got it."

k. "Can you help me to move it into place?"

l. "You seem to be having trouble."

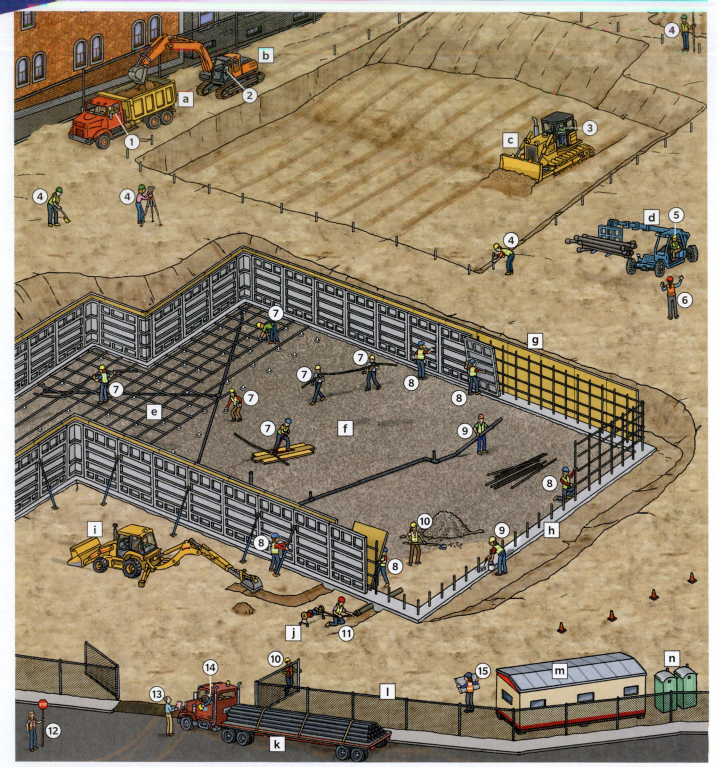

1 dump truck operator
2 excavator operator
3 bulldozer operator
4 surveyor
5 equipment operator
6 construction safety officer
7 concrete worker
8 formwork installer

9 plumber
10 construction laborer
11 electrician
12 flagger
13 jobsite foreman
14 flatbed truck driver
15 construction foreman

a dump truck
b excavator
c bulldozer
d construction forklift
e rebar grid
f gravel
g rebar wall support
h foundation footing

i backhoe
j utility cables
k flatbed truck
l safety barrier fencing
m site trailer
n portable toilets

What occupations do you see at this construction site? What workplace objects do you see?

16 cement truck operator	**21** construction worker	**o** foundation floor	**u** crane truck
17 concrete pump truck operator	**22** concrete finisher	**p** concrete foundation walls	**v** joists
18 crane truck operator	**23** cement mason	**q** boom	**w** support decking
19 steelworker	**24** welder	**r** cement mixer truck	**x** steel plate
20 flatbed truck operator	**25** pipefitter	**s** concrete pump truck	**y** front-end loader
		t hoist	**z** cherry picker truck

1 HVAC technician	**8** pipefitter	**a** roof HVAC unit	**h** base plate
2 roofer	**9** glazier	**b** asphalt carrier	**i** cement tub
3 solar panel installer	**10** tile setter	**c** mop cart	**j** concrete blocks
4 plumber	**11** blockmason	**d** roof vent	**k** handicap ramp
5 construction laborer	**12** concrete laborer	**e** conduit pipe	**l** walkway form
6 project manager	**13** welder	**f** scaffolding	
7 construction supervisor		**g** platform	

What occupations do you see at this construction site?   What workplace objects do you see?

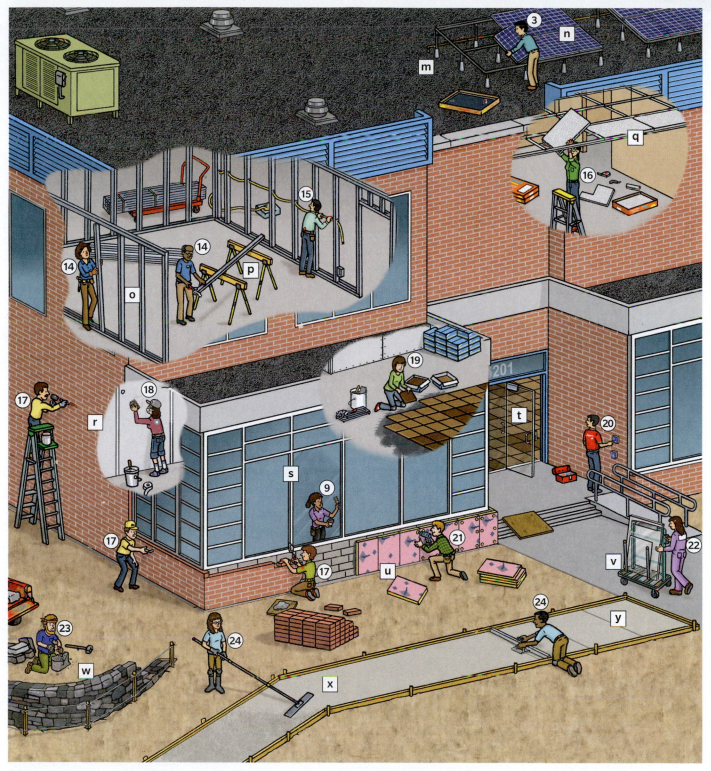

14 carpenter	**20** automatic door installer	**m** solar mounts and rail	**s** window frame
15 electrician	**21** insulation contractor	**n** solar panels	**t** automatic door
16 ceiling tile installer	**22** glass processor apprentice	**o** metal studs	**u** rigid insulation
17 brickmason	**23** stonemason	**p** sawhorse	**v** flat glass trolley
18 plasterer	**24** cement finisher	**q** ceiling track and panel	**w** decorative stone wall
19 tile setter		**r** common bond brick wall	**x** walkway
			y control joints

The scenes on pages 88–91 show four different stages of commercial construction. In your opinion, which stage of the work is the most interesting? the most difficult? Why?

1 excavate a foundation
2 load dirt into a dump truck
3 grade a foundation floor with a bulldozer
4 take exact measurements

5 pound a survey stake
6 point out a safety issue
7 place rebar spacers
8 cut rebar

9 tie rebar
10 connect concrete forms with pins
11 lay PVC* pipe
12 attach support bars to concrete form panels

13 dig a trench for utilities
14 control traffic
15 check a bill of lading
16 read site plans

* PVC = polyvinyl chloride plastic

Look at page 88. What are the workers doing? Describe their actions.

17 pull cement from a cement mixer

18 control a boom and cement flow

19 fill a foundation form

20 strip/remove concrete panels

21 cut a beam to size specification

22 hoist a beam

23 use crane hand signals

24 guide a beam

25 release tie-down straps

26 tighten bolts

27 lay down support decking

28 drive bolts to attach decking to beams

29 spread out concrete

30 level a concrete floor with a screed

31 fill in around a foundation

32 raise the bucket on a cherry picker

Look at page 89. What are the workers doing? Describe their actions.

Job Responsibilities

1. secure a metal mount
2. pour tar into a service bucket
3. mop tar on a roof
4. roll out a cap sheet
5. cut PVC pipe
6. give instructions from blueprints
7. bend conduit
8. erect scaffolding
9. thread a pipe
10. break glass along a score line
11. level a row of cement blocks
12. weld a stair rail
13. drive a stake into the ground to secure a walkway
14. spread gravel
15. lay down mesh wire
16. dump cement

Look at page 90. What are the workers doing? Describe their actions.

17 clip a PVC panel to a rail
18 trim a stud
19 screw a stud into a track channel
20 pull an electrical cable through studs

21 put a ceiling panel on a suspended ceiling track
22 lay brick
23 chisel out cracked brick
24 sand a plastered wall

25 space tile
26 strike a mortar joint
27 apply glazier's putty
28 attach rigid insulation

29 move glass panes
30 break stone
31 smooth a surface
32 cut in control joints

Look at page 91. What are the workers doing? Describe their actions.

1 hard hat
2 safety vest
3 safety sign
4 survey stake and flag
5 marking paint stick
6 range pole
7 surveyor's transit
8 tripod

9 rebar
10 rebar spacer
11 rebar cutter
12 rebar tie tool
13 water supply pipe
14 concrete form support brace
15 safety cone

16 cement discharge hose
17 concrete chute tool
18 torque bolt wrench
19 ratchet tie-down strap
20 industrial impact driver
21 support decking
22 chain wrench
23 hand float

24 power trowel
25 concrete screed
26 welding safety shield
27 metal cutting oxy-fuel torch
28 manhole cover guard
29 traffic safety barrel
30 temporary jack post

Look at pages 88–89 and 92–93. What equipment, tools, and objects do you see?

31 tar mop
32 service bucket
33 cap sheet roll
34 vise stand
35 rubber mallet
36 conduit hand bender
37 gravel rake

38 hand pipe threader
39 concrete block
40 mason line and block
41 glass breaking pliers
42 glass cutter
43 glazier's hammer
44 solar panel

45 tin snips
46 tile cutter
47 marble tile
48 tile spacers
49 handicap door switch
50 cold chisel
51 plaster sanding block

52 knee pads
53 glazier's putty knife
54 rigid insulation fastener
55 brick jointer tool
56 bull float
57 concrete groover

Look at pages 90–91 and 94–95. What equipment, tools, and objects do you see?

1 Two Formwork Installers

A formwork installer is asking a co-worker for material.

A. I need a corner form here.
B. 45-degree or 90-degree?
A. 90 degree.
B. Okay. I'll get one.

2 A Dump Truck Operator & an Excavator Operator

Two equipment operators are coordinating with each other on a task.

A. I think my box is almost full. *Over*.
B. After I dump this bucket, you can pull out. *Over*.
A. Should I send the next truck? *Over*.
B. Yeah, thanks. *Out*.

3 Two Steelworkers

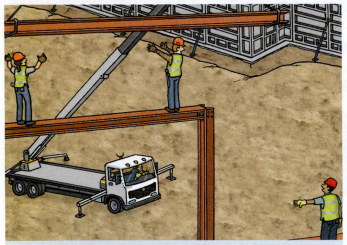

Construction workers are using hand signals to communicate instructions.

A. Give him the hand signal to move the load left.
B. All right.
A. Now have him move it down slowly.
B. Got it. Should I signal him to stop?
A. Yes. Thanks for the help.

4 A Foreman & a Concrete Mason

A foreman is checking on completion of a phase of construction.

A. Is the foundation floor done yet?
B. Yes. We just finished it.
A. How long before we can walk on it? Two days, right?
B. Exactly. You should wait 48 hours.

---

1 You're a worker at a construction site. Ask a co-worker for some material you need.
2 How are these equipment operators communicating with each other?
3 What hand signals do you know? What do they mean?
4 You're a foreman at a construction site. Check on the completion of some work.

5 Two Glaziers

A glazier is asking a co-worker to do a task.

A. Can you cut those panes?
B. Sure. What size do you need?
A. 18 by 22. I need four of them.
B. Okay. Give me 15 minutes.

6 Two Roofers

A roofer is asking a co-worker if a task has been completed.

A. Have you finished sealing all the roof vents?
B. No. I still have to finish a couple.
A. You need to do them before we can mop this area.
B. I'll do them right away.

7 A Construction Laborer & a Solar Panel Installer

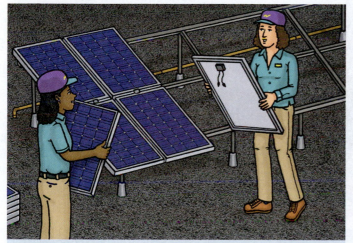

A construction laborer is asking about the scope of a task.

A. How many solar panels do we have to mount?
B. This array will have 24 panels.
A. And then we're done?
B. No. We still have two more arrays to do.

8 An Electrician & a Carpenter

Two workers are coordinating with each other on separate tasks.

A. I'm ready to run the electrical cable in this room.
B. I'm still trimming some studs, but I can do that in the room next door.
A. That would be great.
B. Give me a minute and I'll get out of your way so you can get started.

5 Ask a co-worker to do a task.

6 Ask a co-worker if a task has been completed.

7 Ask a co-worker about the scope of a task.

8 What are other examples of workers needing to coordinate with each other on separate tasks?

A HOW TO EXCAVATE FOR A FOUNDATION

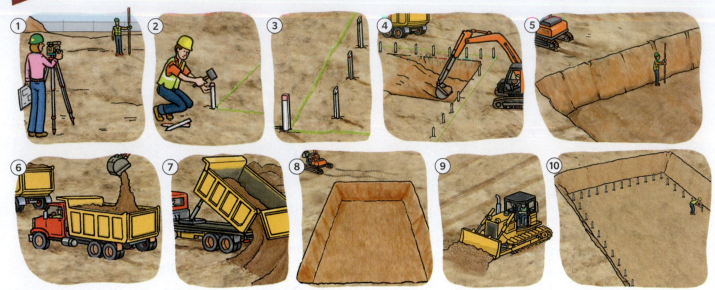

1 Have the surveyor locate the perimeter of the foundation according to the site plan.

2 Mark the corners of the foundation with survey stakes.

3 Put offset stakes approximately four feet from the perimeter line.

4 Start excavating the hole in sections.

5 Excavate the hole to the depth specified by the structural engineer.

6 Transfer the displaced soil into dump trucks.

7 Dump the soil at the soil pile on site for future use.

8 Complete excavating the hole.

9 Grade the foundation floor.

10 Stake the perimeter of the foundation floor for the foundation footings.

B HOW TO POUR A FOUNDATION

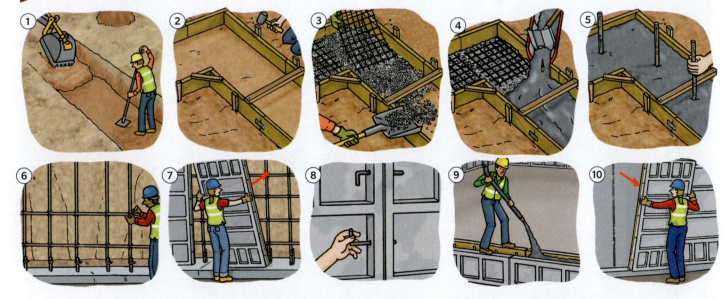

1 Dig and level the footing area.

2 Form foundation footings with lumber.

3 Put down gravel and then metal mesh in the footing area.

4 Fill the footing form with concrete.

5 Put rebar dowels in the concrete every 18 to 24 inches.

6 When the concrete is cured, attach vertical and horizontal rebar to the dowels.

7 Put concrete form panels in place on the footing.

8 Attach the concrete form panels to each other with pins.

9 Pour concrete until all voids are filled.

10 After the concrete is cured, strip off the panels.

C HOW TO INSTALL MODIFIED BITUMEN ROOFING

1 Sweep and pick up any loose debris to prep the roof.
2 Flash any pipes, vents, and supports.
3 Put pieces of tar in the cold vat of the tar kettle.

4 Increase the heat to 450 degrees to turn the tar into liquid form.
5 Transfer the hot liquid tar in a service bucket to the mop cart.
6 Mop hot tar on a section of the roof.

7 Roll out and broom down felt.
8 Mop hot tar onto the felt.
9 Roll out a granulated cap sheet.
10 Fill the pleats with loose granulated fill.

D HOW TO LAY A BRICK WALL

1 Place brick pallets along the length of a wall.
2 Mix mortar.
3 Shovel some mortar onto a piece of wet plywood.

4 Scoop up the mortar and place it on the footing.
5 Set a brick down and tap it until it is level.
6 Set more bricks to complete a course of bricks.

7 Cut away excess mortar.
8 Lay up several courses of brick.
9 Check with a carpenter's level.

1 A Safety Officer & an Equipment Operator

A safety officer is warning about the unsafe use of a machine.

A. Hey!
B. You talking to ME?
A. Yeah! Your load is too heavy! It must be way beyond the safety rating for that forklift.
B. Okay. Thanks for the warning.

2 A Concrete Worker & a Cement Boom Truck Operator

A concrete worker is pointing out a problem with a machine's setting.

A. You set the pump's output too low.
B. I did?
A. Yeah. Jack is having trouble filling all the voids in the foundation form.
B. Okay. I'll speed up the output.

3 A Supervisor & a Construction Laborer

A supervisor is pointing out a problem with the setup of a structure.

A. There's a problem with that scaffolding you're setting up.
B. Oh? What?
A. You left some openings on the second tier platform.
B. Oh, okay. I'll bring up some more planks.

4 Two Tile Setters

A tile setter is asking a co-worker for feedback.

A. Do these tiles look okay to you? Something doesn't look right to me.
B. I don't think you spaced them evenly.
A. You know, you're right.
B. I'd redo this section if I were you.

1 You're a safety officer at a construction site. Warn a worker about a safety problem.

2–3 Point out problems to other workers.

4 Ask a co-worker for feedback (about something you didn't do correctly).

OCCUPATIONS

- automatic door installer
- blockmason
- brickmason
- bulldozer operator
- carpenter
- ceiling tile installer
- cement finisher
- cement mason
- cement truck operator
- concrete finisher
- concrete laborer
- concrete pump truck operator
- concrete worker
- construction foreman
- construction laborer
- construction safety officer
- construction supervisor
- construction worker
- crane truck operator
- dump truck operator
- electrician
- equipment operator
- excavator operator
- flagger
- flatbed truck driver
- flatbed truck operator
- formwork installer
- glass processor apprentice
- glazier
- HVAC technician
- insulation contractor
- jobsite foreman
- pipefitter
- plasterer
- plumber
- project manager
- roofer
- solar panel installer
- steelworker
- stonemason
- structural engineer
- surveyor
- tile setter
- welder

EQUIPMENT, TOOLS, & OBJECTS

- asphalt carrier
- automatic door
- backhoe
- base plate
- boom
- brick jointer tool
- brick pallets
- brick wall
- bull float
- bulldozer
- cap sheet roll
- carpenter's level
- ceiling panel
- ceiling track
- cement
- cement discharge hose
- cement mixer truck
- cement tub
- chain wrench
- cherry picker truck
- cold chisel
- common bond brick wall
- concrete
- concrete block
- concrete chute tool
- concrete form panels
- concrete form support brace
- concrete foundation walls
- concrete groover
- concrete pump truck
- concrete screed
- conduit hand bender
- conduit pipe
- construction forklift
- control joints
- corner form
- course of bricks
- crane truck
- debris
- decorative stone wall
- dowels
- dump truck
- electrical cable
- excavator
- felt
- flat glass trolley
- flatbed truck
- footing area
- footing form
- forklift
- foundation floor
- foundation footing
- foundation form
- front-end loader
- glass breaking pliers
- glass cutter
- glass panes
- glazier's hammer
- glazier's putty knife
- granulated cap sheet
- granulated fill
- gravel
- gravel rake
- hand float
- hand pipe threader
- hand signal
- handicap door switch
- handicap ramp
- hard hat
- hoist
- industrial impact driver
- joists
- knee pads
- lumber
- mason line and block
- manhole cover guard
- marble tile
- marking paint stick
- mason line and block
- metal cutting oxy-fuel torch
- metal mesh
- metal studs
- mop cart
- mortar
- offset stakes
- perimeter/perimeter line
- pins
- pipes
- plank
- plaster sanding block
- platform
- plywood
- portable toilets
- power trowel
- pump
- range pole
- ratchet tie-down strap
- rebar
- rebar cutter
- rebar dowels
- rebar grid
- rebar spacer
- rebar tie tool
- rebar wall support
- rigid insulation
- rigid insulation fastener
- roof
- roof HVAC unit
- roof vent
- rubber mallet
- safety barrier fencing
- safety cone
- safety sign
- safety vest
- sawhorse
- scaffolding
- service bucket
- site trailer
- soil pile
- solar mounts and rail
- solar panel
- steel plate
- studs
- support decking
- survey flag
- survey stake
- surveyor's transit
- tar
- tar kettle
- tar mop
- temporary jack post
- tile cutter
- tile spacers
- tin snips
- torque bolt wrench
- traffic safety barrel
- tripod
- utility cables
- vat
- vents
- vise stand
- walkway
- walkway form
- water supply pipe
- welding safety shield
- window frame

WORKPLACE ACTIONS

apply glazier's putty

attach rigid insulation

attach support bars to concrete form panels

bend conduit

break glass along a score line

break stone

check a bill of lading

chisel out cracked brick

clip a PVC panel to a rail

connect concrete forms with pins

control a boom and cement flow

control traffic

cut a beam to size specification

cut in control joints

cut PVC pipe

cut rebar

dig a trench for utilities

drive a stake into the ground to secure a walkway

drive bolts to attach decking to beams

dump cement

erect scaffolding

excavate a foundation

fill a foundation form

fill in around a foundation

give instructions from blueprints

grade a foundation floor with a bulldozer

guide a beam

hoist a beam

lay brick

lay down mesh wire

lay down support decking

lay PVC pipe

level a concrete floor with a screed

level a row of cement blocks

load dirt into a dump truck

mop tar on a roof

move glass panes

place rebar spacers

point out a safety issue

pound a survey stake

pour tar into a service bucket

pull an electrical cable through studs

pull cement from a cement mixer

put a ceiling panel on a suspended ceiling track

raise the bucket on a cherry picker

read site plans

release tie-down straps

roll out a cap sheet

sand a plastered wall

screw a stud into a track channel

secure a metal mount

smooth a surface

space tile

spread gravel

spread out concrete

strike a mortar joint

strip/remove concrete panels

take exact measurements

thread a pipe

tie rebar

tighten bolts

trim a stud

use crane hand signals

weld a stair rail

WORKPLACE COMMUNICATION

ask a co-worker for feedback

ask a co-worker for material

ask a co-worker if a task has been completed

ask a co-worker to do a task

ask about the scope of a task

communicate instructions using hand signals

coordinate a task with a co-worker

coordinate separate tasks with a co-worker

correct a co-worker

point out a problem to a worker

warn a co-worker about a problem

OCCUPATIONS

 A ▶ **WHAT'S THE OCCUPATION?**

blockmason	ceiling tile installer	construction safety officer	HVAC technician	roofer
brickmason	cement mason	electrician	pipefitter	steelworker
bulldozer operator	construction foreman	flagger	plasterer	stonemason
carpenter	construction laborer	glazier	plumber	surveyor

1. **A.** This person operates a bulldozer.
   B. What is a ___bulldozer operator___?

2. **A.** This person installs ceiling tiles.
   B. What is a _____?

3. **A.** This person lays bricks.
   B. What is a _____?

4. **A.** This person cuts and installs glass.
   B. What is a _____?

5. **A.** This person installs electrical systems.
   B. What is an _____?

6. **A.** This person lays blocks.
   B. What is a _____?

7. **A.** This person installs water and sewer systems.
   B. What is a _____?

8. **A.** This person installs steel beams.
   B. What is a _____?

9. **A.** This person builds things out of wood.
   B. What is a _____?

10. **A.** This person works with stone.
    B. What is a _____?

11. **A.** This person installs heating systems.
    B. What is an _____?

12. **A.** This person applies plaster on walls and ceilings.
    B. What is a _____?

13. **A.** This person measures boundaries around buildings.
    B. What is a _____?

14. **A.** This person installs piping systems.
    B. What is a _____?

15. **A.** This person places barricades in a construction zone.
    B. What is a _____?

16. **A.** This person builds roofs.
    B. What is a _____?

17. **A.** This person is in charge of a construction crew.
    B. What is a _____?

18. **A.** This person performs many different non-skilled tasks.
    B. What is a _____?

19. **A.** This person pours cement.
    B. What is a _____?

20. **A.** This person makes sure working conditions are safe.
    B. What is a _____?

COMMERCIAL CONSTRUCTION

EQUIPMENT, TOOLS, & OBJECTS

B WHAT'S THE ITEM?

__d__	1.	electrical	a.	signal	___ 9.	base	i.	stand	___ 17.	handicap	q.	plans

___ **d** **1.** electrical   **a.** signal   ___ **9.** base   **i.** stand   ___ **17.** handicap   **q.** plans

___ **2.** cement   **b.** wrench   ___ **10.** corner   **j.** roll   ___ **18.** carpenter's   **r.** frame

___ **3.** hand   **c.** cart   ___ **11.** vise   **k.** kettle   ___ **19.** site   **s.** stake

___ **4.** roof   **d.** cable   ___ **12.** tar   **l.** plate   ___ **20.** sanding   **t.** ramp

___ **5.** mop   **e.** panel   ___ **13.** HVAC   **m.** door   ___ **21.** survey   **u.** plate

___ **6.** solar   **f.** tub   ___ **14.** cap sheet   **n.** carrier   ___ **22.** steel   **v.** level

___ **7.** chain   **g.** trailer   ___ **15.** asphalt   **o.** form   ___ **23.** window   **w.** float

___ **8.** site   **h.** vent   ___ **16.** automatic   **p.** unit   ___ **24.** hand   **x.** block

C WHAT DO THEY HAVE IN COMMON?

brick	concrete	foundation	glass	metal	rebar	safety	surveyor	trucks	wood

1. block   form panels   screed

              __concrete__

2. dump   cherry picker   concrete pump

_____

3. floor   footing   form

_____

4. cutter   glazier's hammer   putty knife

_____

5. hard hat   knee pads   vest

_____

6. stake   flag   transit

_____

7. oxy-fuel torch   mesh   studs

_____

8. cutter   spacer   grid

_____

9. pointer tool   pallets   wall

_____

10. plank   lumber   plywood

_____

WORKPLACE ACTIONS

D WHAT'S THE ACTION?

___ **f** **1.** You need to ___ the foundation floor.   **a.** take

___ **2.** Can you ___ this cable through these studs?   **b.** pour

___ **3.** Remember to ___ crane hand signals.   **c.** chisel

___ **4.** It's important to ___ exact measurements.   **d.** pull

___ **5.** You need to ___ some tar into the service bucket.   **e.** raise

___ **6.** I'm trying to ___ out this cracked brick.   **f.** grade

___ **7.** Can you ___ the bucket on the cherry picker?   **g.** use

WORKPLACE ACTIONS

E WHAT DO CONSTRUCTION WORKERS DO?

1. bend _____
  a. brick
  b. conduit
  c. a wall
  d. gravel

2. apply _____
  a. blocks
  b. a stud
  c. putty
  d. panes

3. cut _____
  a. PVC pipe
  b. bolts
  c. scaffolding
  d. a trench

4. load _____
  a. a boom
  b. hand signals
  c. dirt
  d. blueprints

5. control _____
  a. a roof
  b. a wall
  c. stone
  d. a boom

6. erect _____
  a. bricks
  b. scaffolding
  c. a service bucket
  d. gravel

7. break _____
  a. stone
  b. tar
  c. a trench
  d. dirt

8. weld _____
  a. insulation
  b. a boom
  c. a stair rail
  d. concrete

9. dig _____
  a. the roof
  b. a trench
  c. studs
  d. glass

10. mop _____
  a. a pipe
  b. a beam
  c. tar
  d. bolts

11. thread _____
  a. a pipe
  b. concrete
  c. rebar
  d. a window

12. dump _____
  a. spacers
  b. glass
  c. a stud
  d. cement

13. tie _____
  a. tile
  b. cement
  c. rebar
  d. a trench

14. read _____
  a. insulation
  b. site plans
  c. a surface
  d. a surveyor

15. space _____
  a. tiles
  b. cement
  c. a bill
  d. a dump truck

16. tighten _____
  a. stone
  b. putty
  c. brick
  d. bolts

WORKPLACE COMMUNICATION

F WHAT ARE THEY SAYING?

_f_ **1.** ask a co-worker for material

____ **2.** coordinate a task with a co-worker

____ **3.** communicate using hand signals

____ **4.** check on completion of a task

____ **5.** ask a co-worker to do a task

____ **6.** ask about the scope of a task

____ **7.** coordinate on separate tasks

____ **8.** point out a problem with a machine setting

____ **9.** warn about the unsafe use of a machine

____ **10.** point out a problem with the setup of a structure

____ **11.** ask for feedback

a. "Can you cut those panes? I need four of them."

b. "You set the pump output too low!"

c. "Should I send the next truck? *Over.*"

d. "Your load is too heavy! It must be way beyond the safety rating."

e. "There's a problem with the scaffolding you're setting up."

f. "I need a corner form here."

g. "How many solar panels do we have to mount?"

h. "Should I signal him to stop?"

i. "Do these tiles look okay to you?"

j. "Is the foundation floor done yet?"

k. "If you run the electric cables in this room, I'll trim some studs in the room next door."

1 service advisor
2 auto technician
3 shop foreman
4 tire specialist
5 tune-up and electronics specialist
6 automotive exhaust emissions technician
7 brake specialist
8 automotive suspension technician
9 lubrication/lube technician

a parts department
b waiting room
c emergency eyewash station
d diagnostic scanner
e service bay

f charging system analyzer
g tire balance machine
h fluid exchange machine
i jack stand

j auto creeper
k two-post auto lift
l hydraulic floor jack
m tool cart
n tool chest
o service bay pit

What occupations do you see in this auto service department? What workplace objects do you see?

Do you own a car? Where do you take it to be serviced or repaired? Or do you do this yourself?

10 tow truck driver	**16** sunroof installer	**p** flatbed tow truck	**u** trifold doors
11 estimator	**17** window tint	**q** frame pull machine	**v** paint room exhaust
12 frame repairperson	specialist	**r** windshield stand	**w** paint waste drum
13 collision repair technician	**18** auto upholsterer	**s** body dolly	**x** bumper caddy
14 auto body repairperson	**19** auto paint helper	**t** paint room	**y** mixing bench
15 windshield/auto glass technician	**20** auto painter		

What occupations do you see in this auto body repair facility? What workplace objects do you see?

Have you ever needed to use an auto body repair facility? If so, what happened?

1 prepare a work order
2 diagnose an auto problem
3 charge a battery
4 exchange radiator coolant
5 check a restraint system
6 tune up a car
7 drain oil
8 change an oil filter
9 check fluid levels
10 balance a tire
11 mount a tire
12 change a brake pad
13 install a new shock absorber
14 inspect the undercarriage of a car
15 replace a muffler
16 examine a hose for leaks

Look at pages 108–109. What are the workers doing? Describe their actions.

17 lower a car from a tow truck
18 pull a frame to straighten it
19 take off a door panel
20 fill a crack with plastic body filler

21 sand paint off a dented area
22 weld draw pins to a dented area
23 pull out a dent
24 grind down welded draw pins

25 shape an area with a hammer and dollies
26 sand by hand to smooth an area
27 cut a hole in a roof
28 adhere tint film to a window

29 reupholster a ripped seat
30 mask an area and tape it
31 mix paint
32 spray a car panel

1 diagnostic scanner	**7** tire weight	**13** oil dipstick	**18** rubber hose
2 feeler gauge	**8** tire balance clamp	**14** oil filter	**19** hose clamp
3 spark plug	**9** muffler	**15** lift oil drain	**20** shock absorber
4 timing light	**10** muffler clamp	**16** torque wrench	**21** brake pad
5 auto creeper	**11** serpentine belt	**17** rubber mallet	**22** tire pressure gauge
6 air filter	**12** oil filter wrench		

Look at pages 108–111. What equipment, tools, and objects do you see?

23 auto sander	**29** longboard file	**35** body filler	**41** under hood/trunk clip
24 dent hammer	**30** power grinder	**36** auto body spreader	**42** door panel removal tool
25 dome dolly	**31** sanding block	**37** retractable razor scraper	**43** film heat gun
26 anvil dolly	**32** paint thickness gauge	**38** auto body spray gun	**44** window film squeegee
27 slide hammer	**33** upholstery stapler	**39** respirator	**45** window film roll
28 stud welding gun	**34** nibbler	**40** windshield hook tool	

1 A Customer & a Service Advisor

A service advisor is talking with a customer to prepare a work order.

A. My car isn't running right. I don't know what's wrong.

B. When's the last time you had it serviced?

A. It had an oil change about six months ago and it just reached 30,000 miles.

B. Then you're probably due for a tune-up.

2 Two Brake Specialists

Two brake specialists are diagnosing a problem and coordinating tasks.

A. It looks like the front brake pads are worn.

B. How are the rotors?

A. I felt some grooves. They'll have to be machined. I'll take care of that now.

B. Okay. I'll get the new pads from Parts.

3 An Auto Technician & a Service Advisor

An auto tech is describing a problem to a service advisor.

A. There's a problem with the minivan I'm working on.

B. What is it?

A. I checked the fluid levels and the power steering is almost out. I think there's a leak.

B. Okay. I'll let the customer know.

4 An Auto Shop Foreman & an Auto Technician

A shop foreman is checking on the status of a repair job.

A. How's the exhaust system job coming along?

B. I just started it. The muffler and tailpipe need to be replaced.

A. Do you think it'll be finished by closing time?

B. It should be. No problem.

---

1 You're a service advisor. Ask a customer to describe the problem with a car.

2–3 You work in an auto service department. You just diagnosed a problem. Describe it to a co-worker.

4 You're an auto shop foreman. Check on the status of a job.

5 Two Auto Body Repairpeople

Two auto body repairpeople are coordinating tasks.

A. I'm finished pulling out the dent in the fender.
B. Good. I'm still working on this rear quarter panel. Can you grind down the draw pins and then shape the fender?
A. Sure. Will do.

6 Two Frame Repairpeople

Two frame repairpeople are assessing damage and determining a course of action.

A. It looks like there's some sidesway.
B. There's also some sag damage.
A. You're right. I'll take the measurements and locate the factory reference points.
B. Okay. While you do that, I'll lock down the frame.

7 An Auto Painter & an Auto Body Repairperson

An auto painter and an auto body repairperson are coordinating tasks.

A. When will this car be prepped for painting?
B. I've still got a couple of more hours of sanding.
A. Will you be done by noon?
B. Let's say 12:30.

8 Two Collision Repair Technicians

A collision repair tech notices that a co-worker is having a problem.

A. You look like you're having trouble removing that panel.
B. I am.
A. No wonder! You're using a flathead screwdriver!
B. I know. I can't find a door panel removal tool.
A. Wait a minute. I'll get you one.

5–7 You work in an auto body repair facility. Coordinate tasks with a co-worker.
8 Your co-worker is having a problem. Point it out and offer assistance.

A HOW TO CHANGE ENGINE OIL

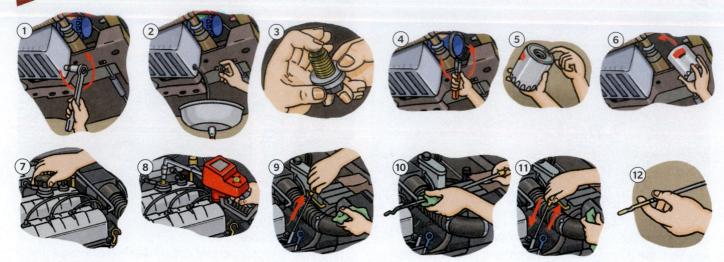

1. Loosen and remove the oil pan plug.
2. Drain the oil.
3. Inspect and replace the oil pan plug.
4. Remove the oil filter.
5. Rub oil on the seal of the new filter.
6. Put on the new filter.
7. Remove the oil filler cap.
8. Add new oil to the manufacturer's specifications.
9. Remove the oil dipstick.
10. Clean the dipstick.
11. Insert and remove the dipstick.
12. Check the dipstick for oil level.

B HOW TO CHANGE A SPARK PLUG

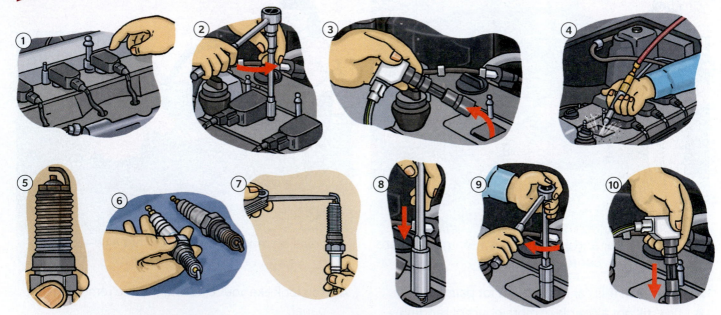

1. Change only one plug at a time.
2. Loosen the screw that holds down the spark plug wire.
3. Remove the spark plug wire.
4. Blow or wipe away any debris from the cylinder.
5. Look for carbon buildup on the electrode end of the plug.
6. Make sure the replacement plug is the same size as the old plug.
7. Check and adjust the gap of the new plug.
8. Insert the plug into the cylinder head.
9. Tighten the plug so it's snug.
10. Push the spark plug wire back on.

C HOW TO FIX A DENT

1 Sand away paint from the dented area.
2 Attach draw pins with a stud welding gun.
3 Use a slide hammer to pull out the dent.
4 Cut down the draw pins.
5 Grind down the draw pins.
6 Shape the area with a dent hammer and dolly.
7 Apply body filler where needed.
8 When the body filler is dry, shape the area with a longboard file.
9 Sand down the area until it's smooth.

D HOW TO PAINT A REPAIRED AREA

1 Clean the repaired area with wax and grease remover.
2 Tape and mask areas not being painted.
3 Apply a primer coat.
4 Rough-sand the area.
5 Apply two base coats of paint.
6 Apply three clear coats.
7 Remove the tape and mask from the covered areas.
8 In two or three days, wet-sand any bumps in the paint.
9 Apply buffing compound.
10 Buff the repaired area until smooth.

1 A Shop Foreman & an Auto Repair Technician

A shop foreman is calling attention to a problem.

A. Did you replace the radiator hose on this vehicle?
B. Yes, I did. Why?
A. There's a leak. You'd better check to see if the clamps are on correctly.
B. Okay. I'll do that right away.

2 Two Auto Repair Technicians

An auto repair tech is asking a co-worker to check his work.

A. Got a minute?
B. Sure. What's up?
A. Could you check something for me? This serpentine belt I installed seems loose.
B. Hmm. It looks like the belt is the wrong size. I always double-check the part number before I replace a belt.

3 Two Auto Body Repairpeople

An auto body repairperson is asking a co-worker for help.

A. I'm having trouble shaping the fender in this area. Am I using the right type of dolly?
B. What are you using?
A. I'm using a dome dolly.
B. That's why you're having trouble. You need to use an anvil dolly.

4 An Auto Painter & an Auto Paint Helper

An auto painter is correcting a helper.

A. Why didn't you mask the hood?
B. I thought we were painting the whole car.
A. No. We're just painting the repaired section.
B. Okay. I'll mask it now.

---

1 You're a shop foreman. Point out a problem to a worker.
2 Ask a co-worker to check your work.

3 Ask a co-worker for help.
4 Give correction to a co-worker.

OCCUPATIONS

auto body repairperson
auto paint helper
auto painter
auto technician
auto upholsterer
automotive exhaust emissions
   technician
automotive suspension technician

brake specialist
collision repair technician
estimator
frame repairperson
lubrication/lube
   technician
service advisor
shop foreman

sunroof installer
tire specialist
tow truck driver
tune-up and electronics
   specialist
window tint specialist
windshield/auto glass
   technician

WORKPLACE LOCATIONS

emergency eyewash
   station
paint room
parts (department)
service bay
service bay pit
waiting room

EQUIPMENT, TOOLS, & OBJECTS

air filter
anvil dolly
auto body spray gun
auto body spreader
auto creeper
auto sander
base coat
battery
body dolly
body filler
brake pad
buffing compound
bumper caddy
car panel
charging system
   analyzer
clamps
cylinder
dent hammer
diagnostic scanner
dipstick
dolly

dome dolly
door panel
door panel removal tool
draw pins
electrode
exhaust system
factory reference points
feeler gauge
film heat gun
filter
flatbed tow truck
flathead screwdriver
fluid exchange machine
fluid level
frame
frame pull machine
grooves
hammer
hose
hose clamp
hydraulic floor jack

jack stand
lift oil drain
longboard file
mixing bench
muffler
muffler clamp
nibbler
oil
oil dipstick
oil filler cap
oil filter
oil filter wrench
oil level
oil pan plug
paint
paint thickness
   gauge
paint waste drum
panel
part number
plastic body filler
plug

power grinder
primer coat
radiator coolant
radiator hose
replacement plug
respirator
restraint system
retractable razor
   scraper
rotors
rubber hose
rubber mallet
sanding block
seal
serpentine belt
shock absorber
slide hammer
spark plug
spark plug wire
stud welding gun
tailpipe
timing light

tint film
tire
tire balance clamp
tire balance machine
tire pressure gauge
tire weight
tool cart
tool chest
torque wrench
tow truck
trifold doors
two-post auto lift
under hood/trunk clip
upholstery stapler
wax and grease
   remover
welded draw pins
window film roll
window film squeegee
windshield hook tool
windshield stand
work order

WORKPLACE ACTIONS

adhere tint film to a window
balance a tire
change a brake pad
change an oil filter
charge a battery
check fluid levels
check a restraint system
cut a hole in a roof
diagnose an auto problem
drain oil

examine a hose for leaks
exchange radiator coolant
fill a crack with plastic body
   filler
grind down welded draw
   pins
inspect the undercarriage
   of a car
install a new shock absorber
lower a car from a tow truck

mask an area and tape it
mix paint
mount a tire
prepare a work order
pull a frame to
   straighten it
pull out a dent
replace a muffler
reupholster a ripped
   seat

sand by hand to smooth an
   area
sand paint off a dented area
shape an area with a
   hammer and dollies
spray a car panel
take off a door panel
tune up a car
weld draw pins to a dented
   area

WORKPLACE COMMUNICATION

ask a co-worker for help
ask a co-worker to check your work
assess damage and determine a
   course of action

call a co-worker's attention to a
   problem
check on the status of a repair job
coordinate tasks with a co-worker
correct a co-worker

deal with a customer's problem
describe a problem to a co-worker
diagnose a problem
observe that a co-worker is having
   a problem

OCCUPATIONS

A ▶ FIND THE RIGHT PERSON!

a. auto glass technician	**g.** automotive suspension technician	**m.** sunroof installer
b. auto paint helper	**h.** brake specialist	**n.** tire specialist
c. auto painter	**i.** collision repair tech	**o.** tow truck driver
d. auto tech	**j.** estimator	**p.** tune-up and electronics specialist
e. auto upholsterer	**k.** service advisor	**q.** window tint specialist
f. automotive exhaust emissions technician	**l.** shop foreman	

___d___ **1.** I've been having a lot of problems with my car. Do you know the name of a good _____?

_____ **2.** The seats in my car are ripped. Do you know a good _____?

_____ **3.** I'm having trouble stopping my car. I need to see a _____.

_____ **4.** My windshield is cracked. Do you know a good _____?

_____ **5.** I've gotten a few flat tires recently. Can you recommend a _____?

_____ **6.** There are fumes coming out the back of my car. I need to take it to a reliable _____.

_____ **7.** My car makes a lot of noise and it's very bumpy when I drive. I need to find a good _____.

_____ **8.** There are several scratches on my car. Do you know a good _____?

_____ **9.** My son assists the auto painter at Jack's Repair Shop. He's an _____.

_____ **10.** I'd like more light in my car. I think I'll contact a _____.

_____ **11.** I was recently in a car accident. I'm fine, but my car is in bad shape. I need to see a _____.

_____ **12.** The spark plugs in my car need to be changed. Can you recommend a good _____?

_____ **13.** If you want to darken the windows in your car, you need to find an experienced _____.

_____ **14.** My car won't start. I need emergency service. Right now I'm waiting and looking for the _____.

_____ **15.** Martin calculates how much car repairs will cost. He's an experienced _____.

_____ **16.** Alex works at an auto body shop. He's in charge of several repairpeople. He's the _____.

_____ **17.** I just arrived at the auto body shop. I'm here to have my car repaired. First, I need to speak with a _____.

WORKPLACE LOCATIONS

B ▶ WHERE ARE THEY?

1. Your car is being repaired in the service (room   technician   bay).

2. Parts are available in the parts (pit   station   department).

3. Maxine is changing the oil in someone's car. She's standing in a service bay (room   pit   station).

4. While your car is being serviced, you can relax in our waiting (room   station   pit).

5. In case of an emergency on the job, go to the emergency eyewash (department   room   station).

EQUIPMENT, TOOLS, & OBJECTS

C ▸ WHAT'S THE ITEM?

_e_	1. base	**a.** filter	____	9. exhaust	**i.** hose	____	17. car	**q.** grinder
____	2. draw	**b.** level	____	10. muffler	**j.** dolly	____	18. feeler	**r.** coat
____	3. oil	**c.** clamp	____	11. rubber	**k.** pad	____	19. grease	**s.** panel
____	4. auto	**d.** chest	____	12. primer	**l.** light	____	20. power	**t.** scanner
____	5. hose	**e.** coat	____	13. brake	**m.** system	____	21. slide	**u.** gauge
____	6. spark	**f.** sander	____	14. timing	**n.** head	____	22. diagnostic	**v.** filler
____	7. tool	**g.** pins	____	15. cylinder	**o.** clamp	____	23. body	**w.** remover
____	8. fluid	**h.** plug	____	16. anvil	**p.** coat	____	24. primer	**x.** hammer

WORKPLACE ACTIONS

D ▸ DANILO'S AUTO REPAIR

The people at Danilo's Auto Repair worked on my car all day today. First, they (mounted   prepared)[1] a work order. They (checked   balanced)[2] the fluid levels and (tuned up   charged)[3] my battery. They (diagnosed   inspected)[4] the undercarriage of my car to make sure everything was okay. They also (drained   welded)[5] the oil, (sprayed   changed)[6] the oil filter, and (mixed   exchanged)[7] the radiator coolant. They (examined   filled)[8] all the hoses for leaks. They (welded   installed)[9] new shock absorbers and (replaced   sanded)[10] my muffler. They also (machined   changed)[11] my brake pads and (reupholstered   rotated)[12] my tires. They did a lot of work!

WORKPLACE COMMUNICATION

E ▸ WHAT ARE THEY SAYING?

_g_ 1. diagnose a problem	**a.** "You'd better check to see if the clamps are on correctly."
____ 2. talk with a customer to prepare a work order	**b.** "I'm still working on this panel. Can you shape the fender?"
____ 3. describe a problem	**c.** "Okay. I'll do that right away."
____ 4. check on the status of a repair job	**d.** "You're probably due for a tune-up."
____ 5. coordinate tasks with a co-worker	**e.** "I'm having trouble shaping the fender."
____ 6. observe that a co-worker is having a problem.	**f.** "You look like you're having trouble removing that panel."
____ 7. give instructions	**g.** "It looks like the front brakes are worn."
____ 8. ask a co-worker to check your work	**h.** "Could you check something for me?"
____ 9. state that you're having a problem	**i.** "How's the exhaust system job coming along?"
____ 10. respond to instructions	**j.** "There's a leak."

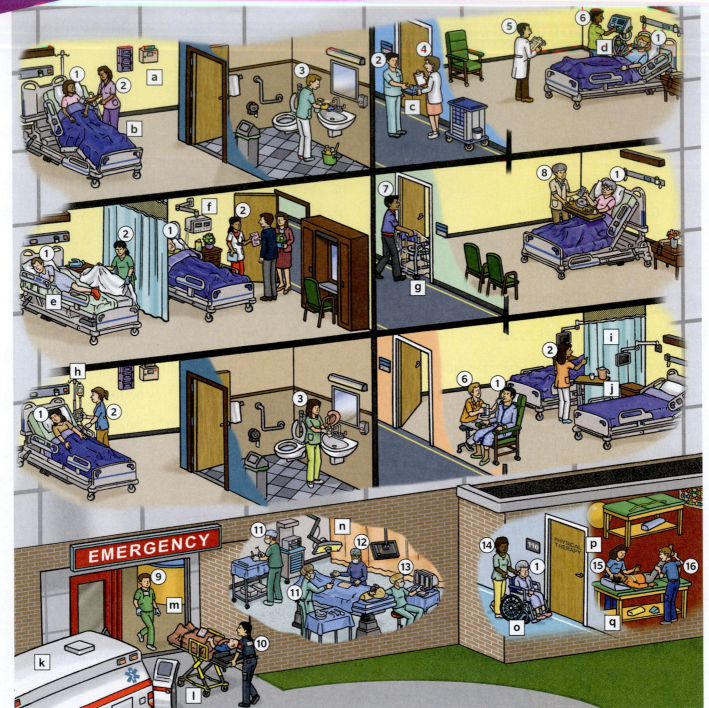

1 patient	8 dietetic technician/aide	a hospital room	h IV* pole/stand
2 CNA*	9 emergency room technician	b hospital bed	i privacy curtain
3 orderly	10 EMT*	c pill cup	j over bed table
4 RN/LPN*	11 surgical technician	d oxygen inhalation equipment	k ambulance
5 doctor	12 surgeon	e bedside rail	l gurney/stretcher
6 respiratory therapist	13 anesthesiologist	f heart/blood pressure monitor	m emergency room entrance
7 medical equipment preparer/certified SPD* technician	14 patient transport attendant	g commode	n surgical suite
	15 physical therapist assistant		o wheelchair
	16 physical therapist		p physical therapy room
			q physical therapy table

* CNA = certified nursing assistant, RN = registered nurse, LPN = licensed practical nurse,
  SPD = sterile processing and distribution, EMT = emergency medical technician, IV = intravenous

What occupations do you see in this hospital?
What workplace objects do you see?

Have you or a family member ever been hospitalized?
If so, what was the situation?

17 client	**20** physical therapist	**r** two-wheel walker	**v** grooming supplies
18 home health aide	**21** visiting nurse	**s** leg bed wedge	**w** raised toilet seat
19 homemaker		**t** lift chair	**x** portable oxygen
		u safety bar	**y** handicap ramp

What home health care occupations do you see?
What home health care objects do you see?

The elderly person in this house lives alone. Home health care workers take care of him. In your opinion, what are some good things or bad things about this situation?

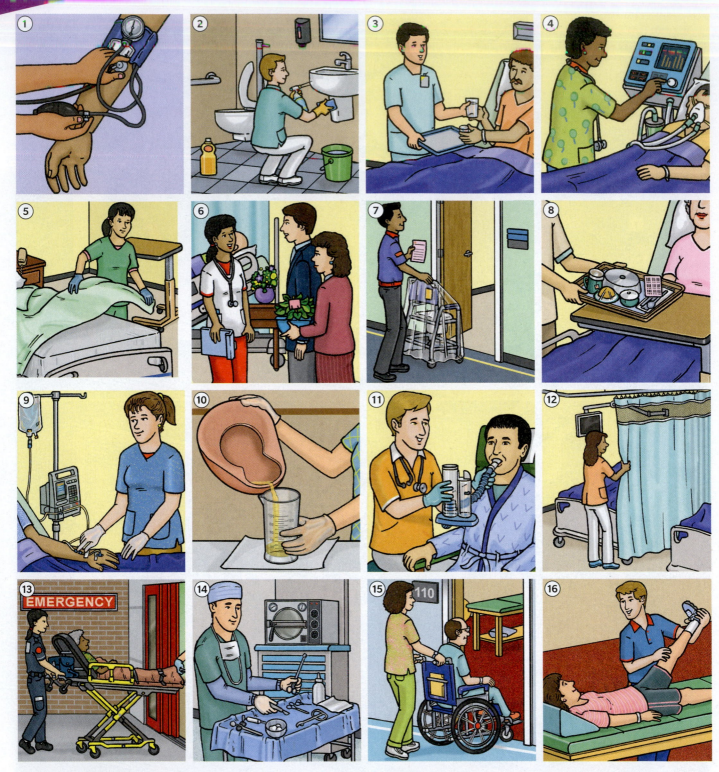

1 take blood pressure
2 sanitize a bathroom
3 administer medication
4 adjust ventilator settings
5 change linens
6 discuss a patient's status with family members
7 bring medical equipment to a patient's room
8 deliver a meal
9 check an IV
10 measure a patient's output
11 do respiratory therapy
12 close a privacy curtain
13 transport a patient to the ER/emergency room
14 set up surgical instruments
15 transport a patient to physical therapy
16 perform physical therapy on a patient

Look at pages 122–123. What are the workers doing? Describe their actions.

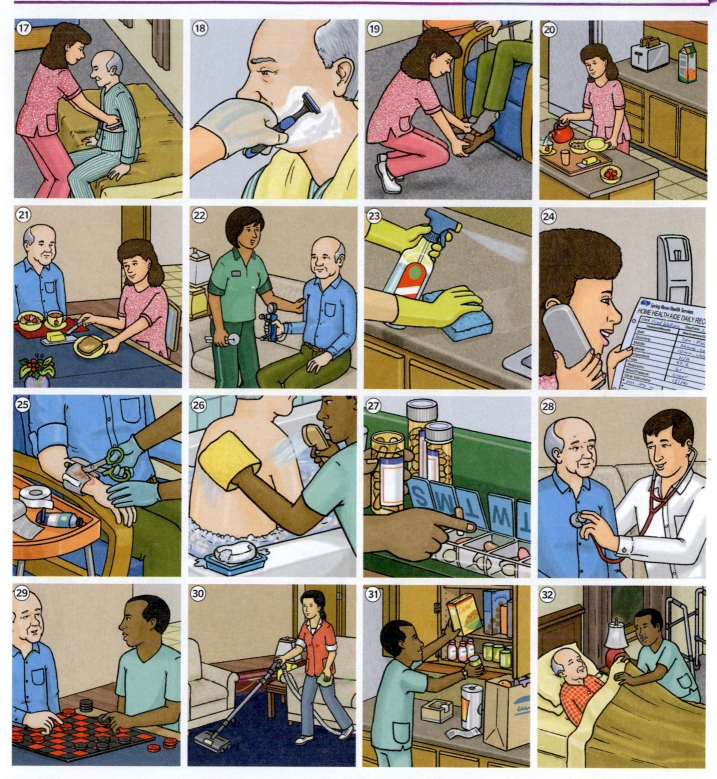

17 help a client get out of bed

18 groom a client

19 dress a client

20 prepare a meal

21 help a client eat

22 evaluate a patient's PT* progress

23 sanitize a counter

24 report on a client's status

25 change a dressing

26 bathe a client

27 organize a client's medication supply

28 check a client's vital signs

29 do activities with a client

30 vacuum and clean the house

31 shop for groceries and put them away

32 put a client to bed

* PT = physical therapy

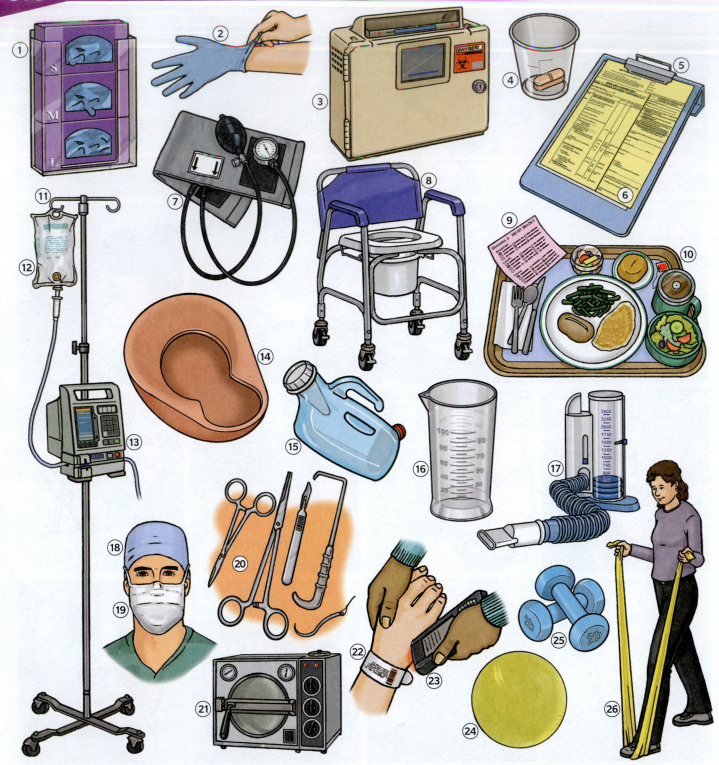

1 glove box dispenser	**8** commode	**15** urine collector	**22** ID wristband
2 disposable gloves	**9** patient's dietary slip	**16** measuring container	**23** ID reader
3 sharps container	**10** patient's low-sodium meal	**17** incentive spirometer	**24** therapy ball
4 pill cup	**11** IV pole/stand	**18** surgical cap	**25** hand weights
5 hospital bed clipboard	**12** IV bag	**19** surgical mask	**26** resistance band
6 patient's chart	**13** infusion pump	**20** surgical instruments	
7 blood pressure cuff	**14** bedpan	**21** autoclave	

Look at pages 122–125. What equipment, tools, and objects do you see?

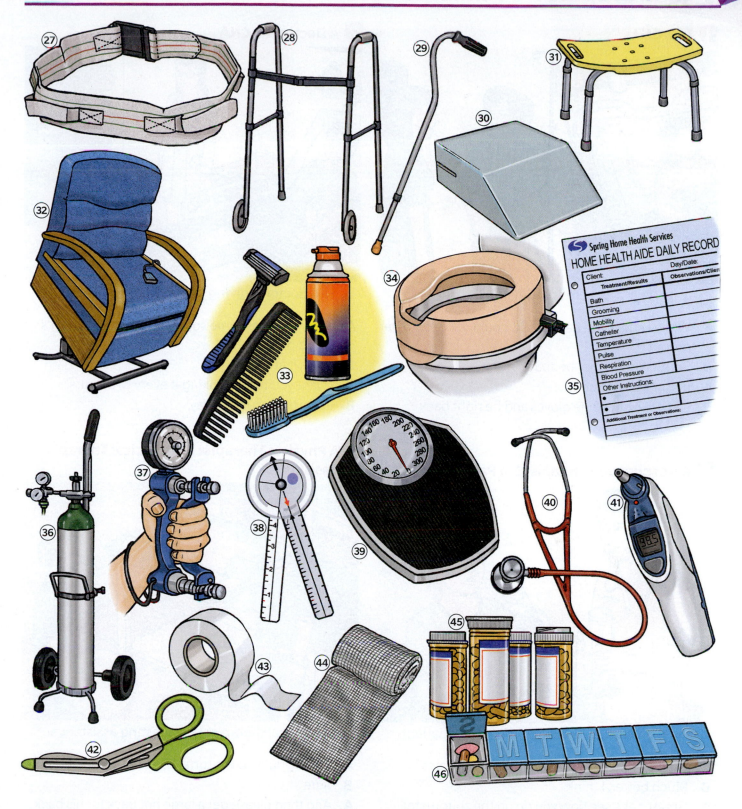

27 gait belt	**32** lift chair	**37** hand dynamometer	**42** medical utility scissors
28 walker	**33** grooming supplies	**38** goniometer	**43** medical tape
29 cane	**34** raised toilet seat	**39** scale	**44** gauze
30 leg bed wedge	**35** daily record sheet	**40** stethoscope	**45** medications
31 bath seat	**36** portable oxygen	**41** tympanic thermometer	**46** weekly pill case

9.4 Workplace Communication

1 Two CNAs

Two CNAs are coordinating tasks.

A. While I check the patient's IV, could you record her output?
B. Sure. Where's her bedpan?
A. It's in the bathroom.
B. Okay. I'll get some gloves and be right back.

2 A Doctor & a CNA

A doctor is giving instructions to a CNA.

A. When's the last time someone took Mr. Chang's blood pressure?
B. I took it at 10 A.M.
A. I want you to start taking it every two hours.
B. Every two hours? Okay.

3 A Respiratory Therapist & a Patient

A respiratory therapist is checking on a patient.

A. How's your breathing today, Mrs. Gonzales?
B. Much better, I think.
A. Great! Let's see how you do on the spirometer.

4 A Physical Therapist & a Physical Therapist Assistant

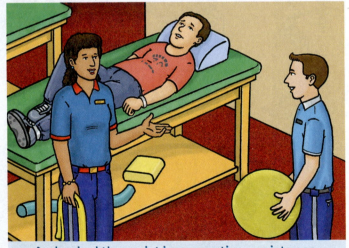

A physical therapist is requesting assistance.

A. Could you help me turn Mr. Green on his side?
B. Sure.
A. And then please get a large hot pack for his back.
B. Okay.

1 You're a CNA in a hospital. Coordinate a patient care task with a co-worker.
2 You're a doctor. Give instructions to a CNA.
3 You work in a hospital. Check on your patient's condition.
4 You're a physical therapist. Ask an assistant for help.

5 A Home Health Aide & a Client

A home health aide is caring for a client.

A. Mr. Watson, are you comfortable?
B. Yes. I'm fine.
A. I'm going to the kitchen to make your lunch. If you need anything, just let me know.
B. I will.

6 A Home Health Aide & a Homemaker

A home health aide is giving instructions to a homemaker.

A. Are you going to vacuum the house today?
B. Yes, I am. Is there anything else you want me to be sure to do?
A. Could you also wash the bathroom floor?
B. Will do.

7 Two Home Health Aides

A daytime home health aide and an overnight home health aide are coordinating during their shift change.

A. I was able to take Mr. Watson for a walk outside this afternoon.
B. That's nice. I think I'll play a board game with him after dinner.
A. He'll enjoy that. And make sure you read to him the letter that arrived from his grandson.
B. I'll do that.

8 A Home Health Aide & a Client

A home health aide is preparing a client for bedtime.

A. It's 9:30, Mr. Watson. Time to get ready for bed.
B. Could I have some dessert first?
A. Mr. Watson, we had dessert after dinner.
B. Oh, yes. We did. I guess it's time for bed.

5 You're a home health aide. Make sure your client is comfortable.

6 Imagine other conversations between a home health aide and a homemaker.

7 You're a daytime home health aide. Coordinate with the overnight aide during your shift change.

8 You're an overnight home health aide. Prepare your client for bedtime.

A HOW TO TAKE BLOOD PRESSURE

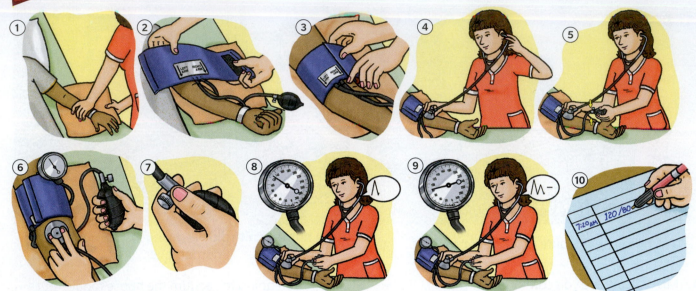

1 Position the patient's arm to be comfortable.
2 Place the cuff on the arm with the artery marker at the brachial artery.
3 Wrap the cuff securely around the arm.
4 Put the diaphragm of the stethoscope on the arm at the brachial artery.

5 Squeeze the bulb to tighten the cuff until you no longer hear a beat.
6 Continue squeezing the cuff until the reading on the gauge is another 30 millimeters.
7 Open the valve and deflate the cuff at a rate of 2 millimeters per second.

8 Stop when you hear the first beat. (That is the systolic pressure.)
9 Continue to deflate the cuff until you hear no beat. (That is the diastolic pressure.)
10 Record the blood pressure reading (systolic over diastolic pressure).

B HOW TO MEASURE A PATIENT'S OUTPUT

1 Wash hands.
2 Put on disposable gloves.
3 Place a paper towel under a measuring container.
4 Drain the patient's urine from the bedpan into the measuring container.

5 Note the amount and color of the urine.
6 Empty the urine into the toilet.
7 Wash and rinse the measuring container and the bedpan.

8 Remove and dispose of the gloves.
9 Wash hands again.
10 Record the patient's output.

C HOW TO AMBULATE A PATIENT WITH A GAIT BELT

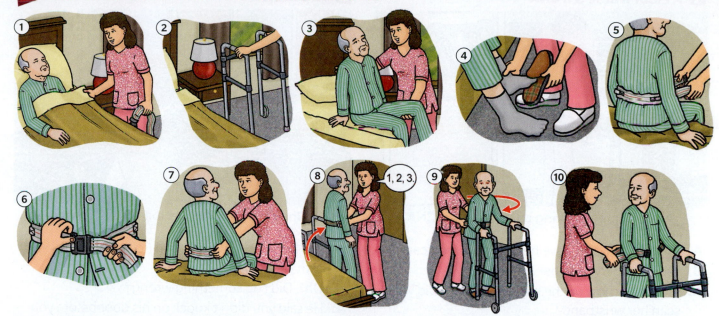

1 Explain the procedure to the client.
2 Position the client's walker at the head of the bed.
3 Help the client into a sitting position.
4 Put on the client's socks and slippers.

5 Place a gait belt around the client.
6 Tighten the gait belt.
7 Grasp the belt with both hands.

8 Count to three and help bring the client to a standing position.
9 Assist the client to pivot and hold onto the walker.
10 Take off the gait belt.

D HOW TO APPLY A CLEAN DRESSING

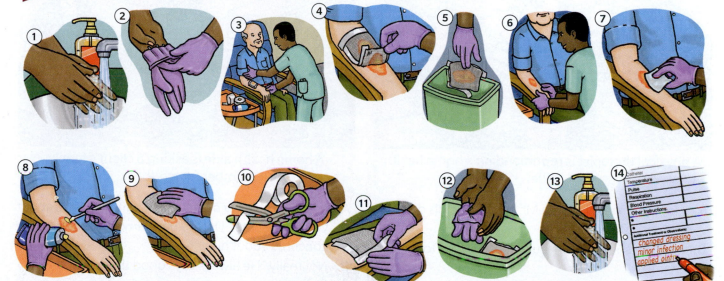

1 Wash hands.
2 Put on disposable gloves.
3 Position the client so the area with the dressing is accessible.
4 Remove the old dressing carefully.
5 Discard the old dressing.

6 Note the color, odor, amount of drainage, and condition of the surrounding skin.
7 Clean the affected area.
8 Apply ointment according to the doctor's instructions.
9 Put clean gauze over the affected area.
10 Cut some adhesive tape.

11 Tape down the new dressing.
12 Remove and discard the gloves.
13 Wash hands again.
14 Record the dressing change, observations of the skin condition, and any client complaints.

1 A Floor Nurse & a CNA

A floor nurse is giving correction to a CNA.

A. Did Mrs. Navarro have her morning medications?
B. Yes. I gave them to her an hour ago.
A. It doesn't show on the medical record. Did you scan her wristband?
B. Oh, no. I forgot.
A. You must always remember to scan a patient's wristband before giving medication.

2 Two CNAs

One CNA is giving feedback to another.

A. You know . . . Mr. Higgins in Room 405 is upset with you today.
B. Oh? Did I do something wrong?
A. He said you didn't knock on his door before you entered his room this morning.
B. I knocked, but he was asleep. I always respect our patients' privacy.
A. Well, I'd apologize to him anyway.

3 A Physical Therapist & a Home Health Aide

A physical therapist is reprimanding a home health aide.

A. Have you been helping Mr. Watson do his daily exercises?
B. I try, but some days he just doesn't want to do them.
A. That's no excuse! You have to make sure he does them every day, or it will affect his progress.
B. Okay. Do you hear that, Mr. Watson? We have to do our exercises daily or you're going to get me into trouble!

4 A Home Health Aide & a Client's Family Member

A home health aide is asking a client's family member for feedback.

A. I'm glad to finally meet you. Your uncle talks about you all the time. Do you have any questions or concerns about his care?
B. Not really. He always says good things about you. Do you have any concerns or advice for me?
A. To be honest, yes. Family members should visit more often. He gets lonely.
B. We'll do that. Thanks.

1 You're a floor nurse in a hospital. Give correction to a CNA.
2 You're a CNA. Give constructive feedback to a co-worker.
3 This physical therapist is angry with the home health aide. Do you think it's fair?
4 You're a home health aide. Have a conversation with a family member of your client.

OCCUPATIONS

anesthesiologist
certified nursing assistant (CNA)
dietetic technician/ aide
doctor
emergency medical technician (EMT)

emergency room technician
home health aide
homemaker
licensed practical nurse (LPN)
medical equipment preparer/ certified sterile processing and distribution (SPD) technician
orderly

patient transport attendant
physical therapist
physical therapist assistant
registered nurse (RN)
respiratory therapist
surgeon
surgical technician
visiting nurse

WORKPLACE LOCATIONS

emergency room (ER)
emergency room entrance
hospital room
patient's room
physical therapy room
surgical suite

EQUIPMENT, TOOLS, & OBJECTS

adhesive tape
ambulance
artery marker
autoclave
bath seat
bedpan
bedside rail
blood pressure cuff
bulb
cane
commode
cuff
daily record sheet
diaphragm
dietary slip
disposable gloves
dressing
gait belt
gauze

glove box dispenser
goniometer
grooming supplies
gurney/stretcher
hand dynamometer
hand weights
handicap ramp
heart/blood pressure monitor
hospital bed
hospital bed clipboard
hot pack
ID reader
ID wristband
incentive spirometer
infusion pump
IV
IV bag
IV pole/stand
leg bed wedge

lift chair
linens
low-sodium meal
measuring container
medical equipment
medical tape
medical utility scissors
medication supply
medications
ointment
output
over bed table
oxygen inhalation equipment
patient's chart
physical therapy table
pill cup
portable oxygen
privacy curtain
raised toilet seat

resistance band
safety bar
scale
sharps container
spirometer
stethoscope
surgical cap
surgical instruments
surgical mask
therapy ball
two-wheel walker
tympanic thermometer
urine collector
ventilator settings
vital signs
walker
weekly pill case
wheelchair
wristband

WORKPLACE ACTIONS

adjust ventilator settings
administer medication
bathe a client
bring medical equipment to a patient's room
change a dressing
change linens
check a client's vital signs
check an IV
close a privacy curtain
deliver a meal

discuss a patient's status with family members
do activities with a client
do respiratory therapy
dress a client
evaluate a patient's PT progress
groom a client
help a client eat
help a client get out of bed

measure a patient's output
organize a client's medication supply
perform physical therapy on a patient
prepare a meal
put a client to bed
report on a client's status
sanitize a bathroom
sanitize a counter

set up surgical instruments
shop for groceries and put them away
take blood pressure
transport a patient to physical therapy
transport a patient to the emergency room
vacuum and clean a house

WORKPLACE COMMUNICATION

ask for feedback
care for a client
check on a patient
coordinate tasks with a co-worker

coordinate work schedules
give correction
give feedback to a co-worker
give instructions

prepare a client for bedtime
reprimand a co-worker
request assistance

OCCUPATIONS

FIND THE MEDICAL CARE SPECIALIST!

anesthesiologist	home health aide	respiratory therapist
CNA	orderly	RN
dietetic aide	patient transport attendant	surgeon
emergency room technician	physical therapist	surgical technician
EMT	physical therapist assistant	visiting nurse

Which medical care specialist . . .

1. diagnoses and treats diseases, ailments, and injuries? _____ RN _____

2. performs emergency medical services outside a hospital? _____

3. makes sure patients have the correct nutrition? _____

4. keeps a patient asleep during surgery? _____

5. helps transport patients to different medical locations? _____

6. evaluates and treats patients with orthopedic problems? _____

7. treats patients with lung and breathing problems? _____

8. cuts into patients' bodies to diagnose and repair problems? _____

9. works under the direction of a physical therapist? _____

10. helps hospital patients perform basic everyday tasks? _____

11. provides medical care for people in their homes? _____

12. prepares the operating room for surgery? _____

13. takes care of ill or disabled patients in their homes? _____

14. works under the supervision of a licensed nurse? _____

15. assists doctors and nurses in the emergency room? _____

WORKPLACE LOCATIONS

WHERE ARE THEY?

1. The ambulance took my husband to the (emergency   patient's) room.

2. Patients are operated on in one of our (surgical suites   patient rooms).

3. Patients with orthopedic problems are treated in the physical therapy (room   entrance).

4. While you're in the hospital, you'll be staying with another patient in a very nice (hospital   emergency) room.

5. The ambulance drove up to the emergency room (entrance   suite).

EQUIPMENT, TOOLS, & OBJECTS

C WHAT'S THE ITEM?

_f_ 1. pill	a. signs	___ 8. ID	h. tape	___ 15. safety	o. marker
___ 2. lift	b. bag	___ 9. hot	i. belt	___ 16. surgical	p. oxygen
___ 3. vital	c. bed	___ 10. medical	j. pack	___ 17. artery	q. bar
___ 4. disposable	d. chair	___ 11. privacy	k. weights	___ 18. bedside	r. supplies
___ 5. hospital	e. gloves	___ 12. gait	l. reader	___ 19. urine	s. rail
___ 6. bed	f. case	___ 13. hand	m. ball	___ 20. grooming	t. cap
___ 7. IV	g. table	___ 14. therapy	n. curtain	___ 21. portable	u. collector

WORKPLACE ACTIONS

D MEDICAL CARE IN ACTION!

1. Please adjust the ___.
   a. bathroom
   b. ventilator settings *(circled)*
   c. client
   d. meal

2. You need to ___ the IV.
   a. vacuum
   b. bathe
   c. check
   d. groom

3. Please transport ___.
   a. the patient
   b. a counter
   c. the house
   d. a patient's status

4. I need to change ___.
   a. the blood pressure
   b. the vital signs
   c. the house
   d. the dressing

5. I can ___ the meal.
   a. perform
   b. prepare
   c. close
   d. sanitize

6. It's time to set up ___.
   a. the instruments
   b. the linens
   c. the client
   d. the groceries

7. I can administer ___.
   a. equipment
   b. patients
   c. medications
   d. the status

8. Can you ___ this meal?
   a. vacuum
   b. help
   c. close
   d. deliver

WORKPLACE COMMUNICATION

E WHAT ARE THEY SAYING?

_g_ 1. coordinate tasks with a co-worker

___ 2. give instructions

___ 3. check on a patient

___ 4. request assistance

___ 5. respond to a request

___ 6. prepare a client for bedtime

___ 7. ask if a task has been done

___ 8. report a problem

___ 9. reprimand someone

___ 10. ask family members for feedback

a. "Could you help me turn Mr. Green on his side?"

b. "Did Mrs. Navarro have her morning medications?"

c. "Time to get ready for bed."

d. "I want you to start taking her blood pressure every two hours."

e. "Do you have any questions or concerns about your uncle's care?"

f. "Mr. Higgins in Room 405 is upset with you."

g. "While I check the patient's IV, could you record her output?"

h. "Will do."

i. "That's no excuse! You have to make sure he does his exercises every day."

j. "How's your breathing today, Mrs. Gonzales?"

1 medical receptionist
2 administrative medical assistant
3 clinical medical assistant
4 medical transcriptionist

5 medical coder
6 EKG* technician
7 doctor/physician
8 physician assistant

* EKG = electrocardiogram

a reception
b medical files
c checkout desk
d doctor/physician scale
e height rod
f office

g lab
h specimen pass-through cabinet
i exam room
j examination table
k EKG machine

What occupations do you see in this medical office?
What workplace objects do you see?

9 dental hygienist	**17** phlebotomist	**a** dental office	**g** X-ray fluoroscopic	**m** phlebotomy lab

9 dental hygienist
10 dental assistant
11 dentist
12 dental lab technician
13 radiology technician
14 radiologist
15 nuclear medicine technician
16 MRI* technician

17 phlebotomist
18 medical lab technician
19 optometrist
20 optometric assistant
21 optical lab technician
22 optician
23 pharmacist
24 pharmacy technician
25 pharmacy assistant

a dental office
b dental chair
c intraoral X-ray camera
d dental X-ray
e dental lab
f radiology imaging center

g X-ray fluoroscopic system
h lead cape
i chest X-ray machine
j X-ray control area
k X-ray film processor
l MRI system

m phlebotomy lab
n diagnostic lab
o vision center
p optometry exam room
q optometry lab
r eyeglass display area
s pharmacy

* MRI = magnetic resonance imaging

What occupations do you see in this medical and dental professional building? What workplace objects do you see?

Where do you go for medical and dental care?

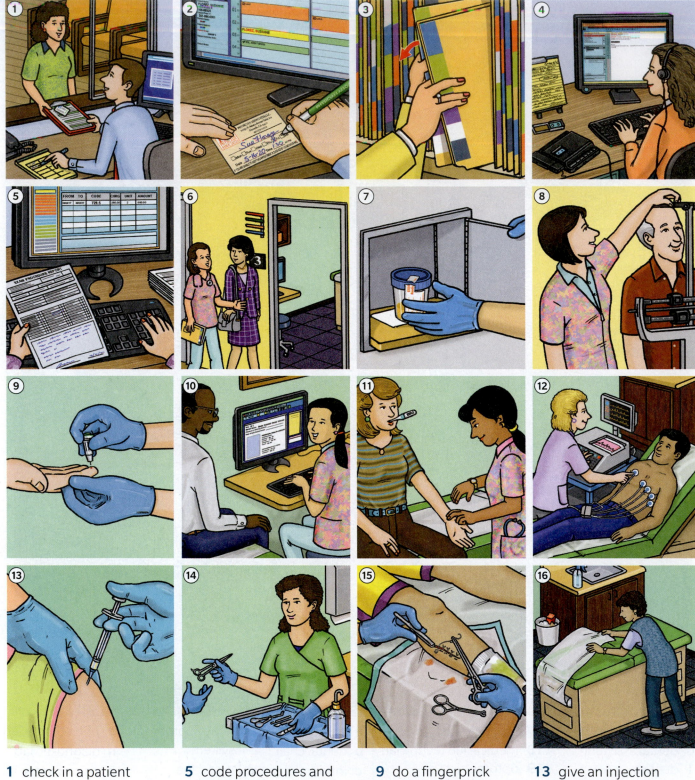

1 check in a patient
2 schedule a patient's next appointment
3 retrieve a medical file
4 transcribe a doctor's notes
5 code procedures and diagnoses
6 escort a patient to an exam room
7 collect a lab specimen
8 measure a patient's height and weight
9 do a fingerprick for a blood test
10 update a patient's medical record
11 take vital signs
12 do an EKG
13 give an injection
14 assist the doctor with a medical procedure
15 suture a wound
16 prepare an exam room for the next patient

Look at pages 136 and 137. What are the health services professionals doing? Describe their actions.

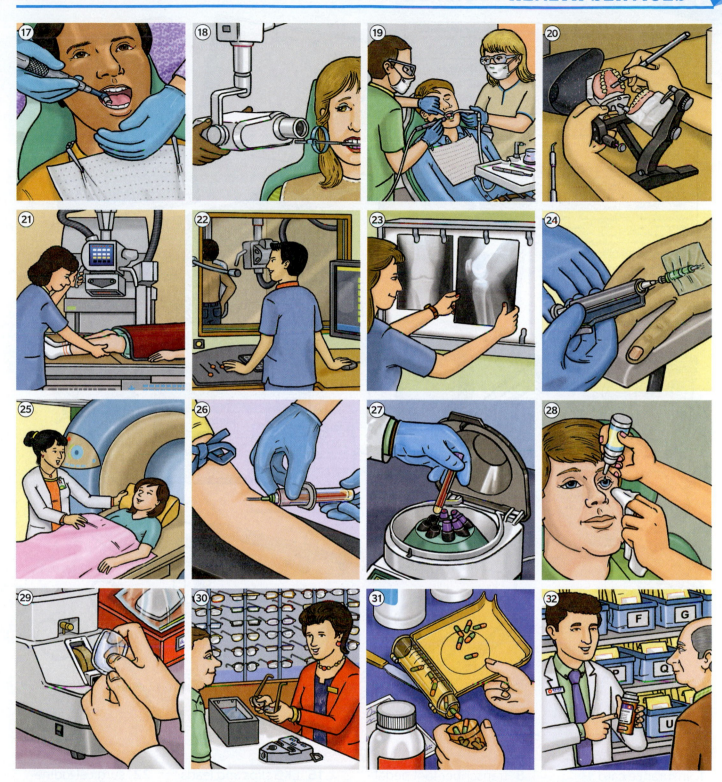

17 clean a patient's teeth
18 take dental X-rays
19 assist the dentist
20 make dentures

21 position a patient for an X-ray
22 take an X-ray
23 read an X-ray
24 inject radiopharmaceutical material

25 prepare a patient for an MRI
26 draw a patient's blood
27 analyze blood samples
28 dilate a patient's eyes

29 grind and polish lenses
30 adjust eyeglass frames
31 fill a prescription
32 give medication instructions

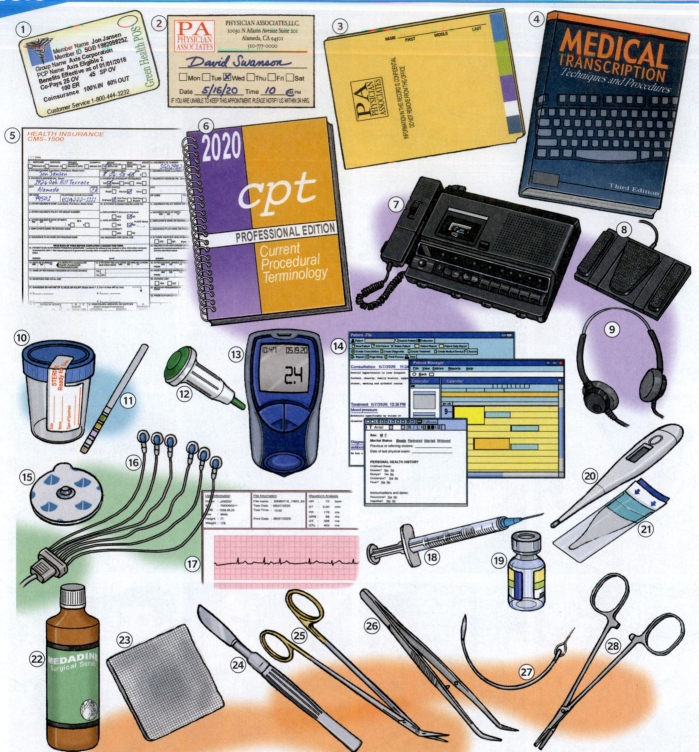

1 insurance card
2 appointment card
3 medical file
4 desk reference book
5 health insurance claim form
6 CPT* reference book
7 transcriber

8 transcriber foot pedal
9 transcriber headphone
10 specimen cup
11 lab specimen test strip
12 disposable lancet
13 handheld blood analyzer
14 medical history software
15 EKG electrode

16 EKG slips and leads
17 EKG reading
18 injection needle
19 vial
20 digital medical thermometer
21 digital thermometer sheath

22 surgical iodine
23 gauze
24 scalpel
25 surgical scissors
26 surgical tweezers
27 surgical suture needle and thread
28 suture clamp

* CPT = Current Procedural Terminology

Look at pages 136–139. What equipment, tools, and objects do you see?

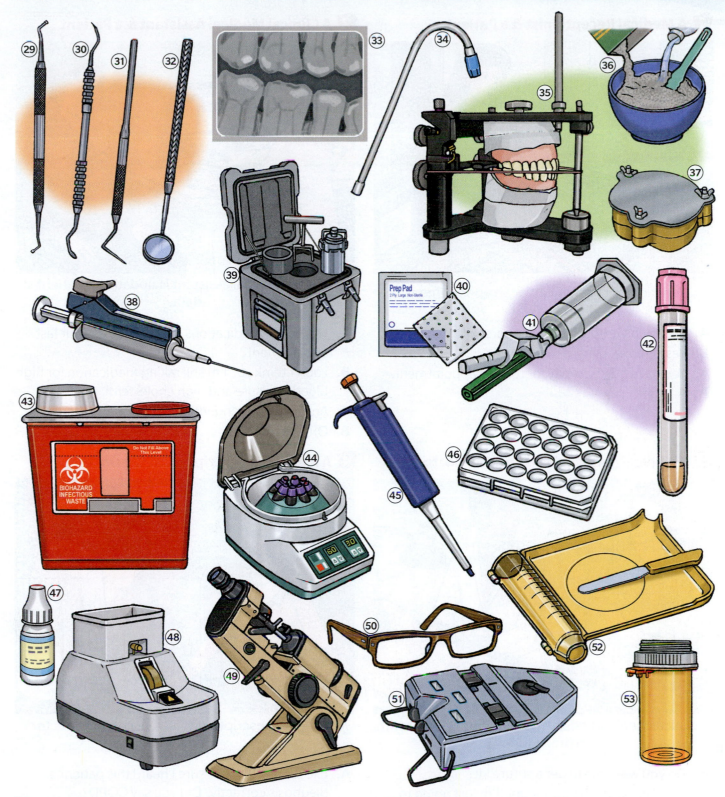

29 dental excavator
30 dental scaler
31 periodontal probe
32 dental mouth mirror
33 bitewing X-ray
34 saliva ejector
35 dentures and articulator

36 dental plaster
37 denture flask
38 tungsten syringe
39 shielded syringe carrier
40 alcohol pad
41 vacutainer holder and needle

42 blood collection tube
43 sharps disposal container
44 centrifuge
45 pipette
46 cell tray
47 eye drops

48 lens edger
49 lensometer
50 eyeglass frame
51 pupillometer
52 pill counting tray and spatula
53 prescription pill bottle

1 A Medical Receptionist & a Patient

A patient is checking in for an appointment.

A. Do you have your insurance card with you?
B. Yes. Here you are.
A. You have a $25 co-pay for today's appointment.
B. All right.

2 A Clinical Medical Assistant & a Patient

A clinical medical assistant is updating a patient's data.

A. Have your medications changed since your last appointment?
B. I don't think so. I'm still taking medication for high blood pressure and high cholesterol.
A. Are you still taking Vitamin E supplements?
B. Oh, yes. I am.

3 A Clinical Medical Assistant & a Doctor

A clinical medical assistant is assisting a doctor with a procedure.

A. Do you want me to get a suture kit?
B. No. That won't be necessary. I'm just going to dress the wound.
A. Okay. I'll get the gauze and tape.
B. Thank you.

4 A Medical Transcriptionist & a Doctor

A medical transcriptionist is transcribing a doctor's notes.

A. Excuse me. I'm not sure I heard this patient's diagnosis correctly. Did you say COPD?
B. Yes. He has chronic obstructive pulmonary disease.
A. That's what I thought. I just wanted to be sure. It was difficult to hear on the recording.

1 You're a medical receptionist. Help a patient check in.
2 You're a clinical medical assistant. Update a patient's data.
3 You're a clinical medical assistant. Help with a procedure.
4 Medicine is full of acronyms like COPD. What other medical acronyms do you know? What do they mean?

5 An Optometrist & an Optometric Assistant

An optometrist is verifying that a patient has been prepped for an exam.

A. Is Mr. Mendoza ready for his exam?
B. Yes, he is.
A. Are his pupils dilated?
B. Yes. They're fully dilated.

6 A Phlebotomist & a Patient

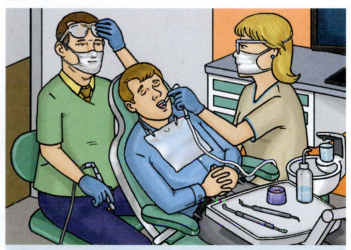

A phlebotomist is doing blood work on a patient.

A. Do you have a preference for which arm I use?
B. Probably the left arm.
A. All right. Let's roll up your sleeve. Yes. That's a very good vein. Make a fist.
B. Okay.

7 A Radiology Technician & a Patient

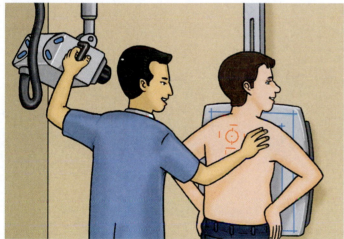

A radiology technician is preparing a patient for an X-ray.

A. Are you comfortable?
B. Yes. I'm okay.
A. All right. Before I take the X-ray, I'll ask you to take a deep breath and hold it until I say, "Exhale."
B. I understand.

8 A Dentist & a Dental Assistant

A dental assistant is assisting a dentist.

A. I've got all the decay out. Suction, please.
B. All right. Are you going to use resin or cement for the filling?
A. I think we'll go with resin.
B. Okay. I'll prepare that.

5–7 What medical exams and tests have you experienced?
8 How often do you go to a dentist's office? Who takes care of you there?

A HOW TO DO PRE-EXAMINATION PROCEDURES

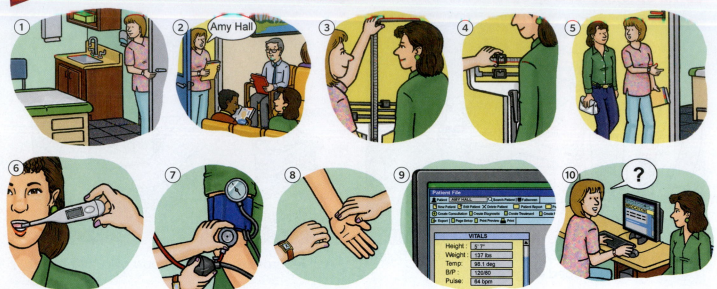

1 Make sure the exam room is clean.
2 Get the patient from the waiting room.
3 Measure the patient's height.
4 Measure the patient's weight.

5 Escort the patient to the exam room.
6 Take the patient's temperature.
7 Take the patient's blood pressure.

8 Take the patient's pulse.
9 Enter the patient's vital signs into the medical record.
10 Ask the patient about any changes in medication.

B HOW TO TAKE AN EKG

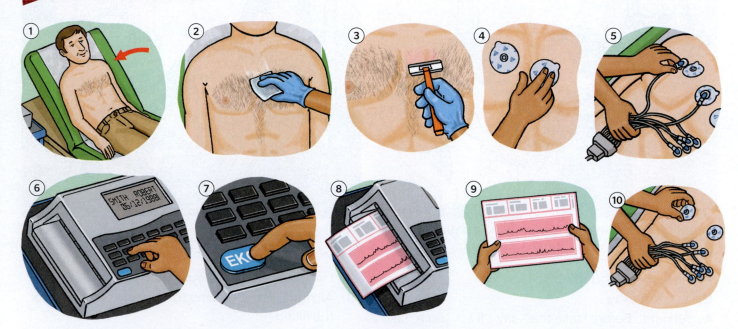

1 Have the patient lie down.
2 Prep the chest by cleaning the skin with an alcohol wipe.
3 If necessary, shave excess hair.
4 Adhere electrode patches to the skin.

5 Attach the clips at the ends of the leads to the correct electrode patches.
6 Input patient information.
7 Start the EKG.

8 Print out the EKG reading.
9 Check the EKG printout.
10 Remove the leads and electrode patches.

C HOW TO COLLECT BLOOD

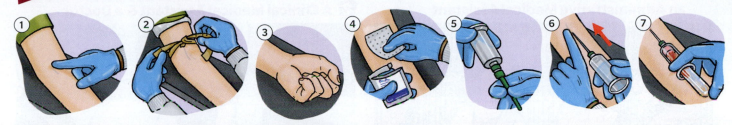
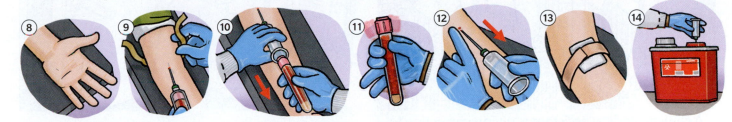

1 Locate a vein.
2 Put a tourniquet on the arm.
3 Have the patient make a tight fist.
4 Clean the skin area.
5 Put a needle on the hub.
6 Insert the needle into the vein.

7 Push a collection tube into the hub to draw blood.
8 Have the patient relax the hand.
9 Release the tourniquet.
10 Remove the collection tube when filled.

11 Shake the tube.
12 Remove the needle and apply pressure.
13 Put gauze and a bandage on the puncture.
14 Dispose of the needle into the sharps container.

D HOW TO TAKE AN X-RAY

1 Put a lead cape on the patient.
2 Position the patient.
3 Position the X-ray lens.
4 Load the film.

5 Go to the control area.
6 Ask the patient to stay still.
7 Take the X-ray.
8 Tell the patient it's okay to move now.

9 Remove the lead cape.
10 Retrieve the film.
11 Process the film.
12 Check the clarity of the X-ray.

**1 A Clinical Medical Assistant &
an Administrative Medical Assistant**

A clinical medical assistant is giving correction to
a co-worker.

A. Excuse me. This is the wrong chart. We have two
Michael Millers—the father and the son.

B. Oh, sorry.

A. It's always a good idea to check the date of birth
when you pull a patient's file.

B. I'll do that in the future.

2 A Clinical Medical Assistant & a Doctor

A clinical medical assistant is asking for feedback.

A. Did I enter the vital signs correctly?

B. Let me see—temperature, blood pressure, radial
pulse. Yes. Everything looks correct.

A. I just wanted to make sure. I'm still getting used to
this new electronic medical record system.

B. We all are.

3 Two X-ray Technicians

An X-ray technician is giving feedback to
a co-worker.

A. This image doesn't look clear. The others seem
fine.

B. I think the patient moved.

A. You should probably redo this one.

B. I agree.

4 A Pharmacist & a Pharmacy Assistant

A pharmacist is giving correction to a pharmacy
assistant.

A. You didn't fill this prescription correctly.

B. I didn't? It's for the 10 milligram tablets, right?

A. Yes. The dosage is correct, but it's supposed to be
for a 90-day supply, not 30 days.

B. Oh. Sorry for the error.

1 You're a clinical medical assistant. Give correction to a co-worker.

2 You're a clinical medical assistant. Ask for feedback (about something you did correctly).

3 You're an X-ray technician. Give feedback to a co-worker about something that needs to be redone.

4 You're a pharmacist. Give correction to an assistant.

OCCUPATIONS

administrative medical assistant	medical coder	optometrist
clinical medical assistant	medical lab technician	pharmacist
dental assistant	medical receptionist	pharmacy assistant
dental hygienist	medical transcriptionist	pharmacy technician
dental lab technician	MRI technician	phlebotomist
dentist	nuclear medicine technician	physician assistant
doctor/physician	optical lab technician	radiologist
EKG technician	optician	radiology technician
	optometric assistant	X-ray technician

WORKPLACE LOCATIONS

checkout desk	optometry exam room
control area	optometry lab
dental lab	pharmacy
dental office	phlebotomy lab
diagnostic lab	radiology imaging center
exam room	reception
eyeglass display area	vision center
lab	waiting room
office	X-ray control area

EQUIPMENT, TOOLS, & OBJECTS

alcohol pad	dentures and articulator	handheld blood analyzer	MRI (system)	surgical scissors
alcohol wipe	desk reference book	health insurance claim form	needle	surgical suture needle and thread
appointment card	digital medical thermometer	height rod	periodontal probe	surgical tweezers
bandage	digital thermometer sheath	hub	pill counting tray	suture clamp
bitewing X-ray	disposable lancet	injection needle	pipette	suture kit
blood collection tube	doctor's notes	insurance card	plaster table	tablet
blood samples	doctor/physician scale	intraoral X-ray camera	prescription	tape
blood test	dosage	lab specimen	prescription pill bottle	transcriber
cell tray	EKG electrodes	lab specimen test strip	pupillometer	transcriber foot pedal
cement filling	EKG machine	lead cape	radiopharmaceutical material	transcriber headphone
centrifuge	EKG printout	leads	resin	tungsten syringe
chart	EKG reading	lens edger	saliva ejector	vacutainer holder and needle
chest Xray machine	EKG slips and leads	lenses	scalpel	vial
clips	electrode patch	lensometer	sharps (disposal) container	X-ray
collection tube	electronic medical record system	medical file	shielded syringe carrier	X-ray film processor
CPT reference book	examination table	medical history software	spatula	X-ray fluoroscopic system
dental chair	eye drops	medical record	specimen cup	X-ray lens
dental excavator	eyeglass frames	medication	specimen pass-through cabinet	
dental mouth mirror	film		surgical iodine	
dental plaster	gauze			
dental scaler				
dental X-ray				
denture flask				

WORKPLACE ACTIONS

adjust eyeglass frames	do a fingerprick for a blood test	make dentures	appointment
analyze blood samples	do an EKG	measure a patient's height and weight	suture a wound
assist a dentist	draw a patient's blood	position a patient for an X-ray	take an X-ray
assist a doctor with a medical procedure	escort a patient to an exam room	prepare a patient for an MRI	take dental X-rays
check in a patient	fill a prescription	prepare an exam room for the next patient	take vital signs
clean a patient's teeth	give an injection	read an X-ray	transcribe a doctor's notes
code procedures and diagnoses	give medication instructions	retrieve a medical file	update a patient's medical record
collect a lab specimen	grind and polish lenses	schedule a patient's next	
dilate a patient's eyes	inject radiopharmaceutical material		

WORKPLACE COMMUNICATION

ask for feedback	give correction to a co-worker	transcribe a doctor's notes
assist a dentist	give feedback to a co-worker	update a patient's data
assist a doctor with a procedure	help a patient check in	verify a patient's readiness for an exam
do blood work on a patient	prepare a patient for an X-ray	

10.8 Skills Check

OCCUPATIONS

A WHO IS IT?

- **a.** administrative medical assistant
- **b.** dental hygienist
- **c.** dental lab tech
- **d.** dentist
- **e.** EKG technician
- **f.** medical coder
- **g.** medical lab tech
- **h.** medical transcriptionist
- **i.** MRI tech
- **j.** nuclear medical tech
- **k.** optician assistant
- **l.** optometrist
- **m.** pharmacist
- **n.** phlebotomist
- **o.** physician assistant
- **p.** radiologist

__a__ **1.** This person checks people in for their appointments.

_____ **2.** This person is a specialist who draws people's blood for testing.

_____ **3.** This person drills teeth and fills cavities in people's mouths.

_____ **4.** This person examines people's eyes.

_____ **5.** This person fills people's medical prescriptions.

_____ **6.** This person performs tests on tissue and blood.

_____ **7.** This person examines and treats patients under the supervision of a licensed physician.

_____ **8.** This person records information about procedures for insurance companies.

_____ **9.** This person takes and interprets X-rays.

_____ **10.** This person administers electrocardiogram tests.

_____ **11.** This person interprets and transcribes medical dictation.

_____ **12.** This person makes dentures to replace people's missing teeth.

_____ **13.** This person performs medical imaging tests.

_____ **14.** This person cleans people's teeth and takes X-rays.

_____ **15.** This person works with eyeglass prescriptions and frames.

_____ **16.** This person uses radioactive materials to diagnose and treat diseases.

WORKPLACE LOCATIONS

B WHERE ARE THEY?

1. When your examination is over, go to the (checkout desk   exam room).

2. Tests are performed in the (diagnostic lab   waiting room).

3. You can look at new frames in the (eyeglass display area   optometric exam room).

4. Blood tests are performed in the (phlebotomy lab   optometry lab).

5. When you arrive at the doctor's office, go to (reception   the control room).

6. Follow me to the (waiting room   exam room). The doctor will be in shortly.

7. Your X-rays will be taken in the X-ray (lab   room).

148

EQUIPMENT, TOOLS, & OBJECTS

C WHAT'S THE ASSOCIATION?

___c___ **1.** drops   frames   lenses

_____ **2.** collection tube   samples   test

_____ **3.** electrodes   printout   reading

_____ **4.** scalpel   suture clamp   surgical scissors

_____ **5.** plaster   excavator   scaler

_____ **6.** MRI   chest X-ray   EKG

_____ **7.** pill bottle   instructions   dosage

a. surgical instruments

b. machines

c. eyes

d. medications

e. EKG

f. blood

g. dental items

WORKPLACE ACTIONS

D HEALTH SERVICES *IN ACTION!*

1. give _____
- **a.** a wound
- **b.** an injection
- **c.** an X-ray
- **d.** an EKG

2. fill _____
- **a.** instructions
- **b.** a procedure
- **c.** a prescription
- **d.** an MRI

3. collect _____
- **a.** a specimin
- **b.** an appointment
- **c.** a fingerprick
- **d.** instructions

4. measure _____
- **a.** X-rays
- **b.** a lab specimin
- **c.** a blood test
- **d.** height

5. suture _____
- **a.** blood samples
- **b.** an injection
- **c.** a wound
- **d.** a prescription

6. grind _____
- **a.** lenses
- **b.** blood
- **c.** eyeglass frames
- **d.** dentures

7. code _____
- **a.** a wound
- **b.** procedures
- **c.** a dentist
- **d.** an exam room

8. retrieve _____
- **a.** an injection
- **b.** a file
- **c.** a patient
- **d.** teeth

WORKPLACE COMMUNICATION

E WHAT ARE THEY SAYING?

___d___ **1.** check in a patient for an appointment

_____ **2.** update a patient's data

_____ **3.** assist with a procedure

_____ **4.** ask for clarification

_____ **5.** verify preparation for a procedure

_____ **6.** give instructions to a patient

_____ **7.** prepare a patient for an X-ray

_____ **8.** give instructions to an associate

_____ **9.** give correction

_____ **10.** ask for feedback

_____ **11.** give feedback

_____ **12.** respond to correction

a. "I'm going to ask you to take a deep breath and hold it in."

b. "Is Mr. Mendoza ready for his exam?"

c. "Make a fist."

d. "You have a $25 co-pay for today's appointment."

e. "This image doesn't look clear. The others seem fine."

f. "This is the wrong chart."

g. "Suction, please."

h. "Have your medications changed since your last appointment?"

i. "Do you want me to get a suture kit?"

j. "Did I enter the vital signs correctly?"

k. "Sorry for the error."

l. "Did you say COPD?"

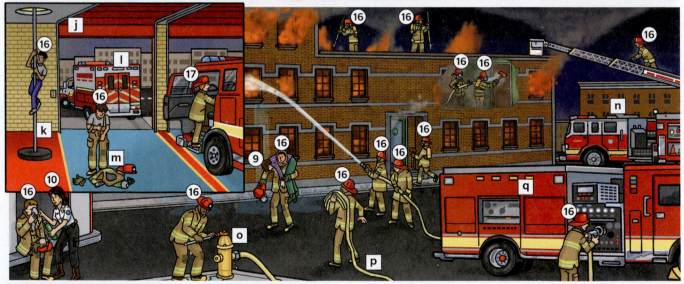

1 911 operator	**10** paramedic	**a** communication center	**j** fire station
2 emergency services dispatcher	**11** detective	**b** animal control vehicle	**k** fire pole
3 police officer	**12** witness	**c** ambulance	**l** EMS* truck
4 suspect	**13** public safety officer	**d** crime scene	**m** turnout gear
5 K9 officer	**14** parking enforcement officer	**e** police station	**n** aerial ladder truck
6 animal control officer	**15** fingerprint analyst	**f** booking area	**o** hydrant
7 forensic identification specialist	**16** firefighter	**g** holding cell	**p** fire hose
8 EMT*	**17** engine chauffeur	**h** interview room	**q** pumper truck
9 victim		**i** forensics lab	

* EMT = emergency medical technician
EMS = emergency medical services

What occupations do you see in these public safety situations? What objects do you see?

18 judge	**27** probation officer	
19 bailiff	**28** TSA* screener	
20 defendant	**29** passenger	
21 public defender	**30** security guard	
22 offender/inmate	**31** school safety officer	
23 corrections officer	**32** asset protection specialist	
24 parole agent	**33** watchman	
25 parolee	**34** security patrol officer	
26 probationer		

a courtroom	**g** walk-through metal detector
b jail cell	**h** surveillance monitoring system
c prison cell	**i** guard house
d security check-in area	**j** security gate
e millimeter wave scanner	**k** security checkpoint station
f carry-on X-ray machine	

* TSA = Transportation Security Administration

How are the public safety services in your community? Describe them.

Is there much crime in your community? Tell about it.

1 chase a suspect
2 apprehend a suspect
3 frisk a suspect
4 handcuff a suspect

5 collect evidence
6 direct traffic
7 catch a dog
8 ticket an illegally parked car

9 fingerprint a suspect
10 interrogate a suspect
11 test evidence
12 dress in turnout gear

13 attach a hose to a hydrant
14 direct a water spray on a fire
15 enter a burning building
16 rescue a victim

Look at pages 150 and 151. What are the public safety workers doing? Describe their actions.

17 escort a defendant
18 search a cell for contraband
19 review conditions of parole
20 check an ankle monitor

21 check photo IDs
22 check an X-ray image of a carry-on bag
23 search carry-on luggage
24 confiscate illegal carry-on items

25 use a handheld metal detector
26 perform a pat-down search
27 view an AIT* screening image
28 search a locker

29 check IDs
30 watch security monitors
31 patrol a building
32 apprehend a shoplifter

* AIT = advanced imaging technology

1 badge	**7** evidence bag	**13** handheld ticket printer	**19** fire hose
2 crime scene tape	**8** piece of evidence	**14** parking citation	**20** nozzle
3 handcuffs	**9** evidence markers	**15** ticket mailing envelope	**21** hydrant spanner wrench
4 bulletproof vest	**10** forensic swab	**16** firefighter helmet	**22** SCBA*
5 gun and holster	**11** taser gun	**17** pike pole	**23** oxygen mask
6 animal snare pole	**12** fingerprint card	**18** fire axe	

* SCBA = self-contained breathing apparatus

Look at pages 150–153. What equipment, tools, and objects do you see?

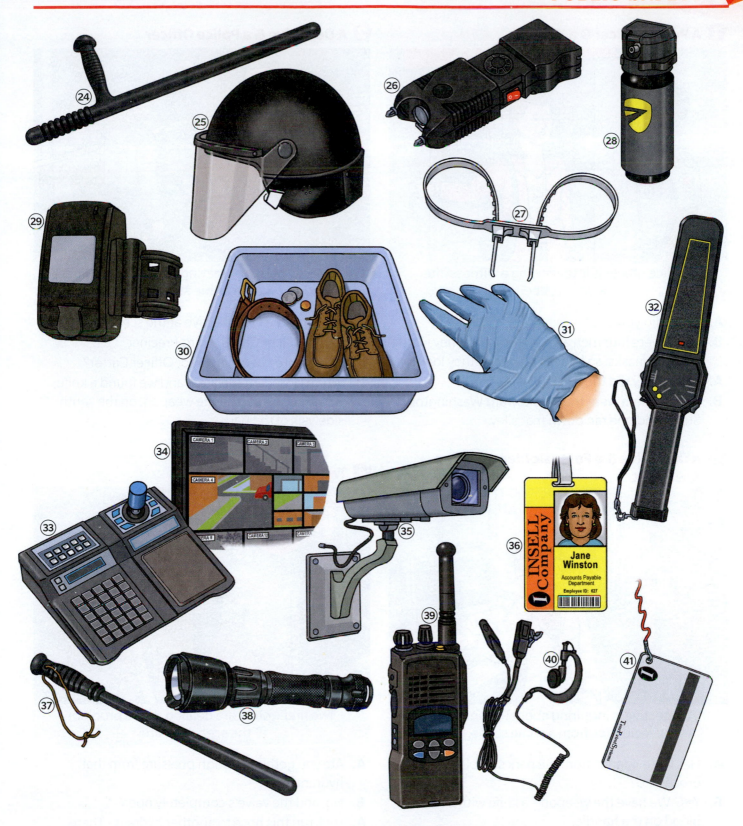

24 baton	**28** defense spray	**32** security wand	**37** nightstick
25 tactical helmet	**29** ankle monitor	**33** security control console	**38** security flashlight
26 stun gun	**30** TSA security tray	**34** security control monitor	**39** two-way radio
27 zip tie handcuffs/ disposable hand restraints	**31** blue nitrate disposable gloves	**35** surveillance camera **36** employee ID badge	**40** radio earpiece **41** guard tour swipe card

1 A Police Officer & a Witness

A police officer is interviewing a witness after a bank robbery.

A. What did you see?

B. There were four men and one woman. They were all wearing masks, so I don't know what they look like.

A. Which way did they go?

B. Four of them went that way toward Washington Street and one ran down that alley.

2 A Detective & a Police Officer

A detective is coordinating with a police officer at a crime scene.

A. Who was the first to arrive at the scene?

B. I was. Officer Carter, Third Precinct.

A. Has the area been secured, Officer Carter?

B. We've closed off the area, and we found a knife, which appears to be the weapon, on the south sidewalk of the park.

3 A Detective & a Forensic Identification Specialist

A detective is inquiring about the analysis of evidence from a crime scene.

A. Has the evidence from the park stabbing been processed?

B. Yes. We have the weapon—a knife with a trace of blood on the handle.

A. Do we have any matches on the fingerprints?

B. Yes. The prints match a Gus Williams, wanted for armed robbery in two states.

4 Two Firefighters

Two firefighters are dealing with a problem at the scene of a fire.

A. Are you getting enough pressure from that hydrant?

B. No, and the valve's completely open.

A. Let's run this hose to another hydrant. There should be another one around the corner.

B. Sure. Right away.

1 You're a police officer. Interview a witness to a crime.
2 You're a detective at a crime scene. Coordinate with a police officer.
3 You're a detective. You're at the forensics lab to inquire about some evidence.
4 You're a firefighter. You and another firefighter are figuring out how to deal with a problem.

5 Two Corrections Officers

Two corrections officers are searching an inmate's cell.

A. Look at this!
B. What did you find?
A. A cell phone under the mattress.
B. That's the second time this month. This inmate is definitely going back to maximum security.

6 A Parole Agent & a Parolee

A parole agent is meeting with a parolee prior to release.

A. Do you have a place to stay and a job lined up?
B. Yes. I'll be staying with my sister, and I'll be working at my uncle's auto body shop.
A. Good. Remember: Under the conditions of your parole, you must contact me within three days if your address or your job changes.
B. I understand.

7 A TSA Agent & a Supervisor

A TSA agent is screening carry-on baggage.

A. Does this look like a curling iron to you?
B. Hard to tell. What do you think?
A. I don't know. It might be a weapon.
B. Baggage check!

8 A Security Guard & a Visitor

A security guard is checking in a visitor.

A. Good morning. May I see an ID, please?
B. Yes. Here you are.
A. All right. Please sign in. Here's a visitor's badge. You need to wear it at all times. And make sure you sign out when you leave the building.
B. Okay. I'll do that. Thank you.

5 You're a corrections officer. You and a co-worker are searching a cell. You just found something.
6 You're a parole agent. What other questions should you ask the parolee?
7 Do you think a TSA agent's job is difficult? Why or why not?
8 You're a security guard. Check in a visitor.

A HOW TO FRISK A SUSPECT

1 Identify yourself as a law enforcement officer.
2 Explain to the suspect, "I'm going to pat you down now."
3 Ask the suspect, "Are you carrying a weapon or anything sharp such as a needle?"
4 Tell the suspect, "Remain standing. Place your hands on your head and spread your legs to more than shoulder width apart."

5 Move behind the suspect. Place one foot between the suspect's legs, in line with the suspect's feet, and the other foot six inches back.
6 Beginning at the top of the suspect's torso, move your hands down both sides of the suspect's body, pulling the clothing and squeezing it.

7 Run your hands down the suspect's chest, back, sides, and arms including the armpits, the nape of the neck, and the waistband.
8 Squat down and repeat the previous two steps on the suspect's legs, feet, abdomen, and crotch. Do not forget the back of the knees and the shoes.
9 If you find a weapon, remove it and place the suspect prone on the ground. Handcuff the suspect and call for backup.

B HOW TO PUT ON FIREFIGHTER TURNOUT GEAR

1 Get into your bunker pants.
2 Pull your bunker pants up by the suspenders.
3 Put your jacket on one arm at a time.

4 Place your Nomex over your head.
5 Zip your jacket and adjust it to the proper position.
6 Put the air mask on your face and pull the straps on the mask until they are secure.

7 Swing the air tank over your shoulders.
8 Latch the waist strap.
9 Put on your gloves and helmet.

C HOW TO SEARCH A PRISON CELL

1 Put on protective gloves.
2 Examine the lights and hiding spots in the ceiling.
3 Remove light covers if necessary.
4 Slide fingertips along the underside of any bars or rails around windows.

5 Remove bedding and look for any cuts or tears.
6 Pick up and check all items on shelves and in drawers.
7 Thumb through books, magazines, and clothing.

8 Investigate all toiletries. Open bottles and squeeze tubes.
9 Put any contraband in a bag.
10 Fill out an inventory sheet.

D HOW TO DO A PAT-DOWN

1 Put on a new pair of gloves.
2 Explain the pat-down procedure to the passenger.
3 Have the passenger spread legs and raise arms outward.
4 Pat down the passenger's hair and head.

5 Use the "front-of-the-hand slide-down technique" to search the neck, along both arms, and down to the waist.
6 Check inside the waistband.
7 Search down from the waist along the inside and outside of both legs.

8 Stand behind the passenger and repeat the pat-down procedure from the head to the legs.
9 Tell the passenger the pat-down is finished.

1 **Two Forensic Identification Specialists**

A forensic identification specialist is correcting a co-worker.

A. Who bagged and tagged this evidence?
B. I did. Is there a problem?
A. Yes. You didn't put an incident number on this bag.
B. Sorry. My mistake.

2 **Two Firefighters**

One firefighter is complimenting another.

A. You did a great job getting that victim out!
B. Tell me about it! He was one heavy guy!
A. You should have called for backup.
B. There wasn't time. The room he was in was about to cave in!

3 **Two TSA Officers**

A TSA officer is giving feedback to a co-worker.

A. You know why that passenger is angry, don't you?
B. No. Why?
A. You didn't explain the pat-down procedure before you started it.
B. I didn't? I must have forgotten. It's been a long day!

4 **An Asset Protection Specialist & a Store Security Guard**

An asset protection specialist is reprimanding a store security guard.

A. Did a guy wearing a brown leather jacket set off the alarm about a minute ago?
B. I don't know. I was helping a customer load a big item into his car.
A. Well, we saw a guy on the security monitors putting some video games under his jacket and exiting here. Don't leave your workstation! Okay?
B. Got it!

In each of these conversations, you're a public safety worker.

1 Give correction to a co-worker.
2 Compliment a co-worker.
3 Give constructive feedback to a co-worker about something not done correctly.
4 Reprimand someone.

OCCUPATIONS

- 911 operator
- animal control officer
- asset protection specialist
- bailiff
- corrections officer
- detective
- emergency medical technician (EMT)
- emergency services dispatcher
- engine chauffeur
- fingerprint analyst
- firefighter
- forensic identification specialist
- judge
- K9 officer
- law enforcement officer
- paramedic
- parking enforcement officer
- parole agent
- police officer
- probation officer
- public defender
- public safety officer
- school safety officer
- security guard
- security patrol officer
- TSA agent
- TSA officer
- TSA screener
- watchman

WORKPLACE LOCATIONS

- booking area
- communication center
- courtroom
- crime scene
- fire station
- forensics lab
- guard house
- holding cell
- interview room
- jail cell
- maximum security
- police station
- prison cell
- security check-in area
- security checkpoint station
- security gate
- workstation

EQUIPMENT, TOOLS, & OBJECTS

- aerial ladder truck
- air mask
- air tank
- AIT screening image
- ambulance
- animal control vehicle
- animal snare pole
- ankle monitor
- badge
- bars
- baton
- blue nitrate disposable gloves
- bulletproof vest
- bunker pants
- carry-on X-ray machine
- contraband
- crime scene tape
- defense spray
- disposable hand restraints
- employee ID badge
- EMS truck
- evidence
- evidence bag
- evidence markers
- fingerprint card
- fingerprints
- fire axe
- fire hose
- fire pole
- firefighter helmet
- forensic swab
- gloves
- guard tour swipe card
- gun and holster
- handheld metal detector
- handheld ticket printer
- handcuffs
- helmet
- hose
- hydrant
- hydrant spanner wrench
- incident number
- inventory sheet
- match
- millimeter wave scanner
- nightstick
- Nomex
- nozzle
- oxygen mask
- parking citation
- photo ID
- piece of evidence
- pike pole
- protective gloves
- pumper truck
- radio earpiece
- rails
- SCBA (self-contained breathing apparatus)
- security control console
- security control monitor
- security flashlight
- security monitor
- security wand
- stun gun
- surveillance camera
- surveillance monitoring system
- tactical helmet
- taser gun
- ticket mailing envelope
- TSA security tray
- turnout gear
- two-way radio
- valve
- visitor's badge
- waist strap
- walk-through metal detector
- water spray
- weapon
- X-ray image
- zip tie handcuffs

WORKPLACE ACTIONS

- apprehend a shoplifter
- apprehend a suspect
- attach a hose to a hydrant
- catch a dog
- chase a suspect
- check an ankle monitor
- check an X-ray image of a carry-on bag
- check IDs
- check photo IDs
- collect evidence
- confiscate illegal carry-on items
- direct a water spray on a fire
- direct traffic
- dress in turnout gear
- enter a burning building
- escort a defendant
- fingerprint a suspect
- frisk a suspect
- handcuff a suspect
- interrogate a suspect
- patrol a building
- perform a pat-down search
- rescue a victim
- review conditions of parole
- search a cell for contraband
- search a locker
- search carry-on luggage
- test evidence
- ticket an illegally parked car
- use a handheld metal detector
- view an AIT screening image
- watch security monitors

WORKPLACE COMMUNICATION

- check in a visitor to a facility
- compliment a co-worker
- coordinate tasks at a crime scene
- correct a co-worker
- deal with a problem at a fire scene
- give feedback to a co-worker
- inquire about the analysis of evidence
- interview a witness
- meet with a parolee
- reprimand a worker
- screen carry-on baggage
- search an inmate's cell

OCCUPATIONS

A WHO AM I?

_f_ 1. "I rescue lost animals."

____ 2. "I enforce the rules and keep order in jails and prisons."

____ 3. "I answer emergency telephone calls."

____ 4. "I collect evidence in a criminal case."

____ 5. "I monitor children in and around school buildings."

____ 6. "I'm in charge of trials in a courtroom."

____ 7. "I collect, analyze, and examine fingerprint evidence."

____ 8. "I use a trained dog to gather criminal evidence."

____ 9. "I make sure the courtroom is safe."

____ 10. "I make sure passengers don't bring dangerous items onto planes."

____ 11. "I analyze physical evidence from crime scenes."

____ 12. "I send police and medical teams to respond to emergencies."

____ 13. "I issue tickets for parking violations."

____ 14. "I watch for suspicious-looking customers in stores."

____ 15. "I supervise released prisoners who still need to be monitored."

a. detective

b. bailiff

c. fingerprint analyst

d. forensic identification specialist

e. emergency services dispatcher

f. animal control officer

g. 911 operator

h. asset protection specialist

i. corrections officer

j. judge

k. parking enforcement officer

l. K9 officer

m. school safety officer

n. parole agent

o. TSA screener

WORKPLACE LOCATIONS

B WHAT'S THE PLACE?

_c_ 1. booking

____ 2. communication

____ 3. crime

____ 4. fire

____ 5. holding

a. center

b. station

c. area

d. cell

e. scene

____ 6. forensics

____ 7. guard

____ 8. interview

____ 9. jail

____ 10. security

f. gate

g. lab

h. cell

i. room

j. house

EQUIPMENT, TOOLS, & OBJECTS

C WHAT DO THEY HAVE IN COMMON?

1. aerial ladder   EMS   pumper   These are types of _____ **trucks** _____.

2. axe   hose   pole   These are related to a _____.

3. flashlight   monitor   wand   These are related to _____.

4. tactical helmet   oxygen mask   turnout gear   These are things you _____.

5. nightstick   stun gun   handheld ticket printer   These are things you _____.

6. fingerprints   visitor's badge   ankle monitor   These provide _____.

WORKPLACE ACTIONS

D PUBLIC SAFETY *IN ACTION!*

apprehend	chase	confiscate	escort	interrogate	review	test	use
attach	collect	direct	frisk	perform	search	ticket	watch

1. Please _____ *escort* _____ the defendant into the courtroom.

2. Charlie, make sure you _____ this water spray on the fire.

3. I'm a security officer in a large department store. Part of my job is to _____ shoplifters.

4. Al, you're new here. Have you learned yet how to _____ the handheld metal detector?

5. There's the suspect! I'll _____ him down the street!

6. Officer Gonzales, you need to _____ the cell for contraband.

7. Make sure you _____ all the evidence at the crime scene.

8. Officer Chen, you need to _____ this suspect to see what information he can give us.

9. I'm your parole officer. Today we're going to _____ the conditions of your parole.

10. We _____ all illegal carry-on items.

11. Can you _____ this hose to the fire hydrant over there?

12. I'll _____ the suspect to see if he's carrying any weapons.

13. We make sure all of our new officers learn to correctly _____ a pat-down search.

14. We _____ all illegally parked cars.

15. At the Apex Company, we carefully _____ all the security monitors.

16. The forensics lab will _____ all the evidence.

WORKPLACE COMMUNICATION

E WHAT ARE THEY SAYING?

e 1. interview a witness to a crime

____ 2. coordinate at a crime scene

____ 3. inquire about evidence

____ 4. deal with a problem at a fire scene

____ 5. search an inmate's cell

____ 6. meet with a parolee

____ 7. screen carry-on baggage

____ 8. check in a visitor

____ 9. respond to correction

____ 10. compliment a co-worker

____ 11. give feedback to a co-worker

____ 12. reprimand someone

a. "Please sign in."

b. "Do you have a place to stay and a job lined up?"

c. "You did a great job getting that victim out!"

d. "Sorry. My mistake."

e. "Which way did they go?"

f. "You didn't explain the pat-down procedure before you started it."

g. "Has the area been secured?"

h. "I found a cell phone under the mattress."

i. "Does this look like a curling iron to you?"

j. "Do we have any matches on the fingerprints?"

k. "Don't leave your workstation! Okay?"

l. "We aren't getting enough pressure from that hydrant."

1 bank security guard
2 customer service associate
3 new account associate
4 financial services rep
5 bank manager
6 auto loan officer

7 mortgage loan officer
8 small business loan officer
9 teller
10 drive-through teller
11 safe-deposit clerk

* ATM = automated teller machine

a ATM*
b information desk
c waiting area
d financial services office
e bank manager's office
f rate display board
g loan department

h check-writing stand
i waiting line
j teller station/window
k teller's money safe
l drive-through window
m vault
n safe-deposit box

What occupations do you see in this bank?
What areas of the bank and what objects do you see?

How often do you go to a bank? What do you do there?

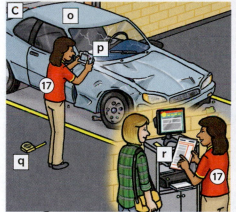

A insurance agency	**12** insurance agent	**19** insurance investigator	**o** damaged vehicle
B insurance company call center	**13** insurance sales agent	**20** sales associate	**p** digital camera
C auto appraisal facility	**14** customer service associate	**21** member services representative	**q** tape measure
D insurance inspection	**15** claims processing specialist	**22** fraud detection associate	**r** repair estimate
E insurance investigation	**16** insurance examiner	**23** collection associate	**s** video camera
F credit card company	**17** auto damage appraiser	**24** collection specialist	**t** digital voice recorder
G collection agency	**18** insurance adjuster	**25** tax preparer	
H tax preparation service			

What insurance and finance occupations do you see?
What insurance and finance offices and situations do you see?
What objects do you see?

Have you ever had to make an insurance claim?
If so, what was the situation?

1   greet a customer
2   establish a new account
3   explain investment account options
4   approve a loan
5   help a customer with an auto loan
6   help a customer with a mortgage application
7   help a customer with a small business loan
8   deposit a customer's check
9   help a customer with a withdrawal
10   prepare a bank check
11   count and band money
12   check a customer's ID
13   handle a commercial customer's deposit
14   reconcile a cash drawer
15   handle drive-through window transactions
16   access a customer's safe-deposit box

Look at pages 164 and 165. What are the people doing? Describe their actions.

17 give an insurance quote
18 obtain customer information
19 review a customer's policy
20 sell insurance

21 assist a customer
22 process a claim
23 review a claim
24 appraise auto damage

25 examine property damage
26 investigate a disability claim
27 activate a credit card
28 handle a customer problem

29 verify transactions
30 call about a late payment
31 collect an unpaid bill
32 prepare a tax return

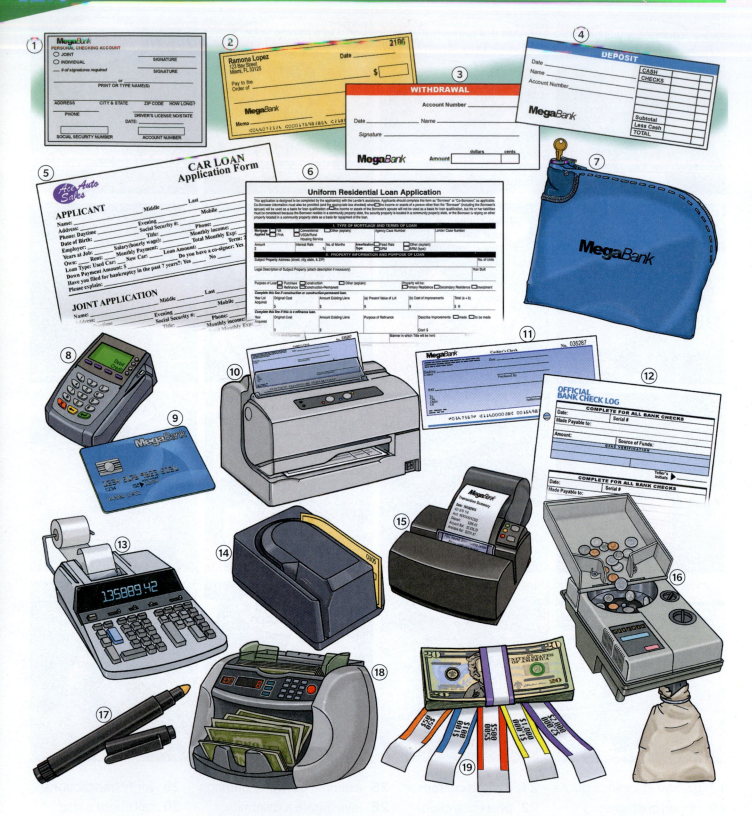

1 signature card
2 check
3 withdrawal slip
4 deposit slip
5 car loan application
6 mortgage application
7 bank deposit bag
8 bank card reader
9 bank card
10 check printer
11 cashier's check
12 bank check log
13 printing calculator
14 check reader
15 bank teller printer
16 coin counter
17 counterfeit detection pen
18 currency counter
19 currency bands

Look at pages 164–167. What equipment, tools, and objects do you see?

20 insurance policy	**23** digital camera	**26** digital voice recorder	**29** 1040 form
21 claim form	**24** measuring wheel	**27** W-2 form	**30** IRS* publication
22 auto repair appraisal	**25** video camera	**28** 1099 form	

* IRS = Internal Revenue Service

1 A Customer Service Associate & a Bank Customer

A customer service associate is greeting a new customer.

A. May I help you?

B. Yes. I'd like to open a checking and savings account.

A. All right. Please take a seat in the waiting area, and our new account associate will be with you shortly.

2 A Customer & a Bank Teller

A bank teller is helping a customer cash a check.

A. I'd like to cash a check.

B. Do you have an account with us?

A. Yes, I do.

B. All right. Please swipe your bank card in the card reader and enter your PIN*.

* PIN = personal identification number

3 Bank Customers & a Loan Officer

A loan officer is helping customers with a mortgage application.

A. We'd like to apply for a mortgage loan.

B. Have you found a home yet?

A. Not yet. But we want to have pre-approval for a loan before we start looking.

B. That's a good idea. Here's a mortgage application. I'll be happy to help you fill it out.

4 A Loan Officer & an Applicant

A loan officer is assisting an applicant with an auto loan application.

A. I'm afraid we have to deny your application for an auto loan.

B. Oh. Why is that?

A. You don't have a sufficient credit history. If someone co-signs the loan, it might be approved.

B. I understand. I just started my first job. I'll ask my parents to be co-signers on the loan.

---

1 You're a new account associate at a bank. Help a new customer open an account.

2 You're a bank teller. Help a customer with a transaction.

3–4 You're a loan officer. Help a customer with a mortgage or auto loan application.

5 An Insurance Policy Holder & a Customer Service Associate

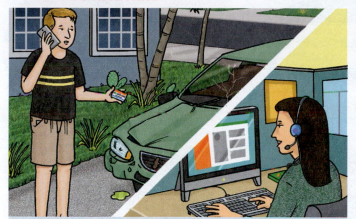

An insurance customer service associate is assisting a customer.

A. Hello. I was in a car accident this morning.
B. Are you injured?
A. No, but my car's front end is damaged.
B. All right. Please give me your name and policy number, and I'll give you a claim number and the location of our nearest appraisal facility.

6 An Insurance Appraiser & a Customer

An insurance appraiser is inspecting damage at a policyholder's home.

A. Aside from the roof and the shutters, is there any other storm damage?
B. Yes. A tree fell onto our storage shed in the backyard.
A. I'll need to go back there and document the damage.
B. Okay. Come this way and I'll show you.

7 A Customer & a Credit Card Member Services Representative

A service representative is assisting a credit card customer.

A. I'm afraid I lost my credit card.
B. When is the last time you used it?
A. Yesterday. I used it at the Big J Department Store.
B. Okay. That's the last transaction our records show for that card number. We'll cancel that card immediately and issue a new one.

8 A Professional Tax Preparer & a Client

A tax preparer is gathering information from a client.

A. Let's start with your income. Do you have a W-2 form from your employer?
B. Yes. Here you are.
A. All right. And did you bring with you any 1099 forms indicating interest and dividends from banks or other institutions?
B. Yes. I brought everything with me.

5 You're an insurance customer service associate. Help a customer who is calling to report a car accident.
6 You're an insurance appraiser inspecting damage. Ask the policyholder for information.
7 Have you ever lost a credit card or other form of identification? Tell about it.
8 Who prepares your tax return? How do you feel about paying taxes?

A HOW TO CASH A CUSTOMER'S CHECK

1 Ask a customer to swipe his or her bank card through the card reader.
2 Ask to see a picture ID.
3 Make sure the front of the check is filled out properly.
4 Make sure the customer has endorsed the check with a signature on the back.

5 Write the customer's ID information on the back of the check.
6 Check the customer's account to verify that funds are available to cover the check amount.
7 Process the check through the check reader.

8 Ask the customer what denominations he or she wants.
9 Count out the money.
10 Give the cash to the customer.

B HOW TO DETECT COUNTERFEIT CURRENCY

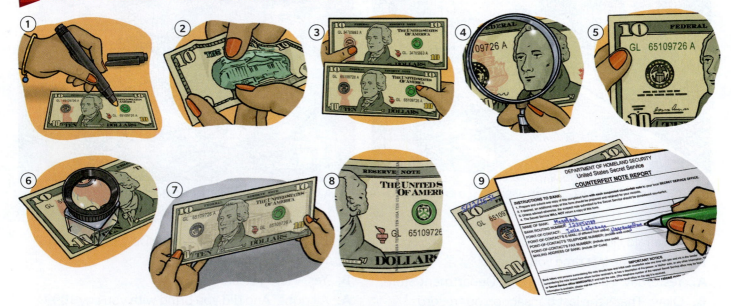

1 Run the counterfeit detection pen across the bill.
2 Feel the texture of the bill.
3 Compare the bill with another of the same denomination.
4 Look carefully at the printing quality.

5 Examine the serial numbers.
6 Look for colored strands in the paper.
7 Hold the bill up to the light and examine the watermark.

8 Look for the security strip running top to bottom.
9 If the bill seems counterfeit, take it out of circulation and report it.

C HOW TO WRITE AN AUTOMOBILE INSURANCE POLICY

1 Review the automobile's title.
2 Record the VIN* number, the year, the make, and the model of the automobile.
3 Ask for the current mileage.
4 Obtain the date of birth, social security number, and driver's license number of each driver to be listed on the policy.

* VIN = vehicle identification number

5 Run a customer background check on each driver.
6 Run a motor vehicle record report on each driver.
7 Explain options for coverages and deductibles.

8 Quote the policy fee and terms.
9 Make copies of the title and driver's license.
10 Collect the premium fee.
11 Provide the customer with proof of insurance.

D HOW TO DO AN AUTO DAMAGE APPRAISAL

1 Ask to see the claimant's driver's license and vehicle registration.
2 Confirm the vehicle's VIN.
3 Record the current odometer reading.
4 Walk around the vehicle and observe any damage.

5 Confirm what damage relates to the claim.
6 Take measurements.
7 Take photographs.
8 Document the damage and the parts and repairs needed.

9 Enter the information in the estimating software, including parts and labor.
10 Give a printed estimate to the claimant.
11 Send the estimate to the claimant's insurance company.

1 **Two Bank Tellers**

A bank teller is asking a co-worker for feedback.

A. Can you take a quick look at this for me?
B. Sure. What is it?
A. I want to make sure I'm following the new procedure correctly for issuing bank checks.
B. Yes. This looks right to me.

2 **A Bank Manager & a New Loan Officer**

A bank manager is giving feedback to a new employee.

A. Could I speak with you for a moment?
B. Sure. What is it?
A. I need to ask you to use a lower voice when you speak with a customer.
B. Oh. Sorry. It's my first day. At my previous bank, loan officers had private offices. I'll keep my voice down. Thanks for telling me.

3 **An Insurance Agency Manager & an Insurance Agent**

A manager is making a suggestion to an insurance agent.

A. What did those customers decide?
B. They're going to insure their new home through our agency.
A. Excellent! Did you tell them about the discount they'll receive if they also insure their autos through us?
B. No, I didn't. I'll call them tomorrow.

4 **A Call Center Supervisor & an Employee**

A supervisor is expressing concern about an employee's job performance.

A. You sounded very angry on that call.
B. The customer was shouting at me because he had been waiting fifteen minutes. He was really nasty!
A. I see. Well, I'm concerned about your tone of voice. I'll review the recorded conversation and get back to you.
B. Okay. You'll hear for yourself. I promise you!

1 You're a bank teller. Ask a co-worker if you're doing something correctly.
2 You're a bank manager. Give constructive feedback to an employee.
3 You're an insurance agency manager. Make a suggestion to one of your agents.
4 You're a supervisor. Express concern about an employee's performance.

OCCUPATIONS

auto damage appraiser
auto loan officer
bank manager
bank security guard
call center supervisor
claims processing specialist
collection associate
collection specialist
customer service associate

drive-through teller
financial services rep
fraud detection associate
insurance adjuster
insurance agency manager
insurance agent
insurance appraiser
insurance examiner
insurance investigator
insurance sales agent

loan officer
member services representative
mortgage loan officer
new account associate
safe-deposit clerk
sales associate
small business loan officer
tax preparer
teller

WORKPLACE LOCATIONS

(auto) appraisal facility
bank manager's office
collection agency
credit card company
drive-through window
financial services office
information desk
insurance agency

insurance company call center
loan department
tax preparation service
teller station/window
vault
waiting area
waiting line

EQUIPMENT, TOOLS, & OBJECTS

1040 form
1099 form
ATM
auto repair appraisal
bank card
bank card reader
bank check
bank check log
bank deposit bag
bank teller printer
car loan application
card reader
cash drawer

cashier's check
check
check endorser
check printer
check reader
check-writing stand
claim form
coin counter
colored strands
counterfeit
counterfeit detection pen
credit card

currency bands
currency counter
customer's policy
damaged vehicle
deposit slip
digital camera
digital voice recorder
driver's license
estimating software
insurance policy
IRS publication
measuring wheel
money

mortgage application
odometer reading
parts
picture ID
PIN
printed estimate
printing calculator
rate display board
records
repair estimate
safe-deposit box
security strip
serial numbers

signature card
tape measure
tax return
teller's money safe
title
unpaid bill
vehicle
vehicle registration
video camera
VIN (number)
W-2 form
watermark
withdrawal slip

WORKPLACE ACTIONS

access a customer's safe-deposit box
activate a credit card
appraise auto damage
approve a loan
assist a customer
call about a late payment
check a customer's ID
collect an unpaid bill
count and band money
deposit a customer's check

establish a new account
examine property damage
explain investment account options
give an insurance quote
greet a customer
handle a commercial customer's deposit
handle a customer problem

handle drive-through window transactions
help a customer with a mortgage application
help a customer with a small business loan
help a customer with a withdrawal
help a customer with an auto loan
insurance inspection

insurance investigation
investigate a disability claim
obtain customer information
prepare a bank check
prepare a tax return
process a claim
reconcile a cash drawer
review a claim
review a customer's policy
sell insurance
verify transactions

WORKPLACE COMMUNICATION

ask a co-worker for feedback
assist a credit card customer
assist an applicant with an auto loan application

express concern about an employee's job performance
gather tax information from a client
give feedback to a new employee
greet a new customer

help a customer cash a check
help a customer with a mortgage application
help a customer with an insurance claim
inspect damage at a policyholder's home
make a suggestion to an employee

OCCUPATIONS

A FIND THE RIGHT PERSON!

a. auto damage appraiser	**f.** customer service associate	**k.** mortgage loan officer
b. auto loan officer	**g.** drive-through teller	**l.** safe-deposit clerk
c. bank manager	**h.** fraud detection associate	**m.** small business loan officer
d. bank security guard	**i.** insurance adjuster	**n.** tax preparer
e. collections specialist	**j.** insurance sales agent	**o.** teller

__n__ **1.** I can help you with your taxes. I'm a _____.

_____ **2.** Martin sells insurance policies. He's an _____.

_____ **3.** The _____ is over there. She will let you into the vault.

_____ **4.** I'm interested in buying a new car. I need to speak with your _____.

_____ **5.** Sam stands at the bank entrance and watches for illegal activity. He's a _____.

_____ **6.** Jane is a _____. She answers questions and handles customer complaints.

_____ **7.** Margaret is in charge of the bank. She's the _____.

_____ **8.** George monitors people's accounts to make sure there is no illegal activity. He's a _____.

_____ **9.** I help people make bank deposits from their cars. I'm a _____.

_____ **10.** If you're interested in buying a new home, you should speak with our _____.

_____ **11.** A _____ attempts to collect money from people who haven't paid back their loans.

_____ **12.** Our _____ will investigate the facts of your car accident and assess the loss or damage.

_____ **13.** Amanda is a _____ at MaxiBank. She helps people deposit and withdraw money from their accounts.

_____ **14.** My brother and I are interested in opening our own bakery. We need to speak with a _____.

_____ **15.** Our _____ will inspect the damage to determine how much we should pay for your loss.

WORKPLACE LOCATIONS

B WHAT'S THE PLACE?

1. Someone at the information (center   desk) will be glad to help you.

2. Look! That teller (station   center) is open.

3. Someone in our loan (facility   department) will assist you.

4. Feel free to sit in our waiting (area   window).

5. My wife just got a job at a call (company   center).

6. To save time, I think I'll go through the drive-through (window   office).

7. Which tax preparation (service   bank) do you recommend?

8. If we don't receive payment soon, we'll have to send this to a collection (desk   agency).

EQUIPMENT, TOOLS, & OBJECTS

C ▶ WHAT'S THE ITEM?

_e_ **1.** 1099   **a.** slip
____ **2.** check   **b.** reading
____ **3.** deposit   **c.** printer
____ **4.** tax   **d.** strip
____ **5.** odometer   **e.** form
____ **6.** security   **f.** license
____ **7.** driver's   **g.** return

____ **8.** insurance   **h.** publication
____ **9.** printed   **i.** drawer
____ **10.** IRS   **j.** bands
____ **11.** colored   **k.** estimate
____ **12.** currency   **l.** bill
____ **13.** unpaid   **m.** policy
____ **14.** cash   **n.** strands

____ **15.** bank card   **o.** application
____ **16.** cashier's   **p.** log
____ **17.** mortgage   **q.** box
____ **18.** repair   **r.** numbers
____ **19.** safe-deposit   **s.** reader
____ **20.** bank check   **t.** estimate
____ **21.** serial   **u.** check

WORKPLACE ACTIONS

D ▶ FINANCE *IN ACTION!*

1. activate ____
   a. information
   b. damage
   c. a credit card
   d. a problem

2. collect ____
   a. a customer
   b. an unpaid bill
   c. a transaction
   d. the cash drawer

3. assist ____
   a. a customer
   b. a loan
   c. an application
   d. a tax return

4. appraise ____
   a. a deposit
   b. a check
   c. money
   d. damage

5. deposit ____
   a. a withdrawal
   b. a check
   c. an insurance quote
   d. property damage

6. process ____
   a. a customer
   b. cash
   c. a claim
   d. money

7. verify ____
   a. transactions
   b. a small business
   c. insurance
   d. taxes

8. obtain ____
   a. auto damage
   b. a problem
   c. colored strands
   d. information

WORKPLACE COMMUNICATION

E ▶ WHAT ARE THEY SAYING?

_d_ **1.** greet a customer
____ **2.** help a bank customer cash a check
____ **3.** help a customer with a loan application
____ **4.** explain a denied auto loan application
____ **5.** assist an insurance customer
____ **6.** inspect damage
____ **7.** assist a credit card customer
____ **8.** gather tax information
____ **9.** ask for feedback
____ **10.** give feedback
____ **11.** respond to feedback
____ **12.** make a suggestion

a. "You don't have a sufficient credit history."
b. "Do you have a W-2 form from your employer?"
c. "I'll give you a claim number."
d. "May I help you?"
e. "We'll cancel that card immediately and issue a new one."
f. "Thanks for telling me."
g. "Please swipe your bank card in the card reader."
h. "I want to make sure I'm following the new procedure correctly."
i. "I'll be happy to help you fill it out."
j. "Did you tell those customers about a discount they'll receive?"
k. "I'll need to go back there and see the tree that fell."
l. "I need to ask you to lower your voice when you speak to a customer."

1 visitor
2 client
3 administrative assistant
4 receptionist
5 delivery person
6 mail clerk

7 office assistant
8 office manager
9 human resource assistant
10 human resource director
11 job applicant

12 accounts payable clerk
13 accounts receivable clerk
14 payroll clerk
15 secretary

a reception
b conference room
c office manager's office
d human resources department
e accounting department
f payroll department

What occupations do you see in this office?
What areas of the office do you see?

16 executive
17 general manager
18 executive assistant
19 executive secretary
20 marketing associate
21 marketing manager

22 sales associate
23 sales manager
24 repair technician
25 file clerk

g executive office
h general manager's office
i executive assistant's office
j marketing department
k sales department

l employee lounge
m mailroom
n copy room
o file room
p supply room

Describe an office you are familiar with. What areas does the office have? Who works there?

1 greet a client
2 ask a visitor to sign in
3 handle an incoming call
4 sign for a delivery

5 prepare meeting materials
6 set up videoconference equipment
7 assign tasks
8 review job applications and resumes

9 interview a job applicant
10 verify company invoices
11 pay invoices
12 process employee forms

13 distribute mail
14 compose correspondence
15 proofread correspondence
16 create a spreadsheet

Look at pages 178 and 179. What are the people doing? Describe their actions.

17 answer the telephone
18 compile information
19 fax a document
20 take shorthand

21 prepare promotional materials
22 update the company's website and social media sites
23 call potential clients
24 take a message

25 sort incoming mail
26 weigh and meter outgoing mail
27 make copies
28 file documents

29 retrieve files
30 put away supplies
31 check inventory
32 make coffee

1 reception station
2 switchboard phone
3 meeting materials
4 presentation easel
5 dry erase board
6 dry erase marker

7 videoconference equipment
8 bulletin board
9 office chair
10 accounts payable software/program
11 accounts payable check
12 invoice

13 Personnel Action Form (PAF)
14 payroll check
15 resume
16 employment application
17 word processing software/program
18 business stationery
19 spreadsheet software/program

Look at pages 178–181. What office equipment, tools, and objects do you see?

20 mail cart
21 water cooler
22 fax machine
23 phone memo
24 office supplies

25 envelopes
26 enclosed bulletin board
27 sales tracking board
28 company website
29 sorting table

30 manila folder
31 hanging file folder
32 file cabinet
33 copy machine/ copier

34 ream of paper
35 postal scale
36 postage meter
37 inventory count sheet
38 coffee maker

1 A Receptionist & an Office Visitor

A receptionist is greeting a visitor.

A. Good morning. May I help you?
B. Yes. I'm here to see Ms. Parsons.
A. Do you have an appointment?
B. Yes, I do.
A. All right. Please sign in and I'll notify her that you're here.

2 An Office Assistant & an Office Manager

An office assistant and manager are prioritizing tasks.

A. Quick question! I'm supposed to clean up the supply room today and also set up the conference room for a meeting. Which do you want me to do first?
B. The meeting is this morning, so I'd set up the conference room first.
A. Okay. Will do.

3 Two Office Assistants

An office assistant is offering to help another.

A. Can I help you set up for the meeting?
B. That would be great. Actually, I need a few more folders and two more copies of the meeting agenda.
A. No problem. I'll take care of it and be right back.
B. Thanks.

4 A Secretary & a Mail Clerk

A secretary is asking about a delivery.

A. Has an express package for me arrived yet?
B. I don't think so. After I distribute the mail, I'll go back to the mailroom and check.
A. Thanks.

---

1 You're a receptionist in an office. Welcome a visitor.
2 You're an office assistant with multiple tasks to do. Ask your manager to prioritize the tasks.
3 You're an office assistant. Offer to help a co-worker.
4 Have you ever sent anything by express mail? If so, what did you send, and why did you send it that way?

5 An Office Clerk & an Administrative Assistant

An office clerk is doing a task for an administrative assistant.

A. I copied and collated the reports.
B. Good. Now please take them to the sales department.
A. Who should I give them to?
B. You can give them to the sales manager or any one of the sales associates.

6 A General Manager & an Executive Assistant

A general manager is asking an executive assistant to place a call.

A. Please place a call to Martin Mendez at Em-Tee Corporation.
B. Certainly.
. . . .
B. I have Mr. Mendez on line 2.
A. Line 2? Thank you.

7 Two Office Assistants

Two office assistants are dealing with a problem.

A. Is the copier broken?
B. I'm fixing a paper jam.
A. Should I come back later?
B. No. I'm almost done. Give me another minute.

8 An Executive & an Administrative Assistant

An executive is giving instructions to an administrative assistant.

A. Is the weekly sales report finished?
B. I'm proofreading it now.
A. Great. I'd like to see it before you send it out. And please print out a hard copy for the boss.
B. All right. It should be ready in about fifteen minutes.

5 You're an administrative assistant. Ask an office clerk to do a task.
6 You're the general manager of a company. Ask your executive assistant to place a call.
7 You're an office assistant. Work with another office assistant to deal with a problem.
8 You're an executive. Give instructions to an administrative assistant.

A HOW TO RESPOND TO AN INCOMING CALL

1 Answer the incoming call with the company's name and a greeting.
2 Listen to the caller's request.
3 Ask who's calling.
4 Transfer the call to the employee's extension.
5 If the employee doesn't pick up, offer to take a message.
6 Take a message.
7 Wish the caller a good day.
8 Give the message to the employee.

B HOW TO PROCESS AN INVOICE

1 Open and review the invoice.
2 Confirm with the appropriate department that the goods were received or the services were performed.
3 Print an A/P* voucher and attach it to a copy of the invoice.
4 Send the A/P voucher and invoice to the appropriate department for approval.
5 Upon receipt of the approved voucher, input the payment information into the system.
6 Print a check.
7 Have the check signed.
8 Mail the check to the vendor.
9 Confirm that the check has been cashed.
10 Apply the deduction to the appropriate account.

* A/P = Accounts Payable

C HOW TO WRITE AND SEND EXECUTIVE CORRESPONDENCE

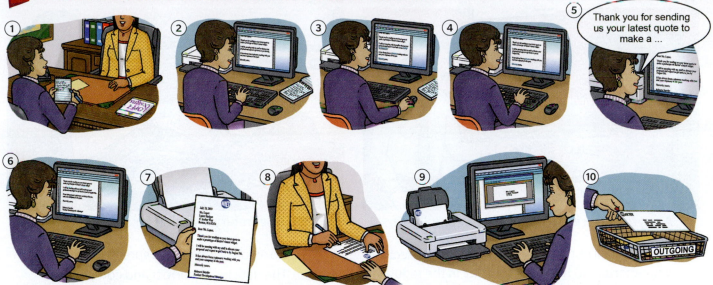

1 Take shorthand dictation from the executive.
2 Write a draft of the letter.
3 Proofread the draft.
4 Make corrections.

5 Read the corrected letter aloud.
6 Make any additional corrections.
7 Print the letter on company stationery.

8 Have the executive sign the letter.
9 Address an envelope.
10 Put the letter in Outgoing Mail.

D HOW TO FAX A DOCUMENT

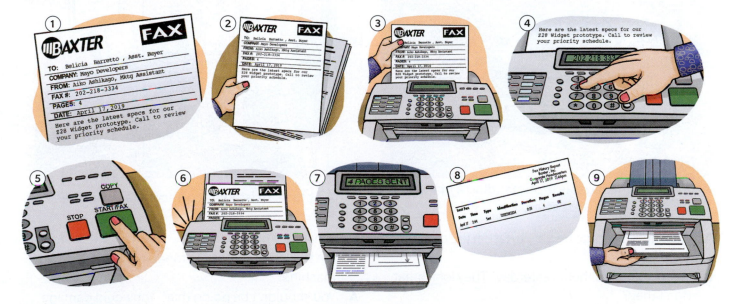

1 Create a cover sheet indicating the recipient, sender, and number of pages.
2 Place the cover sheet on top of the document.
3 Insert the pages into the fax machine feeder facing up or down, according to the machine instructions.
4 Enter the fax number on the machine's keypad.

5 Press the "send" key.
6 Listen for the fax machine tones.
7 Check to confirm that the fax transmission was completed.
8 If desired, print a confirmation page.
9 Remove the pages from the machine.

1 A Payroll Clerk & a New Employee

A payroll clerk is correcting a new employee.

A. You didn't fill out last week's timesheet correctly. You reported 10 hours on Tuesday in the regular hours column.
B. But that's the number of hours I worked on Tuesday.
A. In that case, you should have put 8 hours in the regular hours column and 2 in the overtime column.
B. I see. Last week was my first week here. Now I'll know how to fill it out.

2 A Secretary & an Executive

A secretary is asking for feedback.

A. Did I do an okay job on this spreadsheet?
B. Yes. The data looks correct and complete.
A. How do you like the graph I created?
B. It's excellent! Very clear and colorful.
A. I'm glad you like it. It's a new feature in the updated software.

3 A Marketing Manager & a Marketing Associate

A marketing manager is reprimanding a marketing associate.

A. I just noticed some new pictures on the company's website.
B. Yes. I uploaded them yesterday. They look great, don't they?
A. That's not the point! I need to approve all new content on the site. We don't have approval to use those photos.
B. Oh. I'm really sorry. I'll remove the photos right away.

4 Two Office Assistants

An office assistant is correcting a co-worker.

A. What's going on here?
B. I'm trying to replace the toner in the copy machine.
A. You shouldn't be doing that! You could damage the copier. Only the office manager is authorized to service the machine.
B. Oh, okay. I should have known better. Sorry for this mess!

1 You're a payroll officer. Give correction to a new employee.
2 You're a secretary. Ask for feedback about a task you have accomplished.
3 You're a marketing manager. Reprimand a marketing associate about something that was done incorrectly.
4 You're an office assistant. Give correction to a co-worker.

OCCUPATIONS

accounts payable clerk
accounts receivable clerk
administrative assistant
delivery person
executive
executive assistant
executive secretary
file clerk
general manager
human resource assistant
human resource director
mail clerk
marketing associate
marketing manager
office assistant
office clerk
office manager
payroll clerk
receptionist
repair technician
sales associate
sales manager
secretary

WORKPLACE LOCATIONS

accounting department
conference room
copy room
employee lounge
executive assistant's office
executive office
file room
general manager's office
human resources department
mailroom
marketing department
office manager's office
payroll department
reception
sales department
supply room

EQUIPMENT, TOOLS, & OBJECTS

A/P voucher
accounts payable check
accounts payable software/program
bulletin board
business stationery
check
coffee maker
company stationery
company website
confirmation page
copy machine/copier
correspondence
cover sheet
data
document
draft
dry erase board
dry erase marker
employee forms
employment application
enclosed bulletin board
envelopes
express package
fax machine
fax machine feeder
file cabinet
folder
graph
hanging file folder
hard copy
inventory count sheet
invoice
job application
keypad
mail cart
manila folder
meeting materials
office chair
office supplies
payroll check
Personnel Action Form (PAF)
phone memo
postage meter
postal scale
presentation easel
promotional materials
ream of paper
reception station
resume
sales tracking board
shorthand (dictation)
sorting table
spreadsheet
spreadsheet software/program
switchboard phone
timesheet
toner
videoconference equipment
water cooler
word processing software/program

WORKPLACE ACTIONS

answer the telephone
ask a visitor to sign in
assign tasks
call potential clients
check inventory
compile information
compose correspondence
create a spreadsheet
distribute mail
fax a document
file documents
greet a client
handle an incoming call
interview a job applicant
make coffee
make copies
pay invoices
prepare meeting materials
prepare promotional materials
process employee forms
proofread correspondence
put away supplies
retrieve files
review job applications and resumes
set up videoconference equipment
sign for a delivery
sort incoming mail
take a message
take shorthand
update a company's website and social media sites
verify company invoices
weigh and meter outgoing mail

WORKPLACE COMMUNICATION

ask an assistant to place a call
ask about a delivery
ask for feedback
correct a co-worker
correct a new employee
deal with an office problem
do a task for a co-worker
give instructions
greet a visitor
offer to help a co-worker
prioritize tasks with a co-worker
reprimand a co-worker

13.8 Skills Check

OCCUPATIONS

A MEET THE PEOPLE AT BLAINE ELECTRONICS!

accounts payable	file clerk	office manager
accounts receivable	human resource director	payroll clerk
assistant	mail clerk	receptionist
executive secretary	marketing manager	sales manager

I'm proud and pleased to introduce our wonderful staff here at Blaine Electronics. This is Maria Lopez. She's our _____office manager_____ 1. She supervises our entire administrative staff. Walter Williamson is our _____ 2. He hires people and helps employees who may have problems or conflicts at work. Our _____ 3 clerk is Tania Wong. She receives and pays invoices for goods and services. Her associate, Barry Michaels, is the company's _____ 4 clerk. He makes sure our company has received money owed to us for goods and services we provide.

I'd also like you to meet Rick Santini. He's our _____ 5. Rick manages all of the Blaine Electronics incoming and outgoing mail. Monica Morales is our _____ 6. She's in charge of marketing our company's products and services. Carla Martinez is our _____ 7. She's the one who gives our employees their paychecks.

I'd also like to introduce Jack Perkins. Jack is a _____ 8. He maintains and protects our company's files. Jack reports to Cornelia Jackson, an _____ 9, who provides administrative support to some of our company's executives. Felicia Jones is an office _____ 10. She does a variety of important clerical tasks.

I'd also like you to meet Peter Chen. He's our company's _____ 11. He leads and guides the company's salespeople. And finally, this is Andrea Tyler, our wonderful _____ 12. She answers the telephone and gives information to the public and to our company's customers. I'm very proud of the fine people who work here at Blaine Electronics!

WORKPLACE LOCATIONS

B WHAT'S THE PLACE?

1. There's an important meeting of all the company's executives at 2:00 today in the (copy ~~conference~~) room.
2. You can pick up your check in the (payroll   marketing) department.
3. I'm going to take a break in the (employee lounge   accounting department).
4. Visitors to our company must first go to (the file room   reception).
5. We keep extra paper and pens in the (supply room   executive office).
6. If you want information about job benefits, speak with someone in the (human resources   sales) department.

190

EQUIPMENT, TOOLS, & OBJECTS

C WHAT'S THE ITEM?

_b_	1. manila	a. cabinet	___	7. presentation	g. meter	___	13. payroll	m. package
___	2. cover	b. folder	___	8. coffee	h. easel	___	14. fax machine	n. check
___	3. file	c. cart	___	9. postal	i. marker	___	15. express	o. website
___	4. mail	d. board	___	10. postage	j. maker	___	16. confirmation	p. machine
___	5. bulletin	e. cooler	___	11. business	k. scale	___	17. copy	q. feeder
___	6. water	f. sheet	___	12. dry erase	l. stationery	___	18. company	r. page

WORKPLACE ACTIONS

D OFFICE ADMINISTRATION IN ACTION!

1. distribute ___
   a. shorthand
   (b.) mail
   c. a client
   d. inventory

2. take ___
   a. the telephone
   b. social media sites
   c. a message
   d. a website

3. proofread ___
   a. a client
   b. tasks
   c. a job applicant
   d. correspondence

4. check ___
   a. inventory
   b. a visitor
   c. a call
   d. a chair

5. retrieve ___
   a. tasks
   b. files
   c. an office
   d. the conference room

6. verify ___
   a. telephones
   b. visitors
   c. invoices
   d. the coffee maker

7. update ___
   a. incoming mail
   b. feedback
   c. a website
   d. coffee

8. set up ___
   a. equipment
   b. a ream of paper
   c. incoming mail
   d. shorthand

9. sign for ___
   a. a draft
   b. a graph
   c. a delivery
   d. tasks

WORKPLACE COMMUNICATION

E WHAT ARE THEY SAYING?

_e_	1. greet a visitor	a.	"Can I help you set up for the meeting?"
___	2. prioritize tasks	b.	"That's not the point! I need to approve all new content."
___	3. offer to help	c.	"You didn't fill out last week's timesheet correctly."
___	4. ask about a delivery	d.	"Please take the reports to the sales department."
___	5. assign a task	e.	"Good morning. May I help you?"
___	6. inquire about a problem	f.	"Has an express package for me arrived yet?"
___	7. respond to instructions	g.	"Did I do an okay job on this spreadsheet?"
___	8. correct an employee	h.	"All right."
___	9. ask for feedback	i.	"Set up the conference room first."
___	10. reprimand someone	j.	"Oh, okay. I should have known better."
___	11. respond to correction	k.	"Is the copier broken?"

1 pet sitter	**8** exterminator	**a** pet
2 handyman	**9** locksmith	**b** toolbox
3 home appliance repair technician	**10** dog walker	**c** shelving
4 housekeeper	**11** home entertainment equipment installer	**d** washing machine
5 carpet cleaner	**12** tutor	**e** cleaning supplies
6 nanny	**13** lawn care worker	**f** carpet
7 caregiver	**14** delivery person	**g** carpet cleaning supplies

h snack	**k** carpet cleaning vehicle
i insecticide	**l** lawn care truck
j home entertainment system	**m** delivery truck

What personal service occupations do you see? What objects do you see?

Do you use or perform any of these personal services?

15 senior citizen activities coordinator
16 teacher
17 teacher's aide
18 clerk
19 recreation worker
20 recreation program leader
21 library assistant

22 librarian
23 mail handler
24 mail carrier
25 fitness trainer
26 aerobics instructor
27 child-care worker
28 lawyer
29 paralegal/legal assistant

30 courier/ messenger
31 legal secretary
32 veterinarian
33 veterinary technician
34 tow truck driver
35 funeral attendant
36 funeral director

n senior center
o school
p city hall
q recreation center
r playground
s library
t post office

u health club
v child-care center
w law office
x veterinary clinic
y funeral home

What community service occupations do you see?
What places do you see?

Which of these places are in your community?
Where are they?

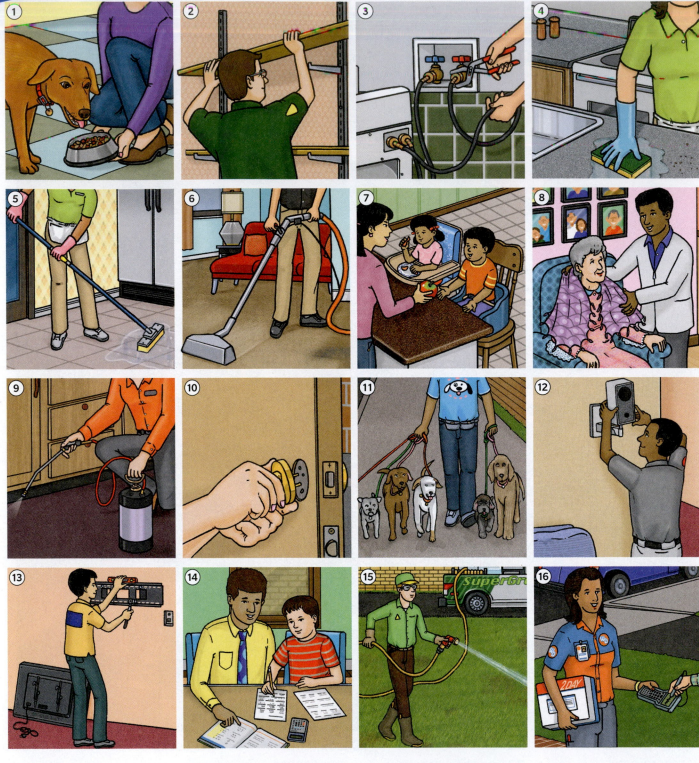

1 feed a pet
2 install shelving
3 repair a washing machine
4 clean a kitchen

5 wash a floor
6 clean a carpet
7 give children a snack
8 provide care

9 spray insecticide
10 install a deadbolt lock
11 walk dogs
12 install speakers

13 mount a TV on a wall
14 tutor a student
15 spray fertilizer
16 deliver a package

Look at pages 192 and 193. What are the people doing? Describe their actions.

17 lead an activity
18 assist a teacher
19 accept a tax payment
20 check out equipment

21 supervise a recreation program
22 sort and shelve books
23 check out library materials
24 sort mail

25 instruct a client on exercise equipment
26 lead an exercise class
27 read to a group
28 do legal research

29 deliver documents
30 give shots
31 tow a vehicle
32 help a family make funeral arrangements

1 pet bowls	**8** hanging utility light	**15** carpet brush	**22** spade bit	**28** TV mount
2 pet food	**9** cleaning supplies	**16** pump sprayer	**23** hole saw	**29** digital level
3 tool caddy	**10** angle broom	**17** bait station	**24** leash	**30** lag bolt
4 screwdriver	**11** sponge mop	**18** bait gun	**25** dog treats	**31** socket wrench
5 pliers	**12** scrub sponge	**19** bait gun holster	**26** wall-mounted	**32** math
6 washing machine	**13** cleaning bucket	**20** deadbolt lock	speaker	worksheet
7 drive belt	**14** carpet spot cleaner	**21** drill	**27** speaker wire	**33** calculator

Look at pages 192–195. What equipment, tools, and objects do you see?

34 bingo cage and ball	**40** book cart	**47** hand weights	**53** messenger bag
35 quiz	**41** book resensitizer	**48** wireless microphone	**54** case law books
36 utility bill	**42** spine label	**49** aerobic steps	**55** vet ear thermometer
37 paid stamp	**43** mail carrier satchel	**50** peg shapes	**56** tow truck
38 ping-pong ball and paddle	**44** flat mail tray	**51** fixed gear bicycle	**57** wheel chock
39 basketball	**45** mailbag	**52** bike lock	**58** hearse
	46 treadmill		**59** casket

1 A Home Appliance Repair Technician & a Customer

A home appliance repair technician is explaining a repair that is needed.

A. I found the problem with your washing machine. The belt is worn out and needs to be replaced.

B. Can you do that today?

A. Oh, yes. I have the part in my truck.

B. How much will that cost?

A. It'll be 50 dollars for the part and 90 dollars labor.

2 An Exterminator & a Customer

An exterminator is asking a customer to describe a pest control problem.

A. So you're having a problem with ants?

B. Yes, mainly in the kitchen—on the counters and on the floor near the cabinets.

A. I'll spray along the baseboard and put some bait traps in the cabinets, and that should take care of the problem.

B. Great! Thanks.

3 A Caregiver & a Client

A caregiver is caring for a client.

A. Mrs. Perez, is there anything I can do for you?

B. Yes. I'm feeling a bit cold.

A. I'll get you a shawl, and then let's play cards.

B. Yes . . . let's play cards. I'd love that.

4 Children & a Nanny

Children and their nanny are disagreeing about their snack.

A. Is it time for our afternoon snack yet?

B. Almost. We're having apples today.

A. Apples?! No! We want ice cream! We want ice cream!

B. Sorry. You know that your parents want you to have fruit as a snack.

A. Oh . . . okay.

1 You're a home appliance repair technician. Explain a repair to a customer.

2 You're an exterminator. Listen to a customer's problem and explain how you'll take care of it.

3 You're a caregiver. Offer to do something for your client.

4 You're a nanny. You and the children you care for are having a disagreement.

5 A Teacher & a Teacher's Aide

A teacher and a teacher's aide are deciding how to do an activity.

A. Do you think we should do this as a whole-class activity?

B. We could. Or what if we divided the class in half?

A. Good idea! I'll work with these students at the front of the room, and you can work with the rest at the back of the room.

6 A Recreation Director & a Recreation Worker

A recreation director is asking a recreation worker about program attendance.

A. How many kids showed up for your after-school program today?

B. There were about 15 kids.

A. That's fewer than usual, isn't it?

B. Yes. I think it's because of the weather.

7 A Librarian & a Library Assistant

A librarian is pointing out a problem to a library assistant.

A. That book drop is really full. It looks like some books have fallen on the floor.

B. I know. There have been a lot of returns this morning.

A. I'll get one of the assistants to bring over a cart and reshelve those items.

B. Thank you.

8 A Veterinarian & a Veterinary Assistant

A veterinarian is giving instructions to a veterinary assistant.

A. How is Buster doing?

B. Okay. I just finished cleaning out the wound.

A. Good. Now please hold him while I do some stitches.

B. All right. I've got him.

5 You're a teacher. Coordinate an activity with your teacher's aide.

6 You're a recreation director. Ask a worker for some information about a program.

7 You're a librarian. Point out a problem to an assistant.

8 You're a veterinarian. Give instructions to an assistant.

A HOW TO CHANGE THE DRIVE BELT ON A WASHING MACHINE

1 Move the washer away from the wall.
2 Unplug the washer from the electrical socket.
3 Turn off the inlet valves.
4 Disconnect the water hoses from the washer.

5 Remove the back panel.
6 Locate and check the belt.
7 Loosen the bolt on the motor bracket.
8 Remove the old belt.
9 Push the motor back into position.

10 Stretch a new belt into place on the pulleys.
11 Tighten the bolt on the motor bracket.
12 Reinstall the back panel.

B HOW TO MOUNT A FLAT-SCREEN TV

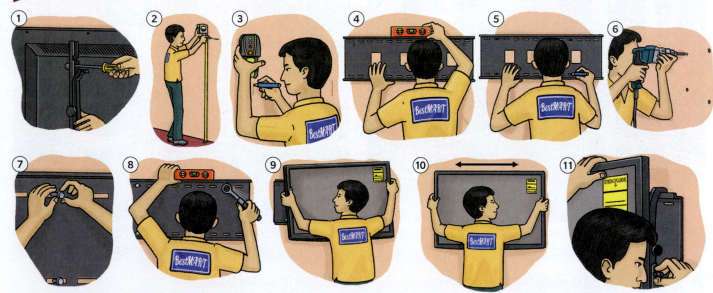

1 Attach monitor brackets to the back of the TV.
2 From the floor, measure and mark the height for the wall plate.
3 Use a stud finder to locate and mark two wall studs that are at least 12 inches apart.
4 While holding the wall plate against the wall at the correct height, use a level to square it to the wall.
5 Mark four holes through the holes in the wall plate.
6 Drill pilot holes to a depth of 2 1/2 inches.

7 Attach the wall plate to the wall using washers and bolts.
8 Recheck the leveling and then tighten the lag bolts with a socket wrench.
9 Lift the TV and hook the brackets to the top rail of the wall plate.
10 Slide the TV left and right to its final position.
11 Lock the latches on the bottom of the brackets to secure the TV.

C HOW TO SHELVE BOOKS IN A LIBRARY

1 Collect books from the book drops.
2 Put the books on a book cart.
3 Check the spine label on each book.
4 Sort the books by their call number onto another cart.

5 Resensitize the books by moving the spine of a book from right to left on the sensitizing machine.
6 Make sure the books remain in the correct order on the cart.
7 Use each book's call number to determine its correct section.

8 Locate each book's section by the signs on the bookshelf ends.
9 Locate a book's home by its exact call number.
10 Place the book on the shelf and bring all books flush with the shelf edge.

D HOW TO TRAIN A CLIENT ON THE USE OF A TREADMILL

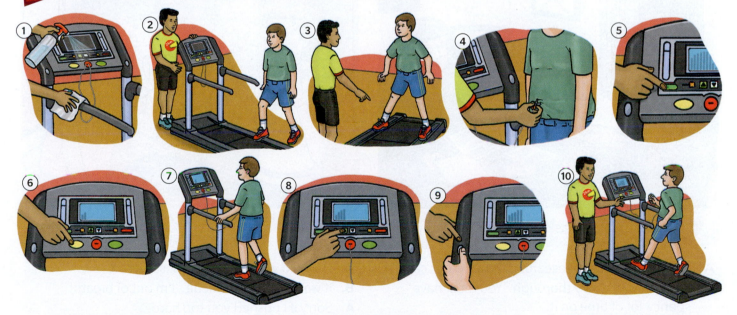

1 Disinfect the treadmill railings and the touchscreen.
2 Have the client get onto the treadmill.
3 Have the client put a foot on each edge of the machine and straddle the belt.

4 Attach the stop chain to the client.
5 Select a workout program and enter all information.
6 Start the belt at the lowest speed.
7 Have the client hold onto the railings and put one foot and then the other onto the belt deck and start walking.

8 Gradually increase the speed.
9 Show the client the heart rate sensors.
10 Have the client walk or run at the desired speed.

1 An Exterminator & a Customer

An exterminator is learning from a customer that a pest control treatment didn't work.

A. So you're still having a problem with ants?
B. Yes. Whatever you sprayed last week didn't work. We still have a lot of ants in the kitchen, and they're really large!
A. They're large? Then you've probably got carpenter ants. I'll spray for those and I'll also place some bait traps around the kitchen.
B. Okay. Thanks.

2 Two Home Entertainment Installers

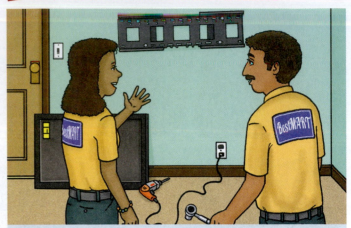

One home entertainment installer is noticing a problem with another's work.

A. That wall plate doesn't look level to me.
B. It doesn't?
A. No. I'd recheck the leveling before you tighten the bolts.
B. Okay. I'll do that.
A. Great. Let me know when you're finished, and I'll help you mount the TV.

3 A Paralegal & a Lawyer

A paralegal is asking for feedback.

A. Did I do a good job researching the Baxter case?
B. Yes. You were very thorough. You must have spent a lot of time on it.
A. I did. I worked all weekend.
B. Well, great job!

4 An Aerobics Instructor & a Client

An aerobics instructor is receiving feedback from a class participant.

A. How did you like today's session?
B. It was much too difficult. I'm out of breath!
A. Sorry if I pushed you too hard.
B. Remember, this is the beginning class, not the advanced level!
A. Thanks for the feedback. I'll keep that in mind.

1 You're an exterminator. Your previous treatment didn't work. Help your customer.
2 You're a home entertainment installer. Notice a problem with the work of your co-worker.
3 You're a paralegal in a law firm. Ask for feedback about something you did well.
4 You're an aerobics instructor. Receive constructive feedback from a class participant.

OCCUPATIONS

- aerobics instructor
- caregiver
- carpet cleaner
- child-care worker
- clerk
- courier/messenger
- delivery person
- dog walker
- exterminator
- fitness trainer
- funeral attendant
- funeral director
- handyman
- home appliance repair technician
- home entertainment equipment installer
- housekeeper
- lawn care worker
- lawyer
- legal secretary
- librarian
- library assistant
- locksmith
- mail carrier
- mail handler
- nanny
- paralegal/legal assistant
- pet sitter
- recreation program leader
- recreation worker
- senior citizen activities coordinator
- teacher
- teacher's aide
- tow truck driver
- tutor
- veterinarian
- veterinary technician

WORKPLACE LOCATIONS

- child-care center
- city hall
- funeral home
- health club
- law office
- library
- playground
- post office
- recreation center
- school
- senior center
- veterinary clinic

EQUIPMENT, TOOLS, & OBJECTS

- aerobic steps
- angle broom
- back panel
- bait gun
- bait gun holster
- bait station
- bait trap
- basketball
- belt
- belt deck
- bike lock
- bingo cage and ball
- bolt
- book cart
- book resensitizer
- bookshelf
- bracket
- calculator
- call number
- carpet
- carpet brush
- carpet cleaning supplies
- carpet cleaning vehicle
- carpet spot cleaner
- case law books
- casket
- chain
- cleaning bucket
- cleaning supplies
- deadbolt lock
- delivery truck
- digital level
- documents
- dog treats
- drill
- drive belt
- electrical socket
- equipment
- exercise equipment
- fertilizer
- fixed gear bicycle
- flat mail tray
- hand weights
- hanging utility light
- hearse
- heart rate sensor
- hole saw
- home entertainment system
- inlet valve
- insecticide
- label
- lag bolt
- lawn care truck
- leash
- level
- library materials
- mail bag
- mail carrier satchel
- math worksheet
- messenger bag
- monitor bracket
- motor bracket
- package
- paid stamp
- part
- peg shapes
- pet bowls
- pet food
- ping-pong ball and paddle
- pliers
- pulley
- pump sprayer
- quiz
- railings
- screwdriver
- scrub sponge
- sensitizing machine
- shelf/shelving
- shots
- snack
- socket wrench
- spade bit
- speaker wire
- speakers
- spine
- spine label
- sponge mop
- tax payment
- tool caddy
- toolbox
- tow truck
- treadmill
- treadmill railings
- truck
- TV mount
- utility bill
- vehicle
- vet ear thermometer
- wall-mounted speaker
- wall plate
- wall stud
- wall stud finder
- washer
- washing machine
- water hoses
- wheel chock
- wireless microphone
- workout program

WORKPLACE ACTIONS

- accept a tax payment
- assist a teacher
- check out equipment
- check out library materials
- clean a carpet
- clean a kitchen
- deliver a package
- deliver documents
- do legal research
- feed a pet
- give children a snack
- give shots
- help a family make funeral arrangements
- install a deadbolt lock
- install shelving
- install speakers
- instruct a client on exercise equipment
- lead an activity
- lead an exercise class
- mount a TV on a wall
- provide care
- read to a group
- repair a washing machine
- sort
- sort and shelve books
- spray fertilizer
- spray insecticide
- supervise a recreation program
- tow a vehicle
- tutor a student
- walk dogs
- wash a floor

WORKPLACE COMMUNICATION

- ask a customer to describe a problem
- ask about program attendance
- ask for feedback
- care for a client
- decide how to do an activity
- disagree about something
- explain a repair that is needed
- give instructions to an assistant
- learn from a customer that a procedure didn't work
- notice a problem with someone's work
- point out a problem to an assistant
- receive feedback

OCCUPATIONS

A WHAT'S MY OCCUPATION?

1. I'm a _____caregiver_____. I take care of people in their homes.
2. I can fix anything! I'm a _____.
3. I deliver packages to homes and businesses. I'm a _____.
4. Are you having a problem with ants in your kitchen? Call me. I'm an _____.
5. I deliver your mail every day. I'm a _____.
6. I assist a teacher in the classroom. I'm a _____.
7. If you're having trouble locking your door, call me. I'm an excellent _____.
8. I take care of small children while their parents are at work. I'm a _____.
9. Are your carpets dirty? I can help you. I'm an experienced _____.
10. I'll be happy to mow your lawn. I'm a lawn care _____.
11. I'll be happy to walk your dogs. I'm a professional _____.
12. I help the librarian in a library. I'm a _____.
13. I work in a lawyer's office. I'm a _____.
14. If your teenager is having problems with mathematics, I can help. I'm a _____.
15. I plan activities for elderly people. I'm a senior citizen activities _____.
16. I can help you with your new sound system. I'm a home entertainment equipment _____.

WORKPLACE LOCATIONS

B WHAT'S THE PLACE?

_c_ 1. law   a. club
___ 2. health   b. hall
___ 3. city   c. office

___ 4. veterinary   d. home
___ 5. funeral   e. center
___ 6. child-care   f. clinic

EQUIPMENT, TOOLS, & OBJECTS

C WHAT'S THE ASSOCIATION?

_c_ 1. bait trap   bait guy   bait gun holster   a. handyman
___ 2. book cart   book resensitizer   call number   b. mail carrier
___ 3. tool caddy   screwdriver   pliers   c. exterminator
___ 4. angle broom   sponge mop   cleaning bucket   d. locksmith
___ 5. deadbolt lock drill   spade bit   e. librarian
___ 6. satchel   flat   bag   f. housekeeper

WORKPLACE ACTIONS

D WHAT'S THE ACTION?

check out	feed	install	repair	supervise
deliver	give	lead	sort	tow
do	help	mount	spray	tutor

1. I _____lead_____ an exercise class for senior citizens.

2. We can _____ a new deadbolt lock tomorrow morning.

3. How often do you _____ library materials?

4. We will _____ fertilizer and insecticide on your lawn.

5. Call us if you need someone to _____ your new TV on your living room wall.

6. I work at the law office of Brown, Wilson, & Moretti. I _____ legal research.

7. We can certainly _____ you make funeral arrangements for your mother.

8. I'm a very responsible pet sitter. I'll _____ your cats and watch them very carefully.

9. I'm a library assistant at the Greenville Public Library. I _____ and shelve books.

10. We can _____ those documents to you by this afternoon.

11. I'll _____ your vehicle to a nearby repair station.

12. We're looking for someone who can _____ a recreation program for teenagers.

13. Our dishwasher is broken. We need to find someone who can _____ it.

14. I _____ students who need help in their science courses.

15. Please _____ the children a healthy snack when they come home from school.

WORKPLACE COMMUNICATION

E WHAT ARE THEY SAYING?

__f__ 1. explain a repair to a customer

_____ 2. inquire about a problem

_____ 3. care for a client

_____ 4. disagree

_____ 5. decide how to do an activity

_____ 6. ask about attendance

_____ 7. point out a problem

_____ 8. give instructions

_____ 9. respond to instructions

_____ 10. ask for feedback

_____ 11. give feedback

a. "Mrs. Perez, is there anything I can do for you?"

b. "Please hold Buster while I do some stitches."

c. "That book drop is really full."

d. "Did I do a good job researching the Baxter case?"

e. "I'll work with these students, and you can work with the others."

f. "The belt on your washing machine is worn out and needs to be replaced."

g. "Today's session was much too difficult!"

h. "Okay. I'll do that."

i. "Apples?! No! We want ice cream!"

j. "So you're having a problem with ants?"

k. "How many kids showed up for your after-school program today?"

1 temp agency owner	**7** cobbler	**14** licensed day-care operator	**a** temp agency/ temporary staffing service	**i** frame shop
2 temporary staffing specialist	**8** baker	**15** child-care worker		**j** barber shop
	9 newsstand proprietor	**16** food truck owner	**b** coffee shop	**k** day-care facility
3 coffee shop owner	**10** photographer	**17** bookstore owner	**c** flower shop	**l** food truck
4 barista	**11** photography assistant	**18** limo* service owner	**d** jewelry store	**m** bookstore
5 floral designer	**12** picture framer	**19** limo* driver/chauffeur	**e** shoe repair shop	**n** limo/limousine service
6 jewelry designer	**13** barber	**20** pet food shop owner	**f** bakery	**o** pet food shop
* limo = limousine		**21** caterer	**g** newsstand	**p** catering service
		22 interior designer	**h** photography studio	**q** interior design studio

What occupations do you see?
What businesses do you see?

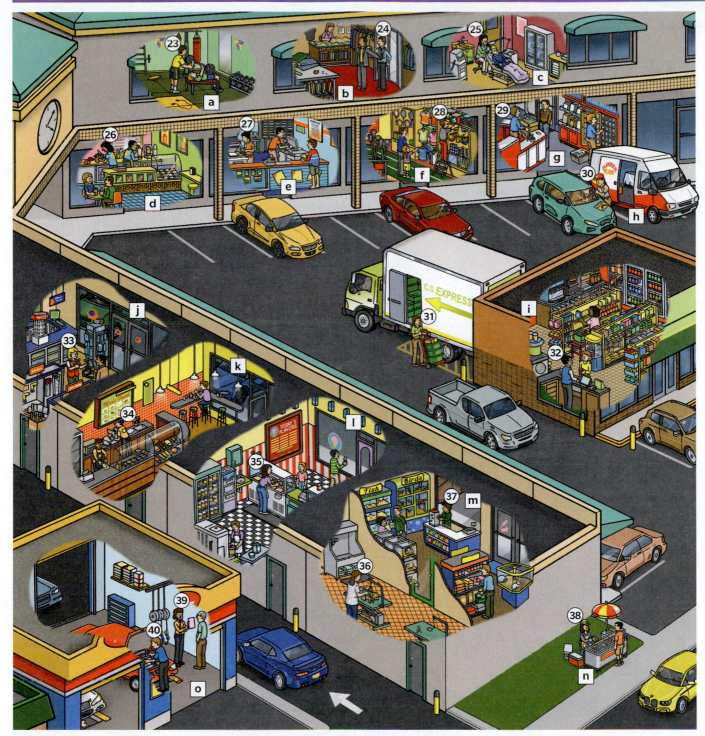

23 personal trainer
24 tailor
25 esthetician
26 smoothie shop owner
27 copy center manager
28 sporting goods store manager
29 mailbox/packaging store manager
30 auto glass repairer

31 jobber/route distributor
32 convenience store owner
33 hardware store manager
34 sandwich shop owner
35 ice-cream shop owner
36 pet groomer
37 pet shop owner
38 food cart vendor
39 auto lube shop owner
40 auto lube shop technician

a personal trainer's studio
b tailor shop
c skin care salon
d smoothie shop
e copy center
f sporting goods store
g mailbox/ packaging store

h mobile auto glass service
i convenience store
j hardware store
k sandwich shop
l ice-cream shop
m pet shop
n food cart
o auto lube shop

Which of these businesses are in your community?   Do you go to any of these businesses? Which ones?

1 find a temporary job for a client
2 greet and check out customers
3 make a flower arrangement
4 design jewelry

5 repair shoes
6 bake pies
7 sell newspapers and magazines
8 do a photo shoot

9 frame a print
10 give a haircut
11 supervise children
12 cook and sell food

13 help customers
14 drive a limo
15 prepare pet food
16 help clients plan an event menu

Look at pages 206 and 207. What are the people doing? Describe their actions.

17 offer fitness training
18 make clothing
19 do skin treatments
20 make smoothies

21 make copies
22 sell sporting goods
23 package items for shipping
24 repair a windshield

25 deliver supplies
26 operate a convenience store
27 sell hardware items
28 make sandwiches

29 serve ice cream
30 groom a dog
31 sell food
32 change oil

1	recruiting software	8	jeweler's anvil	15	dough scraper	22	barber chair	29	bookshelf
2	espresso machine	9	chasing hammer	16	cake pan	23	straight razor	30	book display
3	portafilter	10	cobbler's hammer	17	camera	24	shears/scissors	31	GPS*
4	tamper	11	pincer	18	tripod	25	activity table	32	dog biscuit mold
5	floral scissors	12	magazine	19	softbox light	26	napping mat	33	chafing dish
6	vase	13	newspaper	20	frame	27	griddle	34	serving tray
7	stone gauge	14	rolling pin	21	frame joiner	28	taco shell fryer basket	35	designer display board

* GPS = Global Positioning System navigation device

Look at pages 206–209. What equipment, tools, and objects do you see?

36 exercise ball	**46** stack paper cutter	**56** merchandise container	**65** 3-gallon ice-cream tub
37 wobble board	**47** sports uniform	**57** cups	**66** groomer's table
38 tailor tape	**48** sports equipment	**58** key center	**67** pet nail clippers
39 marking chalk	**49** packing tape dispenser	**59** tool display rack	**68** small animal display
40 pattern scissors	**50** shipping box	**60** disposable gloves	**69** hot dog pushcart
41 application brush	**51** postal box	**61** cutting board	**70** condiment caddy
42 hydration cream	**52** crack opener	**62** portion scale	**71** oil filter wrench
43 smoothie blender	**53** moisture evaporator	**63** sandwich warmer	**72** oil filter
44 add-ins	**54** beverage center	**64** soft-serve ice-cream	**73** oil control gun
45 copier	**55** hand truck	machine	

1 A Job Placement Professional & a Client

A job placement professional is telling a client about a job opportunity.

A. There's a position open at Cole Insurance. They need someone part-time from 10 A.M. to 3 P.M. weekdays.
B. For how long?
A. For three months, but it could turn into a permanent position. Are you interested?
B. Yes. That sounds perfect.

2 A Coffee Shop Owner & a Supplier

A coffee shop owner is ordering supplies.

A. Have you sent out my order yet?
B. No. It won't ship out until the end of the day.
A. Good. I need you to change the quantity of 12-ounce cups on my order. Instead of 6 dozen, I need 12 dozen. Also, please add one more case of filters.
B. Okay. Hold on and I'll get your new total.

3 A Floral Designer & an Assistant

A floral designer is checking on the status of an order.

A. How are you doing with the Mendoza order?
B. I'm almost done. I just need to add some greenery.
A. Great. After you finish, you can put together some Mother's Day bouquets.
B. Okay. I'll make five of them and put them in the display case.

4 A Day-Care Owner & an Employee

A day-care owner is giving instructions to an employee.

A. It's naptime for the two-year olds.
B. They're having their snacks. I'll put them down for their naps as soon as they're finished.
A. Make sure to change their diapers.
B. I'll do that.

1 You're a job placement professional. Tell a client about a job opportunity.
2 You're a coffee shop owner. Order some supplies.
3 You're a floral designer. Give instructions to your assistant.
4 You're a day-care owner. Give instructions to an employee.

5 A Client & a Personal Trainer

A personal trainer is signing up a new client.

A. Is this your own studio?
B. Yes. I opened it a few months ago. Before that, I operated out of my home.
A. Well, your location is very convenient. I think I'd like to sign up for a few sessions.
B. Excellent! Please fill out this enrollment card and I'll explain my services and fees.

6 A Smoothie Shop Employee & the Shop Owner

An employee is reporting a supply shortage to a shop owner.

A. We're running low on some ingredients.
B. What do we need?
A. Strawberries, blueberries, and pineapple chunks.
B. Okay. Bring me the containers when you have a chance and I'll refill them.

7 Two Copy Shop Franchise Owners

Two franchise owners are discussing a work order.

A. Is this a large order?
B. Yes. The customer needs 500 sets of this 20-page document—copied, drilled, and bound.
A. Great! Do we have sufficient paper for that?
B. Yes, we do. I think I'll start on it right away.

8 A Convenience Store Owner & a Route Distributor

A store owner is asking about missing delivery items.

A. I don't see the Veggie Bars.
B. Yeah, I know. They're backordered. I should have some for your next delivery.
A. I hope so. They've been a great seller.
B. Tell me about it! Every store on my route can't get enough of them!

5 You're a personal trainer. Sign up a new client.
6 You work in a smoothie shop. Tell the shop owner about a supply shortage.
7 You work in a copy shop. Make sure you have enough supplies for a work order.
8 You're a convenience store owner. Discuss an order with your route distributor.

A   HOW TO START A SMALL BUSINESS

1 Write a business plan.
2 Test your idea or product.
3 Choose a business location.
4 Obtain financing.
5 Decide on a business structure.

6 Decide on a business name.
7 Register the business with federal, state, and local agencies.
8 Obtain the necessary licenses and permits.

9 Contact suppliers.
10 Construct the business facility.
11 Open the business.

B   HOW TO OPEN A FOOD TRUCK BUSINESS

1 Decide on a specific type of food to sell.
2 Check for available locations.
3 Receive a food handler's ID and certification.
4 Obtain equipment.
5 Plan your menu.
6 File a sales tax and use permit.
7 Fill out a food vending application.

8 Find local suppliers.
9 Sign up for mobile credit card processing.
10 Promote your location through advertising, signage, and social media.
11 Begin operating your business.
12 Be prepared for food/health inspections.

SMALL BUSINESS, FRANCHISE OWNERSHIP, & ENTREPRENEURSHIP

C HOW TO OPEN A FRANCHISE BUSINESS

1 Explore the types of franchises that fit your interests, skills, experience, and budget.
2 Contact franchises that interest you.
3 Call ahead and visit existing franchise locations.
4 Find a suitable location for your franchise.
5 Decide on a franchise and submit the franchise application package.
6 When approved by the franchisor, read and review the franchise disclosure document with an attorney.

7 Attend the franchise's "Discovery Day" to meet the management and ask questions.
8 Execute the franchise agreement.
9 Attend franchisor training sessions.
10 Obtain necessary permits and insurance.
11 Hire and train staff.
12 Have your Grand Opening!

D A DAY OPERATING A SMALL BUSINESS

1 Lead a morning meeting with your employees.
2 Make sure all employees are dressed appropriately and ready for work.
3 Before opening, make sure the sales floor is in order.

4 Open the store.
5 Check inventory on the sales floor and in the stockroom.
6 Deal with suppliers.
7 Take care of accounts payable. Pay bills and supplier invoices.
8 Handle customer complaints.

9 Calculate the payroll.
10 Create the next week's employee work schedule.
11 At the end of the business day, close out the register.
12 Close the store.

1 A Coffee Shop Owner & a Barista

A coffee shop owner is correcting a barista.

A. You need to listen more carefully when customers give you their orders.
B. Is there a problem?
A. Yes. This customer ordered a *spiced* latte, and you're making an *iced* latte!
B. Oh. Sorry about that.

2 A Limo Service Owner & a Driver

A limo service owner is reprimanding a driver.

A. It's time for you to pick up the Peterson wedding party.
B. I know. I'm leaving right now.
A. Oh no you're not! Look at that limo! It's filthy! I've been getting complaints about the cleanliness of your vehicle. You really need to shape up!
B. I apologize. I'll get the car cleaned right now. I promise it won't happen again.

3 An Esthetician & a Client

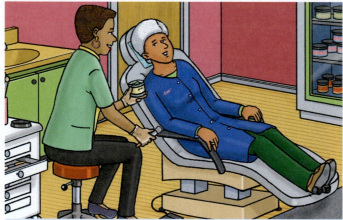

An esthetician is asking a client for feedback.

A. How does that facial mask feel?
B. It's much better than last time.
A. I changed to 95% organic enzyme cream.
B. I can really feel the difference. This is very relaxing.

4 A New Employee & an Ice-Cream Shop Owner

A new employee is asking a shop owner for feedback.

A. Excuse me. Is this the right amount of ice cream for the kid-sized cone?
B. No. That's too much. The kid size is about half a scoop. The regular size is one full scoop like you've got there.
A. Oh, okay. I just wanted to make sure.
B. You're doing a great job on your first day! Feel free to ask when you have any questions.

1. You're a coffee shop owner. Give correction to a barista.
2. You're a limo service owner. Reprimand a driver.
3. You're an esthetician. Ask a client for feedback.
4. You're a new employee at an ice-cream shop. Ask the owner for feedback about something you're doing.

OCCUPATIONS

auto glass repairer
auto lube shop owner
auto lube shop technician
baker
barber
barista
bookstore owner
caterer
child-care worker
cobbler
coffee shop owner
convenience store owner
copy center manager
esthetician

floral designer
food cart vendor
food truck owner
hardware store manager
ice-cream shop owner
interior designer
jewelry designer
jobber/route distributor
licensed day-care operator
limo driver/chauffeur
limo service owner
mailbox/packaging store manager
newsstand proprietor

personal trainer
pet food shop owner
pet groomer
pet shop owner
photographer
photography assistant
picture framer
sandwich shop owner
smoothie shop owner
sporting goods store manager
tailor
temp agency owner
temporary staffing specialist

EQUIPMENT, TOOLS, & OBJECTS

3-gallon ice-cream tub
activity table
add-ins
application brush
barber chair
beverage center
book display
bookshelf
bouquet
cake pan
camera
chafing dish
chasing hammer
cobbler's hammer
condiment caddy
cone
copier
crack opener
cups
cutting board
designer display board
diaper
disposable gloves
document
dog biscuit mold
dough scraper
employee work schedule
enzyme cream
espresso machine

event menu
exercise ball
facial mask
filters
floral scissors
flower arrangement
food handler's certification
food handler's ID
food vending application
frame
frame joiner
franchise agreement
franchise application package
franchise disclosure document
GPS
greenery
griddle
groomer's table
hand truck
hardware items
hot dog pushcart
hydration cream
ingredients
inventory
invoice
jeweler's anvil

jewelry
key center
latte
license
magazine
marking chalk
menu
merchandise container
moisture evaporator
napping mat
newspaper
oil
oil control gun
oil filter
oil filter wrench
packing tape dispenser
paper
pattern scissors
payroll
permit
pet food
pet nail clippers
pies
pincer
portafilter
portion scale
postal box
print
recruiting software

register
rolling pin
sales tax and use permit
sandwich warmer
scoop
serving tray
shears/scissors
shipping box
small animal display
smoothie
smoothie blender
snack
soft-serve ice-cream machine
softbox light
sporting goods
sports equipment
sports uniform
stack paper cutter
stone gauge
straight razor
taco shell fryer basket
tailor tape
tamper
tool display rack
tripod
vase
windshield
wobble board

WORKPLACE LOCATIONS

auto lube shop
bakery
barber shop
bookstore
business facility
business location
catering service
coffee shop
convenience store
copy center
day-care facility
flower shop
food cart

food truck
frame shop
franchise location
hardware store
ice-cream shop
interior design studio
jewelry store
limo/limousine service
mailbox/packaging store
mobile auto glass service
newsstand
personal trainer's studio

pet food shop
pet shop
photography studio
sales floor
sandwich shop
shoe repair shop
skin care salon
smoothie shop
sporting goods store
stockroom
tailor shop
temp agency/temporary staffing service

WORKPLACE ACTIONS

bake pies
change oil
cook and sell food
deliver supplies
design jewelry
do a photo shoot
do skin treatments
drive a limo
find a temporary job for a client
frame a print
give a haircut

greet and check out customers
groom a dog
help clients plan an event menu
help customers
make a flower arrangement
make clothing
make copies
make sandwiches
make smoothies
offer fitness training
operate a convenience store

package items for shipping
prepare pet food
repair a windshield
repair shoes
sell food
sell hardware items
sell newspapers and magazines
sell sporting goods
serve ice cream
supervise children

WORKPLACE COMMUNICATION

ask a client for feedback
ask a shop owner for feedback
ask about missing delivery items
check on the status of an order

correct an employee
discuss a work order
give instructions to an employee
order supplies

report a supply shortage
reprimand an employee
sign up a new client
tell a client about a job opportunity

OCCUPATIONS

A WHAT ARE THEIR JOBS?

auto glass repairer	barber	caterer	esthetician	photographer
baker	barista	cobbler	interior designer	tailor

1. I want to find someone to take pictures of our family. Can you recommend a good **photographer**?
2. Max has repaired boots and shoes for the past thirty years. He's everybody's favorite _____.
3. The windshield on my car is broken. Do you know a good _____?
4. Kelly is the best _____ at Carla's Coffee Shop.
5. I've been having problems with the skin on my face. Can you recommend a good _____?
6. I know a wonderful _____ who can help you decorate your house.
7. Mustafa cuts men's hair. He's a very popular _____.
8. These pants are too long. They need to be shortened. Do you know a good _____?
9. We need to plan the menu for my daughter's wedding. Can you recommend a _____?
10. Bora's cakes and pies are incredible! Everybody agrees that she's the best _____ in town!

B WHAT ARE THEIR JOB TITLES?

1. Timothy is a personal ((trainer) owner).
2. Amanda is a pet (groomer framer).
3. I'm looking for a limo (vendor driver).
4. We need a good floral (designer operator).
5. I work as a route (repairer distributor).
6. I'm looking for a picture (framer technician).
7. Omar is a temp agency (tailor owner).
8. Amy is a photography (barista assistant).
9. Ramil is a food cart (vendor chauffeur).
10. I'm a temporary staffing (designer specialist).
11. I'm a newsstand (groomer proprietor).
12. I'm a licensed day-care (operator distributor).

C WE LOVE OUR JOBS!

auto lube	hardware store	jewelry	route	sporting goods

All the people in our family have interesting jobs. My sister, Denise, is very creative. She's a _____ **jewelry** _____ [1] designer. My brother, Mark, is an experienced _____ [2] shop technician. Victor, my husband, is a _____ [3] distributor. And I've had two wonderful jobs. I used to be a _____ [4] store manager. Now I'm a _____ [5] manager. We all love what we do!

WORKPLACE LOCATIONS

D WHAT'S THE PLACE?

| agency | cart | center | floor | service | shop | store | studio |

1. We have more than five salespeople to help customers on our store's sales _____ **floor** _____.

2. Can you recommend a reliable limousine _____?

3. I just bought some beautiful paintings. Do you know a good frame _____?

4. In your opinion, what's the best hardware _____ in this city?

5. I just wrote a short story and I'd like to make a few copies. Is there a copy _____ nearby?

6. Let's walk over to the food _____ and get a sandwich and something to drink.

7. My friend just opened an interior design _____.

8. I just sent my resume to a temp _____.

EQUIPMENT, TOOLS, & OBJECTS

E WHAT ARE THEY SAYING?

___k___ 1. You'll find newspapers and magazines at a _____.

_____ 2. You'll find a straight razor and shears at a _____.

_____ 3. You'll find a portafilter and tamper at a _____.

_____ 4. You'll find an exercise ball and wobble board at a _____.

_____ 5. You'll find a rolling pin and dough scraper at a _____.

_____ 6. You'll find a tripod and softbox light at a _____.

_____ 7. You'll find a napping mat and activity table at a _____.

_____ 8. You'll find marking chalk and pattern scissors at a _____.

_____ 9. You'll find a key center and tool display rack at a _____.

_____ 10. You'll find an oil control gun and oil filter at an _____.

_____ 11. You'll find a vase and floral scissors at a _____.

_____ 12. You'll find a griddle and fryer basket in a _____.

_____ 13. You'll find a chafing dish and serving tray at a _____.

_____ 14. You'll find an application brush and hydration cream at a _____.

_____ 15. You'll find a blender and add-ins at a _____.

_____ 16. You'll find a postal box at a _____.

_____ 17. You'll find a stone gauge and anvil at a _____.

_____ 18. If you're looking for part-time work, you should contact a _____.

a. day-care facility
b. personal trainer's studio
c. auto lube shop
d. photography studio
e. catering service
f. hardware store
g. temp agency
h. coffee shop
i. jewelry store
j. barber shop
k. newsstand
l. skin care salon
m. bakery
n. mailbox store
o. food truck
p. tailor shop
q. flower shop
r. smoothie shop

WORKPLACE ACTIONS

F ▸ BUSINESS *IN ACTION!*

1. repair _____
   a. fitness training
   b. customers
   c. a windshield ⟲
   d. oil

2. do _____
   a. a store
   b. skin treatments
   c. a tripod
   d. items

3. frame _____
   a. a print
   b. a pet
   c. supplies
   d. clothing

4. sell _____
   a. a job
   b. a work schedule
   c. sales tax
   d. sporting goods

5. prepare _____
   a. a job
   b. pet food
   c. hardware
   d. sporting goods

6. bake _____
   a. cups
   b. smoothies
   c. pies
   d. clothing

7. make _____
   a. a photo shoot
   b. a blender
   c. scissors
   d. copies

8. groom _____
   a. a dog
   b. pet nail clippers
   c. inventory
   d. a blender

9. change _____
   a. pies
   b. copies
   c. oil
   d. children

10. package _____
    a. customers
    b. items
    c. a dog
    d. a limo

11. help _____
    a. hardware
    b. packages
    c. shoes
    d. customers

12. offer _____
    a. fitness training
    b. a newsstand
    c. auto glass
    d. a convenience store

13. cook _____
    a. a food truck
    b. arrangements
    c. supplies
    d. food

14. greet _____
    a. sporting goods
    b. treatments
    c. customers
    d. copies

15. supervise _____
    a. shoes
    b. customers
    c. the stockroom
    d. children

16. serve _____
    a. oil
    b. ice cream
    c. jewelry
    d. items

WORKPLACE COMMUNICATION

G ▸ WHAT ARE THEY SAYING?

_c_	**1.** tell a client about a job opportunity	**a.** "We're running low on some ingredients."
___	**2.** order supplies	**b.** "Make sure to change their diapers."
___	**3.** check on the status of an order	**c.** "There's a position open at Cole's Insurance."
___	**4.** give instructions	**d.** "I don't see the Veggie Bars."
___	**5.** sign up a new client	**e.** "Is this a large order?"
___	**6.** report a supply shortage	**f.** "Please add one more case of filters."
___	**7.** discuss a work order	**g.** "Is this the right amount of ice cream for the kid-sized cone?"
___	**8.** ask about missing delivery items	**h.** "I promise that won't happen again."
___	**9.** correct an employee	**i.** "How are you doing with the Mendoza order?"
___	**10.** respond to correction	**j.** "Please fill out this enrollment card."
___	**11.** ask for feedback	**k.** "You need to listen more carefully when customers give you their orders."

Travel Agency

1 travel agent
2 customer

Airport

3 taxi driver/ cab driver
4 curbside check-in agent
5 skycap
6 wheelchair agent
7 passenger
8 ticket agent
9 TSA screener
10 gate agent
11 food service worker
12 cabin serviceperson
13 baggage handler
14 line service technician
15 flight attendant
16 first officer
17 pilot
18 ground crew member

Auto Rental Agency

19 auto rental agent
20 shuttle driver
21 service agent

a taxicab
b check-in counter
c baggage scale
d security check-in area
e boarding gate
f podium
g gangway
h cabin
i food service lift truck
j bag tug and baggage cart
k mobile baggage conveyor
l cockpit/flight deck
m reservation counter
n shuttle bus

What occupations do you see?
What places and objects do you see?

Are you familiar with an airport near you? If so, describe it.

Hotel

22 valet
23 bellhop
24 doorman
25 guest
26 front desk clerk
27 concierge
28 housekeeper
29 housekeeping manager
30 room service attendant
31 hotel maintenance worker
32 event planner
33 event coordinator
34 houseperson
35 banquet manager
36 busperson
37 banquet server

Tourism

38 group tour guide
39 tour bus driver
40 tour escort

o hotel entrance
p lobby
q front desk
r elevator
s guest floor
t guest room
u function room/ banquet room
v retractable wall
w tour bus
x drop off/ pickup area
y tourist site
z information plaque

Describe a hotel or a motel you are familiar with.   Describe a tourist site in or near where you live.

1 make travel arrangements
2 drop off a passenger at the airport
3 load luggage onto a baggage cart
4 provide wheelchair assistance

5 check a passenger's ticket and ID
6 print a boarding pass
7 weigh and tag luggage
8 check a boarding pass and ID

9 stow/secure a food cart
10 load baggage
11 check overhead compartments
12 direct aircraft

13 demonstrate safety/ emergency procedures
14 drive a shuttle
15 give a customer a rental agreement
16 record mileage and gas level

Look at pages 222 and 223. What are the people doing? Describe their actions.

Our hotel guest needs a table for two at 8 P.M.

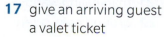

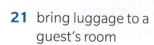

17 give an arriving guest a valet ticket

18 welcome an arriving guest

19 check in a guest

20 review a departing guest's folio

21 bring luggage to a guest's room

22 make reservations for a hotel guest

23 make up a room

24 inspect a room

25 deliver food

26 design an event floor plan

27 coordinate an event

28 set up for an event

29 supervise wait staff

30 serve meals

31 operate a tour bus

32 lead a tour

1. GDS*/travel agency software
2. travel brochures
3. trip itinerary
4. taxi meter
5. receipt
6. skycap baggage cart
7. skycap cap
8. airline ticket
9. baggage tag
10. ticket jacket
11. baggage scale
12. boarding pass
13. boarding pass validator
14. in-flight meal
15. airline food cart
16. seat belt demo unit
17. oxygen mask demo unit
18. life vest demo unit
19. onboard safety card
20. aviation hearing protectors
21. marshaling wands
22. ground crew safety vest
23. car rental agreement
24. car rental keys
25. handheld check-in terminal & printer

* GDS = Global Distribution System

Look at pages 222–225. What equipment, tools, and objects do you see?

26 valet ticket	**33** guest folio	**39** amenities basket	**46** server's tray
27 valet key stand	**34** concierge desk	**40** room service tray	**47** folding tray stand
28 luggage cart	**35** local menus	**41** event lighting	**48** water pitcher
29 doorman cap	**36** local attraction	**42** event backdrop	**49** hand count clicker
30 doorman whistle	brochures	**43** function table	**50** wireless transmitter &
31 guest room card key	**37** housekeeper's cart	**44** pipe and drapes	wireless receiver
32 card key encoder	**38** hanging card	**45** plate cover	**51** tour guide flag

1 A Travel Agent & a Customer

A travel agent is assisting a customer with a trip.

A. Here are all your travel documents—your airline tickets and your vouchers for ground transportation, hotels, and the meals included in your tour package.
B. Is that everything we need?
A. Don't forget your passports and visas. Your passports are up to date, right?
B. Yes, they are. Thanks very much for your help.

2 A Ticket Agent & a Passenger

A ticket agent is checking in a passenger for a flight.

A. How many pieces of luggage are you checking in today?
B. Just this one. I hope it isn't too heavy.
A. Let's see. It's 38 pounds. That's two pounds under the baggage weight allowance, so you're fine.
B. Great! Thanks.

3 Two Baggage Handlers

Two baggage handlers are coordinating to complete a task.

A. Is this all the luggage?
B. No. There are a few additional bags coming from some late check-ins. I'll radio to see if they're going to make this flight.
B. They better hurry! This "baby's" out of here in a few minutes!

4 A Shuttle Bus Driver & an Auto Rental Agent

A shuttle bus driver is coordinating with an auto rental agent.

A. This is Shuttle Bus 3. I'm about to head back to the terminal. *Over.*
B. Wait about two minutes. I'm finishing up with a family of five. They're running late for a flight leaving from Terminal B. *Over.*
A. Got that. *Roger.*

1 You're a travel agent. Assist a customer with a trip.
2 You're an airline ticket agent. Check in a passenger.
3 You're a baggage handler. Coordinate a task with a co-worker.
4 You're a shuttle bus driver for an auto rental agency. Coordinate your route with an agent.

5 A Front Desk Clerk & a Hotel Guest

A front desk clerk is checking in a hotel guest.

A. Welcome to the Grand Hotel! May I ask what name your reservation is under?
B. Yes. The name is Henderson.
A. Welcome, Ms. Henderson. I see you'll be staying with us for two nights. Is that correct?
B. Yes.
A. All right. May I see a form of photo identification and a credit card, please?

6 A Housekeeping Supervisor & a Housekeeper

A housekeeping supervisor is checking on the status of work completed.

A. Have you finished cleaning all the rooms in this section?
B. All of them except Room 219. There's still a *Do Not Disturb* sign on the door.
A. Okay. They should be checking out by noon. You can move to the next section and I'll let you know when the room is ready for cleaning.

7 A Banquet Server & a Banquet Manager

A banquet server is reporting a problem to a banquet manager.

A. A guest at Table 8 says he requested a vegetarian meal.
B. All right. I'll let the kitchen know to prepare another one. Please let the guest know we're taking care of it.
A. Okay. I'll let him know right away.
B. Good. And please apologize for the oversight.

8 A Tour Bus Driver & a Passenger

A tour bus driver is reassuring a passenger.

A. Can I leave my jacket on the bus?
B. Yes. I'll be here the whole time you're taking the tour.
A. Thank you. I just wanted to make sure.
B. I understand. Enjoy the tour, and make sure you take lots of pictures when you get to the top. It's a beautiful view!

5 You're a front desk clerk in a hotel. Check in a guest.
6 You're a housekeeping supervisor in a hotel. Check with a housekeeper about work completed.
7 You're a banquet server. Report a problem to your manager.
8 You're a tour bus driver. Respond to a passenger's request or concern.

16.5 On-the-Job Instructions

A HOW TO CHECK IN AN AIRLINE PASSENGER

1 Ask for the passenger's ticket or reservation information.
2 Locate the reservation in the reservation system.
3 Check the passenger's photo ID or passport.
4 Have the passenger put any baggage on the scale.
5 Weigh the baggage.
6 Collect any excess baggage fee, if required.
7 Print the boarding pass and baggage tag.
8 Put the baggage tag on the baggage.
9 Place the baggage on the conveyor belt.
10 Give the boarding pass to the passenger.
11 Tell the passenger the boarding time and departure gate.

B HOW TO PREPARE THE CABIN FOR TAKEOFF

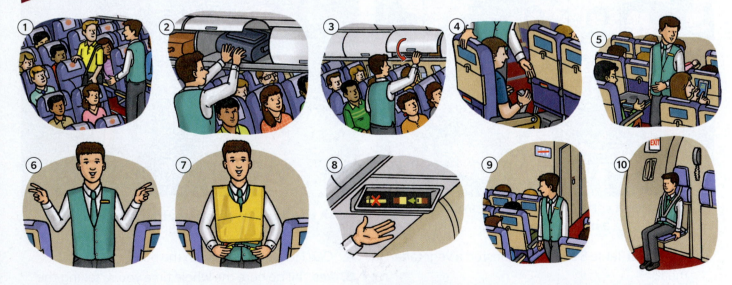

1 Make sure all passengers are seated.
2 Check that all carry-on bags are stored correctly in the overhead bins.
3 Close the overhead bins.
4 Check that passengers' seat belts are fastened, seat backs and tray tables are in their upright positions, and carry-on items are stored properly under the seats.
5 Instruct passengers that portable electronics have to be turned off.
6 Point out the locations of emergency exits.
7 Demonstrate the use of safety equipment.
8 Explain the in-flight smoking and seat belt regulations.
9 Do a final cabin and lavatory walk-through.
10 Sit in your jump seat and prepare for takeoff.

C HOW TO REGISTER A HOTEL GUEST

1 Welcome the guest.
2 Ask the guest's name.
3 Find the guest's reservation in the reservation system.
4 Confirm the length of stay and type of room.

5 Ask for a photo ID and a credit card.
6 Swipe the guest's credit card.
7 Print out the reservation record.
8 Have the guest initial the length of stay and room rate on the reservation record and sign at the bottom.

9 Encode the room key card.
10 Give the room key card and any hotel information to the guest.

D HOW TO SET UP FOR A BANQUET EVENT

1 Dress the tables. (Make sure the tablecloths are clean and pressed, with no rips, fading, or burns.)
2 Check the banquet manager's instructions for the design selected for the event.
3 Fold napkins neatly according to the design selected for the event.
4 Place dinner plates two inches from the edge of the table.
5 Place utensils needed for each course of the meal at each place setting.

6 Place dishes and glasses at each place setting.
7 Inspect all utensils, dishes, and glasses for spots or blemishes.
8 Place a bread basket in the center of each table. (Make sure they are free of fraying and crumbs.)
9 Get into uniform for the event.
10 Be at your post at least 15 minutes before the event is scheduled to begin.
11 Make sure all service setup is complete before the doors are opened for the event.

1 A Skycap & a Curbside Check-in Attendant

A skycap is pointing out a problem to a curbside check-in attendant.

A. Did you just check in this passenger's bags?
B. Yes. Is there a problem?
A. There sure is! Her dog carrier isn't checked baggage. It's carry-on!
B. Oh! I'll retrieve it right away.

2 An Auto Rental Agent & a Service Agent

An auto rental agent is pointing out a problem to a service agent.

A. Did you service the blue hybrid?
B. Yes. I just did.
A. You forgot to fill the gas tank. That's the second time today.
B. Sorry. I'll do it right away.

3 A Banquet Manager & a Server

A banquet manager is giving positive feedback to a server.

A. Is this your section?
B. Yes, it is. Is there a problem?
A. No, on the contrary. I want you to know that some guests at one of your tables just complimented you for being very friendly and helpful.
B. That's great to hear. Thank you.

4 A Tour Guide & a Tourist

A tour guide is asking a tourist for feedback.

A. Are you enjoying our tour today?
B. It's okay, but could you lower the microphone volume? It's really loud! And the driver is going way too fast!
A. Thank you for letting me know. I'll lower the volume and I'll speak to the driver.
B. Thanks.

---

1 You're a skycap at an airport. Point out a problem to a curbside check-in attendant.
2 You're an auto rental agent. Point out a problem to a service agent.
3 You're a banquet manager. Give positive or negative feedback to a server.
4 You're a tour guide. Ask a tourist for feedback.

OCCUPATIONS

- auto rental agent
- baggage handler
- banquet manager
- banquet server
- bellhop
- busperson
- cabin serviceperson
- concierge
- curbside check-in agent
- doorman
- event coordinator
- event planner
- first officer
- flight attendant
- food service worker
- front desk clerk
- gate agent
- ground crew member
- group tour guide
- hotel maintenance worker
- housekeeper
- housekeeping manager
- houseperson
- line service technician
- pilot
- room service attendant
- service agent
- shuttle driver
- skycap
- taxi driver/cab driver
- ticket agent
- tour bus driver
- tour escort
- travel agent
- TSA screener
- valet
- wheelchair agent

WORKPLACE LOCATIONS

- boarding gate
- cabin
- check-in counter
- cockpit/flight deck
- concierge desk
- departure gate
- drop off/ pickup area
- emergency exit
- front desk
- function room/ banquet room
- gangway
- guest floor
- guest room
- hotel entrance
- lobby
- reservation counter
- security check-in area
- terminal
- tourist site

EQUIPMENT, TOOLS, & OBJECTS

- aircraft
- airline food cart
- airline ticket
- amenities basket
- aviation hearing protectors
- bag tug and baggage cart
- baggage
- baggage scale
- baggage tag
- bags
- boarding pass
- boarding pass validator
- bread basket
- car rental agreement
- car rental keys
- card key encoder
- carry-on bag
- conveyor belt
- credit card
- dinner plate
- do not disturb sign
- dog carrier
- doorman cap
- doorman whistle
- elevator
- event backdrop
- event lighting
- excess baggage
- folding tray stand
- food cart
- food service lift truck
- function table
- gas level
- gas tank
- GDS/travel agency software
- ground crew safety vest
- guest folio
- guest room card key
- hand count clicker
- handheld check-in terminal & printer
- hanging card
- housekeeper's cart
- hybrid
- ID
- in-flight meal
- information plaque
- jump seat
- lavatory
- life vest demo unit
- local attraction brochures
- local menus
- luggage
- luggage cart
- marshaling wands
- microphone
- mileage
- mobile baggage conveyor
- onboard safety card
- overhead bin
- overhead compartment
- oxygen mask demo unit
- passport
- photo identification
- pipe and drapes
- place setting
- plate cover
- podium
- portable electronics
- receipt
- rental agreement
- reservation record
- reservation system
- retractable wall
- room key card
- room service tray
- safety equipment
- scale
- seat belt demo unit
- server's tray
- shuttle/shuttle bus
- skycap baggage cart
- skycap cap
- spot/blemish
- tablecloth
- taxi meter
- taxicab
- ticket
- ticket jacket
- tour bus
- tour guide flag
- travel brochures
- tray table
- trip itinerary
- utensils
- valet key stand
- valet ticket
- vegetarian meal
- visa
- voucher
- water pitcher
- wheelchair
- wireless transmitter & wireless receiver

WORKPLACE ACTIONS

- bring luggage to a guest's room
- check a boarding pass and ID
- check a passenger's ticket and ID
- check in a guest
- check overhead compartments
- coordinate an event
- deliver food
- demonstrate safety/emergency procedures
- design an event floor plan
- direct aircraft
- drive a shuttle
- drop off a passenger at the airport
- give a customer a rental agreement
- give an arriving guest a valet ticket
- inspect a room
- lead a tour
- load baggage
- load luggage onto a baggage cart
- make reservations for a hotel guest
- make travel arrangements
- make up a room
- operate a tour bus
- print a boarding pass
- provide wheelchair assistance
- record mileage and gas level
- review a departing guest's folio
- serve meals
- set up for an event
- stow/secure a food cart
- supervise wait staff
- weigh and tag luggage
- welcome an arriving guest

WORKPLACE COMMUNICATION

- ask for feedback
- assist a customer with a trip
- check in a hotel guest
- check in a passenger for a flight
- check on the status of work completed
- coordinate completion of a task
- coordinate tasks with a co-worker
- give positive feedback
- point out a problem
- reassure a passenger
- report a problem

OCCUPATIONS

A WHAT'S MY OCCUPATION?

| bellhop | busperson | concierge | doorman | housekeeper | skycap | valet |

1. I assist passengers with their luggage at the airport. I'm a _____ skycap _____.

2. I welcome people when they walk into our hotel. I'm a _____.

3. I set up and clean tables at hotel banquets. I'm a _____.

4. I park people's cars at a hotel. I'm a _____.

5. I can get you theater tickets and make dinner reservations for you. I'm a _____ in a hotel.

6. I make the beds and clean people's rooms in a hotel. I'm a _____.

7. I assist hotel guests with their luggage. I'm a _____.

B WHAT ARE THEIR JOB TITLES?

__d__ 1. I can help you rent a car at the airport. I'm an auto rental _____.

_____ 2. I make sure airline passengers are safe and comfortable. I'm a flight _____.

_____ 3. I check people in when they arrive at the hotel. I'm a front desk _____.

_____ 4. I plan when and where events take place. I'm an event _____.

_____ 5. I make sure that everything at an event takes place successfully. I'm an event _____.

_____ 6. Welcome! My name is Gus. I'll be your tour bus _____.

_____ 7. I take groups of people on organized trips. I'm a group tour _____.

_____ 8. I load and unload luggage at the airport. I'm a baggage _____.

_____ 9. I'm in charge of all the rooms in a hotel. I'm the housekeeping _____.

_____ 10. I service airplanes when they're on the ground. I'm a ground crew _____.

_____ 11. I assist the pilot on an airplane. I'm the first _____.

_____ 12. I check carry-on bags at the airport. I'm a TSA _____.

_____ 13. I bring people their food at large events. I'm a banquet _____.

_____ 14. I clean airplanes between flights. I'm a cabin _____.

_____ 15. I direct planes when they arrive and leave. I'm a line service _____.

_____ 16. I fix things that are broken in hotel rooms. I'm a hotel maintenance _____.

a. planner
b. guide
c. worker
d. agent
e. screener
f. clerk
g. member
h. driver
i. attendant
j. technician
k. officer
l. serviceperson
m. coordinator
n. server
o. handler
p. manager

WORKPLACE LOCATIONS

C WHAT'S THE PLACE?

__b__ 1. departure   a. site
_____ 2. guest   b. gate
_____ 3. tourist   c. room

_____ 4. flight   d. desk
_____ 5. concierge   e. entrance
_____ 6. hotel   f. deck

_____ 7. emergency   g. site
_____ 8. reservation   h. exit
_____ 9. tourist   i. counter

EQUIPMENT, TOOLS, & OBJECTS

D WHAT'S THE ITEM?

_d_	1. airline	a. cart		___ 6. baggage	f. card		___ 11. dog	k. table
___	2. food	b. table		___ 7. jump	g. tag		___ 12. boarding	l. belt
___	3. gas	c. meter		___ 8. room key	h. basket		___ 13. skycap	m. carrier
___	4. taxi	d. ticket		___ 9. overhead	i. seat		___ 14. conveyor	n. pass
___	5. function	e. tank		___ 10. bread	j. bin		___ 15. tray	o. cap

WORKPLACE ACTIONS

E WHAT DO TRAVEL & HOSPITALITY WORKERS DO?

1. lead ____
- a. a room
- (b.) a tour
- c. a cart
- d. food

2. direct ____
- a. mileage
- b. a menu
- c. aircraft
- d. brochures

3. operate ____
- a. a tour bus
- b. a floor plan
- c. a boarding pass
- d. an ID

4. drop off ____
- a. arrangements
- b. a gas tank
- c. an overhead bin
- d. a passenger

5. make ____
- a. aircraft
- b. a carry-on bag
- c. reservations
- d. utensils

6. make up ____
- a. arrangements
- b. a room
- c. a hotel
- d. a bus

7. weigh ____
- a. luggage
- b. a tour
- c. a gas tank
- d. a receipt

8. check in ____
- a. a hotel
- b. a valet
- c. a guest
- d. an event

9. supervise ____
- a. wait staff
- b. hotel rooms
- c. menus
- d. IDs

10. coordinate ____
- a. a guest
- b. an event
- c. a receipt
- d. a ticket

11. provide ____
- a. a blemish
- b. an emergency
- c. excess baggage
- d. assistance

12. record ____
- a. mileage
- b. a microphone
- c. food
- d. a wait staff

WORKPLACE COMMUNICATION

F WHAT ARE THEY SAYING?

_d_	1. assist a customer with a trip	a. "I'll be here the whole time you're taking the tour."
___	2. check in a passenger for a flight	b. "A guest at Table 8 says he requested a vegetarian meal."
___	3. coordinate a task with a co-worker	c. "May I ask what name your reservation is under?"
___	4. check in a hotel guest	d. "Here are all your travel documents."
___	5. check on the status of work completed	e. "Are you enjoying our tour today?"
___	6. report a problem	f. "How many pieces of luggage are you checking in today?"
___	7. reassure a passenger	g. "You forgot to fill the gas tank."
___	8. point out a problem	h. "Have you finished cleaning all the rooms in this section?"
___	9. give positive feedback	i. "Wait about two minutes before you head back to the terminal."
___	10. ask for feedback	j. "Thank you for letting me know."
___	11. respond to feedback	k. "Some guests just complimented you for being very friendly and helpful."

Publishing

1 author/writer
2 desktop publisher
3 illustrator
4 graphic designer
5 publication assistant
6 technical writer
7 web designer

Printing

8 prepress technician

* CTP = computer
to plate

9 digital press operator
10 finisher

Advertising & Marketing

11 art director
12 assistant art director
13 graphic designer
14 copywriter
15 creative director
16 client

Print Journalism

17 reporter
18 interviewee

19 photojournalist
20 staffer
21 assignment editor
22 researcher/archivist
23 intern
24 assistant copy editor
25 online content
producer
26 web developer
27 digital editor
28 digital staff writer
29 columnist

a CTP* plate maker
b digital press
c electric paper cutter
d binder
e art director's office
f creative department
g conference room
h assignment board
i assignment desk
j newsroom
k web development
department

What occupations do you see in publishing, printing, advertising & marketing, and print journalism?
What objects do you see?

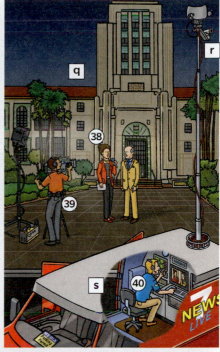

Television Broadcasting	**38** field reporter	**Music Production**	**l** TV studio	**s** ENG news truck
30 camera operator	**39** field camera	**43** musician	**m** anchor desk	**t** radio studio
31 newscaster	operator	**44** sound	**n** green screen/	**u** broadcast booth
32 meteorologist/	**40** ENG* operator	technician	chroma key screen	**v** recording studio
weather reporter	**Radio Broadcasting**	**45** singer	**o** production floor	**w** live room
33 floor manager	**41** radio	**46** recording	**p** PCR*	**x** vocal booth
34 newscast producer	broadcaster	engineer	**q** remote location	**y** control room
35 program director	**42** radio broadcast	**47** assistant	**r** microwave antenna	**z** mixing board
36 broadcast technician	technician	recording		
37 sound engineer		engineer		

* ENG = electronic news gathering
PCR = production control room

What occupations do you see in television broadcasting, radio broadcasting, and music production?
What objects do you see?

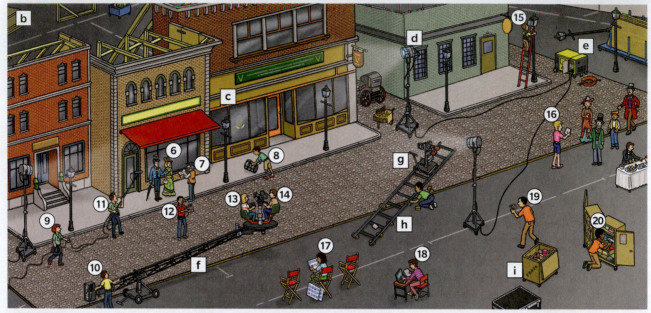

Movie Production

1 screenwriter
2 story analyst/ script reader
3 actor
4 assistant casting director
5 casting director
6 actress
7 director
8 on-set dresser

9 sound assistant
10 gaffer
11 boom operator
12 clapper
13 camera operator
14 assistant camera operator
15 grip
16 set production assistant
17 assistant director

18 writer assistant
19 prop master
20 assistant prop master
21 producer
22 assistant producer
23 film editor
24 assistant film editor
25 recording mixer
26 Foley artist

a casting agency
b soundstage
c set
d set lighting
e generator
f camera crane
g camera dolly
h camera dolly track

i prop cart
j production board
k post production department
l Foley room

What occupations do you see in movie production?
What objects do you see?

Theater

27 set designer
28 set painter
29 scenic artist
30 set carpenter
31 lighting technician
32 assistant set designer
33 sound technician
34 director
35 actor
36 actress
37 stage manager
38 assistant stage manager
39 choreographer
40 assistant choreographer
41 dancer
42 conductor
43 musician
44 board operator

* CAD = computer assisted design

Architecture

45 architect
46 architectural model maker
47 draftsperson
48 CAD* operator

Fine & Applied Arts

49 sculptor
50 portrait painter
51 abstract artist
52 glassblower
53 ceramicist

Fashion

54 fashion designer
55 assistant fashion designer
56 pattern maker
57 photography assistant
58 fashion model
59 fashion photographer
60 buyer
61 assistant buyer

m lighting grid
n backdrop
o set
p scissor arm lift
q backstage
r wing
s stage
t orchestra pit
u architectural firm
v sculpture studio
w artist's studio
x glass studio
y ceramic studio
z fashion design house

What occupations do you see in theater, architecture, fine & applied arts, and fashion? What objects do you see?

Which areas of communication and the arts on pages 236–239 are most interesting to you? Why?

1 write a manuscript
2 lay out a page
3 do an illustration
4 design a publication
5 operate printing equipment
6 trim printed documents
7 bind documents
8 create graphics
9 write ad copy
10 give a presentation to clients
11 do an interview
12 take news photographs
13 write a news story
14 edit copy
15 write a column
16 create website content

Look at page 236. What are the people doing? Describe their actions.

17 operate a studio camera
18 read the news
19 report the weather
20 give timing cues to on-air talent

21 direct a TV program
22 switch video feeds
23 monitor sound levels
24 do an on-location report

25 operate a field camera
26 engineer a remote news feed
27 do a radio broadcast
28 engineer a radio broadcast

29 play an instrument
30 hook up sound equipment
31 sing
32 engineer a recording session

Look at page 237. What are the people doing? Describe their actions.

1 write a script
2 evaluate a script
3 audition
4 take direction

5 adjust lighting
6 dress a set
7 operate a camera
8 prepare a production slate

9 operate a boom microphone
10 manage sound cables
11 handle props
12 note changes in a script

13 update a production schedule
14 edit a film
15 mix audio
16 create sound effects

Look at page 238. What are the people doing? Describe their actions.

17 build a stage set
18 paint scenery
19 set up stage lighting
20 mark a stage

21 rehearse
22 demonstrate a dance routine
23 set up sound equipment
24 build an architectural model

25 draft building plans
26 sculpt
27 paint a portrait
28 blow glass
29 make pottery

30 lay out a garment pattern
31 take fashion photographs
32 select clothing designs for a store

Look at page 239. What are the people doing? Describe their actions.

1 desktop publishing software
2 illustration
3 illustrator's supplies
4 PMS* color swatches
5 typeface samples
6 technical illustration

   * PMS = Pantone Matching System

7 digital press ink cartridge
8 tape binding machine
9 wire binding machine
10 paper drill
11 graphics software
12 presentation projector
13 presentation remote
14 reporter's notebook
15 photojournalist vest

16 word processing software
17 web analytics software
18 studio digital video camera
19 production room headphones
20 ENG microwave antenna
21 portable area light
22 field camera

23 dynamic microphone (mic)
24 shotgun microphone
25 condenser microphone
26 microphone shield
27 microphone preamp
28 guitar preamp
29 audio cable
30 guitar amplifier

Look at pages 236–237 and 240–241. What equipment, tools, and objects do you see?

31 screenplay	**37** production slate	**43** lighting gels
32 MOS* camera	**38** film editing software	**44** stage marking tape
33 boom pole	**39** rerecording software	**45** floor microphone
34 boom microphone	**40** Foley floor	**46** music stand
35 storyboard	**41** Fresnel light	**47** CAD software
36 script	**42** scoop light	**48** track drafting machine
MOS = motor only shot		**49** compass

50 architectural scale	**59** glass shears
51 calipers	**60** mallet
52 pottery wheel	**61** riffler rasp
53 studio easel	**62** pattern tracing wheel
54 painting knife	**63** pattern shears
55 paint	**64** dressmaker form
56 artist's brushes	**65** form curve ruler
57 blowpipe	**66** light meter
58 marver table	

Look at pages 238–239 and 242–243. What equipment, tools, and objects do you see?

1 A Graphic Designer & a Publication Assistant

A graphic designer and publication assistant are coordinating on a project.

A. How do you like this typeface for the publication's cover page?
B. I think it looks great.
A. Is everything ready to send out for approval?
B. Not yet. We're still waiting for the cover illustration.
A. I'll e-mail the illustrator and find out when we can expect to receive the art.

2 A Finisher & a Digital Press Operator

A finisher is checking with a digital press operator on the status of a job.

A. Are you almost done with that print run?
B. It's about half done.
A. Okay. Let me know when it's finished.
B. Will do.

3 An Advertising Copywriter & an Assistant Art Director

An advertising copywriter and assistant art director are brainstorming ideas for an advertisement.

A. What kind of dog is the art department thinking of for the pet food campaign?
B. The research department suggests a golden retriever or a chihuahua.
A. I'd go with the chihuahua. And for the ad copy, I'm thinking of "Happy dogs for happy times." What do you think?
B. How about "Happy dogs for happy homes"?
A. Great suggestion!

4 A Reporter & a Photojournalist

A reporter and photojournalist are preparing to go out on an assignment.

A. Did you get the message? They're sending us out to cover a fire downtown.
B. Yeah. I got it. Where's the fire?
A. In an empty warehouse on Front Street.
B. Give me a minute to grab my equipment and I'll meet you at the van.

1. You're a graphic designer. Coordinate on a project with a publication assistant.
2. You work in a printing company. Check with a co-worker on the status of a job.
3. You're an advertising copywriter. Brainstorm ideas for an advertisement with a co-worker.
4. How do you learn about local news, such as fires, in your community?

5 A Floor Manager & a Newscaster

A floor manager is giving timing cues to the on-air talent.

A. Okay, everybody. We have 10 seconds until air time.
B. Is my tie on straight?
A. Yes. It's fine. And we're on the air in 5, 4, 3, 2, 1!
B. Good evening. I'm Keith McGee, with Diane Martinez, and here are today's top stories.

6 An ENG Operator & a Field Reporter

An ENG operator and a field reporter are preparing to do a live remote broadcast.

A. Can you give me a sound level?
B. "I'm reporting from City Hall and speaking with the mayor about tonight's council meeting." How's that?
A. That's fine. We'll be going live in about one minute.
B. One minute? Okay. Mayor Wilkins, we'll be going live in about one minute.

7 A Radio Announcer & a Broadcast Technician

A radio announcer and a broadcast technician are coordinating during a commercial break.

A. Are we going to the traffic report from Gina after a commercial break?
B. There's a problem with Gina's connection.
A. Okay. Let's do the weather forecast first.
B. Fine. And then we'll do the traffic report after that.

8 A Musician & a Recording Engineer

A musician and a recording engineer are troubleshooting and resolving a problem.

A. We're getting some feedback in here.
B. Any idea where it's from?
A. I think it's from the studio monitor.
B. Okay. I'll lower the volume. How's that?
A. Feedback's gone. Thanks.

5 Do you watch the news on television? If so, what news programs do you watch?
6 You're a TV news field reporter. Interview a public official.
7 How do you get information about the weather forecast?
8 What's your favorite kind of music? How do you listen to it?

Workplace Communication

9 An Assistant Casting Director & an Actress

An assistant casting director is preparing an actress to read for an audition.

A. Next!

B. Hello. My name is Melanie Mitchell. I have some head shots for you.

A. Thank you. Melanie, you're auditioning for the part of Sarah. She's a strong and proud woman who works in an auto factory. Are you ready to start?

B. Yes. I'm all set.

10 A Camera Operator & an Assistant

A camera operator is asking an assistant for a camera part.

A. I'll need the macro lens for the next scene.

B. It's in Crate 7. Right?

A. Yes. It should be next to the zoom lens.

B. Okay. I'll get it now.

11 A Set Dresser & a Prop Manager

A set dresser is pointing out a problem during a movie shoot.

A. Wait a minute! We're not ready to shoot this scene yet. There's supposed to be a coffee mug on the kitchen table.

B. That's right. According to the prop list, there's supposed to be a white coffee mug.

A. Do we have that?

B. Someone is bringing it now.

12 A Film Editor & an Assistant Film Editor

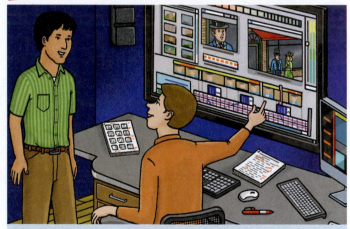

A film editor and an assistant are discussing how to edit a scene.

A. Are you almost finished with the scene you're editing?

B. Yes. Here, take a look! Do you think it should end at this frame, or should it run about two seconds longer?

A. Let's go with the extra two seconds, and the director can decide where to cut it.

B. I agree. That's what I'll do.

9 Imagine you're an actress or actor. What part in a famous movie do you wish you had played?

10–11 You're working at a movie shoot. Ask a co-worker for something or point out a problem.

12 You're editing an important scene in a famous movie. Discuss how to edit it with an assistant.

13 A Set Carpenter & a Set Painter

A set carpenter and set painter are coordinating tasks in a scene shop.

A. I just finished building the steps, so they're ready to be painted.

B. Do you know what color they're supposed to be?

A. No. You'll have to check the set design plan.

B. Got it.

14 A Lighting Technician & an Assistant Set Designer

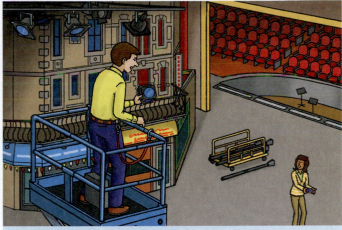

A lighting tech is making a suggestion to an assistant set designer.

A. Hey, Marsha! Are you sure there are supposed to be so many blue gels in the back of the lighting grid?

B. I guess so, if that's what's on the light plot.

A. Well, if you ask me, a mix of blue and red gels would look better.

B. Good suggestion. I'll text the set designer and let you know what she says.

15 An Architect & a Draftsperson

An architect is checking with a draftsperson on the progress of a job.

A. How's your progress on the floor plans?

B. Pretty good. They're almost ready.

A. When do you think you'll be able to start on the elevations?

B. I'll probably start them tomorrow. They should be ready by Friday or at the latest next Monday.

16 A Fashion Designer & an Assistant Designer

A fashion designer and an assistant are attempting to solve a problem.

A. Hmm. Something's not right. I think this dress has too full a look.

B. I agree. What if we reduced the waistline?

A. Sure. Let's try that. We'll need to revise the sample pattern.

B. I'll start on it right away.

13–14 You're working on a theater production. Make a suggestion to another worker.

15 You're an architect. Check on the progress of a job.

16 You're a fashion designer. Work with an assistant to solve a problem.

A HOW TO DESIGN AND PREPARE A PUBLICATION USING DESKTOP PUBLISHING SOFTWARE

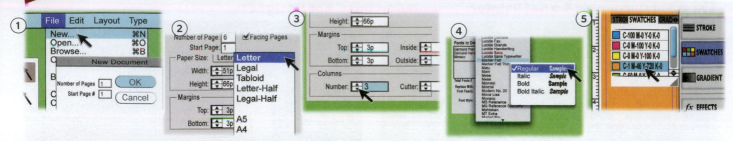

1 Create a new document file in the software program.
2 Specify settings for page size and margins.
3 Design the page layout (such as number of columns).
4 Choose fonts, sizes, and styles.
5 Choose colors for document pages.
6 Create text frames and write or import text.
7 Import photos and graphics.
8 Make other layout changes as needed.
9 Save the document file.
10 Upload the file to the printing company.

B HOW TO ENGINEER A RECORDING SESSION

1 Mark floor positions in the live room.
2 Position the musicians' instruments.
3 Set up microphones for the musicians and instruments.
4 Make sure all the microphones and instruments are plugged in.
5 Set up microphones in the vocal booth.
6 Have the musicians and singers get set for sound checks.
7 Do a sound check for each instrument.
8 Adjust instrument positions and sound levels as needed.
9 Do a sound check for each vocalist.
10 Adjust vocalist positions, microphones, and sound levels as needed.
11 Do a full sound check sample.
12 Record the session.

C HOW TO OPERATE A BOOM MICROPHONE

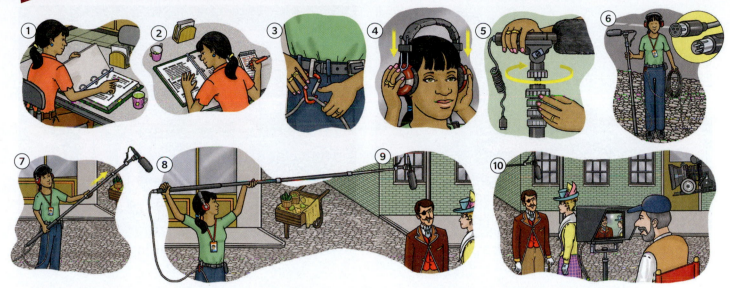

1 Memorize the script and the director's notes.
2 Note the lines that you are responsible to pick up.
3 Clip a carabiner to your belt to run cables through.
4 Put on your headphones.
5 Attach a shotgun microphone with a wind buster to the boom pole.
6 Make sure the boom pole has extra-long XLR* cables.

   * XLR = external line return

7 Telescope the boom pole.
8 Keep the boom above your head in an "H" position.
9 Point the shotgun microphone directly at the sound source.
10 Get the microphone as close as possible to the actors, but out of the frame of the shot.

D HOW TO BRING A NEW CLOTHING DESIGN TO MARKET

1 Review the designer's final sketches.
2 Make a sample prototype.
3 Make corrections and adjustments to the sample.
4 Make a pattern.
5 Order fabric.
6 Make a finished sample.
7 Get the designer's approval of the finished piece.
8 Make any changes requested by the designer.
9 Hire a model.
10 Arrange a fashion shoot in a photo studio.
11 Show the piece in a fashion show.
12 Take orders from buyers.

1 A Press Operator & a Finisher

A press operator is pointing out a possible error to a finisher.

A. Hold on!
B. What's the matter?
A. I think that booklet is supposed to be tape bound, not spiral bound.
B. Really? I'll double-check the work order. Thanks for the heads up.

2 An ENG Operator & a Reporter

An ENG operator is apologizing for making a mistake.

A. Wait a minute! I have no sound! We'll have to start again.
B. What's the problem?
A. My bad! I forgot to open your mic. Sorry.
B. I apologize, Mr. Mayor. We'll have to start the interview again.

3 A Movie Director & a Boom Operator

A movie director is reprimanding a boom operator.

A. Cut! You with the boom mic, what's your name?
B. Harold.
A. Harold, you're holding the mic too low! It's in the shot!
B. I'm so sorry. It won't happen again.

4 An Assistant Choreographer & a Choreographer

An assistant choreographer is asking for feedback about a dance number.

A. Well, what do you think?
B. I like it. I like what you're doing with the choreography, and I love the new ending.
A. Great! We've been rehearsing it for several hours.
B. The work shows.

1 You work at a printing company. Point out a possible error to a co-worker.
2 You're a broadcasting engineer. Apologize for a mistake you made.
3 You're a movie director. Reprimand someone on the set.
4 You're an assistant choreographer. Ask for feedback about a dance number.

OCCUPATIONS

abstract artist
actor
actress
architect
architectural model maker
art director
assignment editor
assistant art director
assistant buyer
assistant camera operator
assistant casting director
assistant choreographer
assistant copy editor
assistant director
assistant fashion designer
assistant film editor
assistant producer
assistant prop master

assistant recording engineer
assistant set designer
assistant stage manager
author/writer
board operator
boom operator
broadcast technician
buyer
CAD operator
camera operator
casting director
ceramicist
choreographer
clapper
columnist
conductor
copywriter
creative director
dancer
desktop publisher

digital editor
digital press operator
digital staff writer
director
draftsperson
ENG operator
fashion designer
fashion model
fashion photographer
field camera operator
field reporter
film editor
finisher
floor manager
Foley artist
gaffer
glassblower
graphic designer
grip
illustrator
intern
lighting technician
meteorologist/ weather reporter

musician
newscast producer
newscaster
on-set dresser
online content producer
pattern maker
photography assistant
photojournalist
portrait painter
prepress technician
press operator
producer
program director
prop manager
prop master
publication assistant
radio announcer
radio broadcast technician
radio broadcaster
recording engineer
recording mixer
reporter

researcher/ archivist
scenic artist
screenwriter
sculptor
set carpenter
set designer
set dresser
set painter
set production assistant
singer
sound assistant
sound engineer
sound technician
staffer
stage manager
story analyst/ script reader
technical writer
web designer
web developer
writer assistant

WORKPLACE ACTIONS

adjust lighting
audition
bind documents
blow glass
build a stage set
build an architectural model
create graphics
create sound effects
create website content
demonstrate a dance routine
design a publication
direct a TV program
do a radio broadcast
do an illustration
do an interview
do an on-location report
draft building plans

dress a set
edit a film
edit copy
engineer a radio broadcast
engineer a recording session
engineer a remote news feed
evaluate a script
give a presentation to clients
give timing cues to on-air talent
handle props
hook up sound equipment
lay out a garment pattern
lay out a page
make pottery
manage sound cables

mark a stage
mix audio
monitor sound levels
note changes in a script
operate a boom microphone
operate a camera
operate a field camera
operate a studio camera
operate printing equipment
paint a portrait
paint scenery
play an instrument
prepare a production slate
read the news
rehearse
report the weather

sculpt
select clothing designs for a store
set up sound equipment
set up stage lighting
sing
switch video feeds
take direction
take fashion photographs
take news photographs
trim printed documents
update a production schedule
write a column
write a manuscript
write a news story
write a script
write ad copy

COMMUNICATION & THE ARTS

WORKPLACE LOCATIONS

architectural firm
art director's office
artist's studio
backstage
broadcast booth
casting agency
ceramic studio

conference room
control room
creative department
fashion design house
Foley room
glass studio
live room

newsroom
orchestra pit
photo studio
post production
   department
printing company
production control
   room (PCR)

production floor
radio studio
recording studio
remote location
sculpture studio
set
soundstage

stage
TV studio
vocal booth
web development
   department
wing

EQUIPMENT, TOOLS, & OBJECTS

anchor desk
architectural scale
artist's brushes
assignment board
assignment desk
audio cable
backdrop
binder
blowpipe
boom microphone
boom pole
cables
CAD software
calipers
camera
camera crane
camera dolly
camera dolly track
carabiner
chisel
compass
condenser
   microphone
CTP plate maker
desktop publishing
   software
digital press

digital press ink
   cartridge
director's notes
document file
dressmaker form
dynamic microphone
   (mic)
electric paper cutter
ENG microwave
   antenna
ENG news truck
fabric
field camera
film editing software
finished piece
finished sample
floor microphone
Foley floor
form curve ruler
frame
Fresnel light
generator
glass shears
graphics software
green screen/
   chroma key screen
guitar amplifier

guitar preamp
headphones
illustration
illustrator's supplies
instruments
light meter
lighting gels
lighting grid
mallet
manuscript
marver table
microphone
microphone
   preamp
microphone shield
microwave antenna
mixing board
MOS camera
music stand
page layout
paint
painting knife
paper drill
pattern
pattern shears
pattern tracing
   wheel

photojournalist vest
photos and graphics
PMS color swatches
portable area light
portrait
pottery wheel
presentation projector
presentation remote
printing equipment
production board
production room
   headphones
production slate
prop cart
props
prototype
reporter's notebook
rerecording software
scenery
scissor arm lift
scoop light
screenplay
script
set
set lighting
shot
shotgun microphone

sketch
software program
sound cables
sound equipment
sound level
sound source
stage marking tape
storyboard
studio camera
studio digital video
   camera
studio easel
tape binding
   machine
technical illustration
text frame
track drafting
   machine
typeface samples
web analytics
   software
wind buster
wire binding
   machine
word processing
   software
XLR cables

WORKPLACE COMMUNICATION

apologize for making a mistake
ask a co-worker for a part to a
   piece of equipment
ask for feedback
brainstorm ideas with a co-worker
check on a co-worker's progress
check on the status of a job

coordinate tasks with a co-worker
discuss with a colleague how to
   do a task
give timing cues to a performer
make a suggestion
point out a possible error in
   someone's work

point out a problem
prepare someone to read for an audition
prepare to do a live remote broadcast
prepare to go out on an assignment
reprimand a worker
troubleshoot and resolve a problem
work with a colleague to solve a problem

OCCUPATIONS

A WHAT ARE THEIR JOB TITLES?

1. Dave is a board (model   ~~operator~~) in a theater.
2. Sharon is a technical (maker   writer).
3. Oscar is a portrait (painter   reporter).
4. Tony is a fashion (model   master).
5. Carla is a weather (designer   reporter).
6. Lorenzo works as a floor (manager   publisher) in a TV studio.
7. Jane is a copy (operator   editor) in a newsroom.

8. Ahmed is a prop (master   technician) for movie productions.
9. Christine is a script (director   reader).
10. Richard is a desktop (reporter   publisher).
11. Anya is a sound (engineer   manager).
12. Marcus is a graphic (designer   operator).
13. Leo is a pattern (model   maker) in a fashion design house.
14. Terry is a radio (broadcaster   carpenter).

B WHAT DO THEY HAVE IN COMMON?

These are types of . . .

assistants	designers	directors	editors	operators	technicians

1. web   set   graphic
   designers

2. assignment   film   copy
   _____

3. lighting   sound   pre-press
   _____

4. board   boom   digital press
   _____

5. casting   creative   program
   _____

6. sound   writer   photography
   _____

These are related to . . .

fashion	journalism	movies	sound	television	theater

7. reporter   copy editor   assignment editor
   _____

8. director   gaffer   clapper
   _____

9. stage manager   choreographer   board operator
   _____

10. recording mixer   Foley artist   boom operator
    _____

11. designer   model   photographer
    _____

12. camera operator   meteorologist   broadcast technician
    _____

C WHAT'S THE PLACE?

_e_ 1. Can you recommend a good architectural _____?

_____ 2. Let's look over the plans in the art director's _____.

_____ 3. I was recently contacted by a well-known casting _____.

_____ 4. The director just walked into the control _____.

_____ 5. Does your band like our new recording _____?

_____ 6. Can you recommend a good printing _____?

_____ 7. We'll be doing the interview with the mayor at a remote _____.

_____ 8. The announcer just walked into the broadcast _____.

_____ 9. I just got a new job in a post production _____.

_____ 10. The entire orchestra is now in the orchestra _____.

_____ 11. We just found a very creative new fashion design _____.

_____ 12. Make sure everything is all set on the production _____.

a. agency
b. booth
c. company
d. department
e. firm
f. floor
g. house
h. location
i. office
j. pit
k. room
l. studio

EQUIPMENT, TOOLS, & OBJECTS

D WHAT'S THE ITEM?

_c_ 1. audio   a. stand
_____ 2. paper   b. dolly
_____ 3. music   c. cable
_____ 4. mixing d. floor
_____ 5. Foley   e. level
_____ 6. sound   f. drill
_____ 7. camera g. board

_____ 8. page   h. lighting
_____ 9. digital   i. desk
_____ 10. set   j. wheel
_____ 11. painting k. layout
_____ 12. pottery l. program
_____ 13. software m. knife
_____ 14. anchor   n. press

_____ 15. architectural o. brushes
_____ 16. paper   p. preamp
_____ 17. camera   q. scale
_____ 18. artist's   r. shears
_____ 19. green   s. crane
_____ 20. pattern   t. screen
_____ 21. guitar   u. cutter

WORKPLACE ACTIONS

E THE SAME ACTION

_d_ 1. *Graphics & sound effects* are things you _____.

_____ 2. *Radio broadcasts & recording sessions* are things you _____.

_____ 3. *Presentations & timing cues* are things you _____.

_____ 4. *Cameras & boom microphones* are things you _____.

_____ 5. *Sound equipment & stage lighting* are things you _____.

_____ 6. *Photographs & directions* are things you _____.

_____ 7. *Scripts & news stories* are things you _____.

a. give
b. take
c. set up
d. create
e. write
f. engineer
g. operate

F THE ARTS *IN ACTION!*

1. bind _____
a. props
b. documents *(circled)*
c. a microphone
d. a stage

2. direct _____
a. glass
b. the stage
c. a TV program
d. the weather

3. edit _____
a. a film
b. a client
c. lighting
d. props

4. hook up _____
a. scenery
b. a schedule
c. a script
d. equipment

5. mix _____
a. scenery
b. a camera
c. audio
d. a script

6. build _____
a. an interview
b. sound
c. a set
d. the orchestra

7. handle _____
a. props
b. paper
c. paint
d. a film

8. paint _____
a. a script
b. scenery
c. stage lighting
d. a news story

9. demonstrate _____
a. a dance routine
b. a film
c. the news
d. a schedule

10. report _____
a. sound effects
b. a broadcast
c. the weather
d. direction

11. select _____
a. the stage
b. the orchestra pit
c. direction
d. designs

12. design _____
a. a light
b. a publication
c. a camera
d. a recording session

13. read _____
a. a set
b. a portrait
c. a studio
d. the news

14. mark _____
a. a newscaster
b. a stage
c. a reporter
d. direction

15. trim _____
a. an instrument
b. a set
c. a document
d. the weather

16. update _____
a. a schedule
b. a stage
c. an orchestra
d. a studio

WORKPLACE COMMUNICATION

G WHAT ARE THEY SAYING?

_h_ **1.** check on the status of a job

_____ **2.** give timing cues

_____ **3.** coordinate tasks

_____ **4.** troubleshoot a problem

_____ **5.** ask for a part

_____ **6.** point out a problem

_____ **7.** ask for advice

_____ **8.** make a suggestion

_____ **9.** check on a co-worker's progress

_____ **10.** identify a problem

_____ **11.** point out a possible error

_____ **12.** apologize for a mistake

_____ **13.** reprimand a worker

_____ **14.** ask for feedback

a. "I think the feedback is from the studio monitor."

b. "How's your progress on the floor plans?"

c. "Do you think the scene should end at this frame?"

d. "Well, what do you think?"

e. "I think that booklet is supposed to be tape bound, not spiral bound."

f. "Let's do the weather forecast first and then we'll do the traffic report."

g. "Something's not right. This dress has too full a look!"

h. "Are you almost done with that print run?"

i. "Wait a minute! We're not ready to shoot this scene yet."

j. "You're holding the mic too low! It's in the shot!"

k. "We have 10 seconds until air time."

l. "If you ask me, a mix of blue and red gels would look better."

m. "I'll need the macro lens for the next scene."

n. "I apologize, Mr. Mayor. We'll have to start the interview again."

1 telecommunications lineperson
2 line installer
3 cell tower climber
4 phone company installer
5 cable company installer
6 security/fire alarm installer
7 telecommunications technician

a utility pole
b digger derrick truck
c bucket truck
d cable spool/cable reel
e reel loader truck
f ride-on trencher
g trench

h cell tower
i modem
j smoke detector/alarm
k alarm control box
l telephone interface box
m CMTS* relay junction pedestal

* CMTS = cable modem termination system

What telecommunications occupations do you see?
What objects do you see?

> You are now eligible for our upgraded service package, including phone, Internet, and HDTV.

8 satellite TV installer	**14** 711 relay client	**n** satellite dish
9 PBX* installer	**15** TTY/TDD* 711 relay operator/ 711 communication assistant	**o** satellite receiver
10 voice communication analyst		**p** multiline phone
11 central office technician		**q** PBX trunk
12 611 customer service assistant	**16** telecommunications sales associate	**r** distribution frame
13 mobile phone customer		**s** central relay office

t 611 call center	
u 711 call center	
v TTY device	
w telecommunications sales center	

* PBX = private branch exchange (a private telephone switchboard)TTY/
  TDD = teletypewriter/text telephone

What kind of phone, TV, or alarm services do you have where you live?
What companies supply these services?

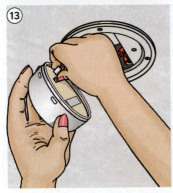

1 drill a hole for a pole
2 set a pole in place
3 climb a pole
4 attach a cable to a strain suspension insulator

5 dig a trench
6 pull cable
7 lay down conduit
8 feed cable through conduit

9 backfill a trench
10 wire an RJ11* telephone socket outlet
11 drop coaxial cable down a wall
12 install a residential modem

13 install a smoke detector
14 program a cable remote
15 hook up an alarm control box
16 test an uninstalled phone line

* RJ11 = registered jack 11

Look at pages 258 and 259. What are the people doing? Describe their actions.

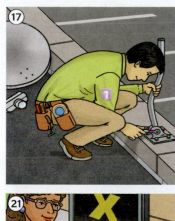

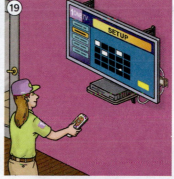

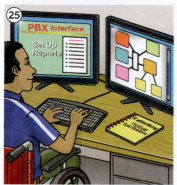

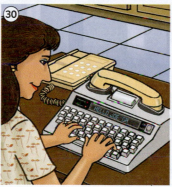

17 attach a satellite dish mounting arm

18 connect a feedhorn to a dish

19 program a satellite receiver

20 connect a phone to a wall outlet

21 code in phone features

22 attach a handset to a speaker phone

23 screw on a PBX trunk

24 attach phone lines to a PBX trunk

25 customize PBX software

26 test lines

27 pull out a switch

28 create a customer service case number

29 reply to a customer's online question

30 type in a message

31 read a message

32 offer an upgrade

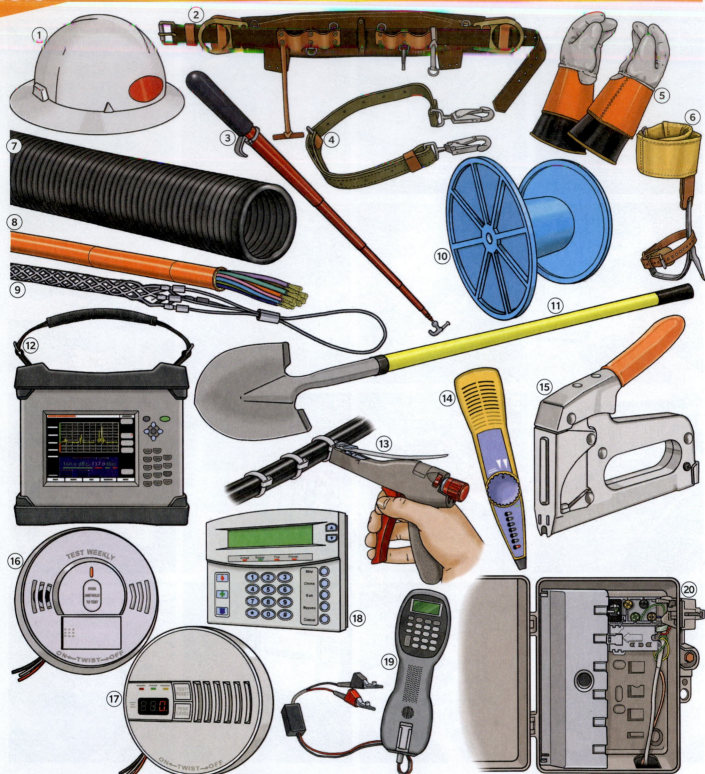

1	lineman hard hat	6	pole climber	11	long handle shovel	16	smoke detector/alarm
2	lineman belt	7	conduit	12	PIM* tester	17	carbon monoxide detector/alarm
3	hot stick	8	fiber optic cable	13	cable tie gun	18	alarm system keypad
4	pole strap	9	pulling grip	14	toner probe	19	line test handset
5	rubber safety gloves	10	cable spool/cable reel	15	staple gun	20	network interface box

* PIM = passive intermodulation

Look at pages 222–225. What equipment, tools, and objects do you see?

21	satellite dish	27	coaxial connector	33	handset
22	feedhorn	28	remote	34	PBX trunk
23	roof mount	29	receiver	35	cable stripper
24	digital compass	30	PBX management software	36	cordless drill
25	multiswitch	31	telephone RJ wall plate	37	frequency meter
26	coaxial cable	32	PBX multiline phone	38	TDD/TTY device/text telephone

1 Two Telecommunications Installers

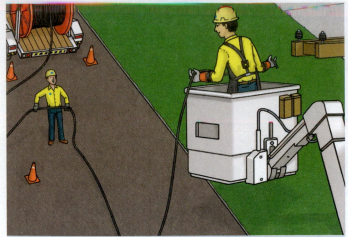

Two telecommunications installers are coordinating a task.

A. How much cable are you going to need?
B. I'll need you to feed me about 50 feet.
A. I'd better check to see if there's enough left on this spool.
B. Okay. Thanks.

2 Two Fiber Optic Cable Installers

Two fiber optic cable installers are working on an installation.

A. Is the trench finished yet?
B. Yes. Just finished it.
A. Good. I'll start laying down the conduit.
B. And I'll get ready to feed the cable.

3 Two Cable Installers

Two cable installers are working on an installation.

A. What rooms are we hooking up for cable?
B. The family room on the first floor and the three bedrooms upstairs.
A. So should I run a line up to the attic?
B. Yes. And then you can drop a line for each bedroom.

4 Two Phone Company Installers

Two phone company installers are troubleshooting a problem.

A. I'm not getting a dial tone on any of the extensions in the house.
B. And I don't have a dial tone at the network interface either.
A. You'd better call the central office and see if the line is activated.
B. Will do.

1–3 You're working on a telecommunications installation. Coordinate a task with a co-worker.
4 You're a phone company installer. Troubleshoot a problem with a co-worker.

5 A PBX Installer & a Voice Communication Analyst

A PBX installer is getting information needed to do an installation.

A. How many voicemail boxes will you need?
B. We currently have 23 employees, and there will be two new hires next month.
A. Okay. I'll set you up with 25, and I can show you how to add more.
B. Great.

6 Two Satellite TV Installers

NO SATELLITE FOUND

Two satellite TV installers are coordinating an installation.

A. I'm not getting a signal yet.
B. I still have to adjust the dish to its satellite coordinates.
A. Sorry. I thought you were ready.
B. Another five minutes and I'll be finished up here.

7 A Customer Service Assistant & a Mobile Phone Customer

A customer service assistant is helping a mobile phone customer with a problem.

A. How can I help you?
B. I got a message saying I've reached my text limit for this month and I'll be charged extra for each additional text.
A. Let me check. It looks like your account doesn't have unlimited texting, and you've used your monthly allowance.
B. Can I change my plan to unlimited texting?
A. Of course. Let me set that up for you.

8 A 711 Relay Operator & a Caller

A 711 relay operator is assisting a caller.

A. Good morning. Relay operator 1328.
B. Hello. Could you please dial 521-643-1918?
A. Sure. One moment.
B. Could you let her know that it's her grandson calling?
A. Okay. Hold on.

---

5 You're installing an office telecommunications system. Get information you need from an office worker.
6 Is satellite TV common in your area? What are the different ways you can watch TV programs?
7 You're a mobile phone company customer service assistant. Help a customer with a problem.
8 Are you familiar with TTY telephone services? Why are they important?

A   HOW TO DIG A TRENCH AND LAY CABLE

1 Prepare and mark the site.
2 Make sure all components are on site.
3 Dig the trench to the required depth.
4 Lay down the innerduct conduit.
5 Feed cable from the cable spool.
6 Connect a grip to the cable.
7 Pull the cable through the conduit.
8 Put conductive marker tape on the conduit.
9 Backfill the trench.
10 Inspect the workmanship.

B   HOW TO INSTALL A SECURITY SYSTEM

1 Install the main control board.
2 Place door sensors on all entry doors.
3 Install window sensors on the first floor windows.
4 Install motion detectors in high-traffic areas.
5 Install the indoor siren.
6 Install smoke alarms in every bedroom, outside each sleeping area, and on every level of the home.
7 Install carbon monoxide alarms near sleeping areas.
8 Run wiring from each location back to the main control board.
9 Install a control panel next to the entry door.
10 Test all door and window sensors and motion detectors.
11 Test the smoke and carbon monoxide alarms.
12 Show the homeowner how to set passcodes and use the system.

C HOW TO INSTALL A SATELLITE DISH

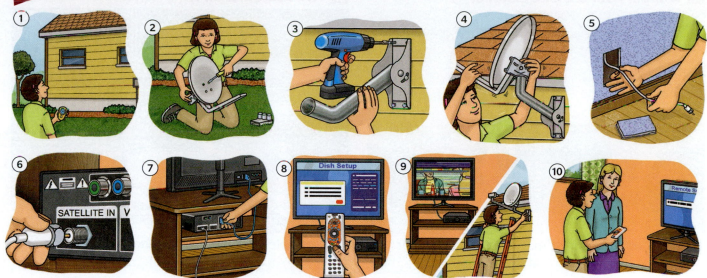

1 Choose a location for the dish on the structure.
2 Assemble the dish.
3 Fasten the mounting bracket to the building.
4 Attach the dish to the mounting bracket.

5 Feed a coaxial cable from the dish to the inside locations.
6 Connect the coaxial cable to the receiver.
7 Attach the TV to the receiver.
8 Program the dish setup through the TV.

9 If there are reception problems, check the dish alignment.
10 Program the remote control for the customer.

D HOW TO RELAY A 711 CALL FROM A HEARING-IMPAIRED PERSON

1 Let the person know that he or she is receiving a call from a hearing-impaired person.
2 Give your operator number.
3 Ask if the person has received a relay call in the past.

4 Let the person know the caller will be typing and you will read the words aloud.
5 Tell the person it will be time to speak after you say, "Go ahead."
6 Tell the person you will then type the words so the caller can read them.

7 Tell the person to speak directly to the caller and end with "Go ahead."
8 Connect the parties.

1 A Supervisor & a Line Installer

A supervisor is reprimanding a line installer for a job safety issue.

A. Hey! Get back down now!
B. What's the problem?
A. Your safety is frayed! Don't you check your equipment?
B. I guess I missed that. Thanks.

2 Two Cable Installers

Two cable installers are dealing with a customer complaint.

A. The homeowner's mad. We have to go back in.
B. What's the problem?
A. You programmed his remote, but you didn't teach him how to use it.
B. I did!
A. Well, do it again. He says he's going to call the central office and complain.

3 A Supervisor & a PBX Installer

A supervisor is checking on a PBX installer's work.

A. Have you finished programming all the office extensions?
B. Yes. I just finished.
A. Did you remember to program the privacy feature on the conference room extension?
B. Oh. I forgot. I'll do that right now.

4 A Supervisor & a Telecommunications Sales Associate

A supervisor is complimenting a sales associate.

A. You did a good job on that last call.
B. Thank you. I could tell the customer was frustrated.
A. Well, from what I heard, you handled that call perfectly.
B. I'm glad you think so.

1 You're a supervisor at a telecommunications installation. Reprimand a line installer for a job safety issue.
2 Have you ever had a problem with a cable or other installation where you live? Describe it.
3 You're a supervisor working at an office telecommunications installation. Check on an installer's work.
4 Have you ever called a communications company for help with a problem? Tell about your experience.

OCCUPATIONS

611 customer service
  assistant
711 communication
  assistant
711 relay operator
cable (company) installer
cell tower climber
central office technician
customer service assistant
fiber optic cable installer

line installer
PBX installer
phone company installer
satellite TV installer
security/fire alarm
  installer
telecommunications
  installer
telecommunications
  lineperson

telecommunications
  sales associate
telecommunications
  technician
TTY/TDD 711 relay
  operator/
  711 communication
  assistant
voice communication
  analyst

WORKPLACE LOCATIONS

611 call center
711 call center
central office
central relay office
telecommunications sales center

EQUIPMENT, TOOLS, & OBJECTS

alarm control box
alarm system keypad
bucket truck
cable
cable reel
cable remote
cable spool
cable stripper
cable tie gun
carbon monoxide
  alarm/detector
cell tower
CMTS relay junction
  pedestal
coaxial cable
coaxial connector
conductive marker tape
conduit
control panel
cordless drill

customer service case
  number
dial tone
digger derrick truck
digital compass
distribution frame
door sensor
extensions
feedhorn
fiber optic cable
frequency meter
grip
handset
hot stick
indoor siren
innerduct conduit
line test handset
lineman belt
lineman hard hat
long handle shovel

main control board
modem
motion detector
mounting bracket
multiline phone
multiswitch
network interface
network interface box
passcode
PBX management
  software
PBX multiline phone
PBX trunk
phone features
phone line
PIM tester
pole
pole climber
pole strap
pulling grip

receiver
reel loader truck
remote/remote
  control
residential modem
ride-on trencher
RJ11 telephone
  socket outlet
roof mount
rubber safety
  gloves
satellite coordinates
satellite dish/dish
satellite dish
  mounting arm
satellite receiver
signal
smoke alarm/
  detector
speaker phone

spool
staple gun
strain suspension
  insulator
switch
TDD/TTY device/
  text telephone
telephone interface
  box
telephone RJ wall
  plate
toner probe
trench
uninstalled phone
  line
upgrade
utility pole
voicemail box
wall outlet
window sensor

WORKPLACE ACTIONS

attach a cable to a strain
  suspension insulator
attach a handset to a
  speaker phone
attach a satellite dish
  mounting arm
attach phone lines to a
  PBX trunk
backfill a trench
climb a pole
code in phone features

connect a phone to a
  wall outlet
connect a feedhorn to
  a dish
create a customer
  service case number
customize PBX software
dig a trench
drill a hole for a pole
drop coaxial cable down
  a wall

feed cable through conduit
hook up an alarm control box
install a residential modem
install a smoke detector
lay down conduit
offer an upgrade
program a cable remote
program a satellite receiver
pull cable
pull out a switch

read a message
reply to a customer's online
  question
screw on a PBX trunk
set a pole in place
test an uninstalled phone line
test lines
type in a message
wire an RJ11 telephone socket
  outlet

WORKPLACE COMMUNICATION

assist a caller
check on a colleague's work
compliment a sales associate
coordinate tasks with a co-worker

deal with a customer complaint
get information needed to do a job
help a customer with a problem

reprimand a worker on a job safety issue
troubleshoot a problem
work on an installation with a co-worker

OCCUPATIONS

A WHAT ARE THEIR JOBS?

611	analyst	cable	installer	lineperson	technician
711	associate	climber	line	PBX	TV

1. I install cable TV service in people's homes. I'm a _____cable_____ company installer.

2. I inspect cell phone towers. I'm a cell tower _____.

3. I set up office telephone systems. I'm a _____ installer.

4. I install security and fire alarm systems. I'm a security and fire alarm _____.

5. I'm a _____ customer service assistant. Contact me if you're having telephone problems.

6. I attach lines from telephone poles to the insides of buildings. I'm a _____ installer.

7. I set up satellite television systems in homes and businesses. I'm a satellite _____ installer.

8. I set up telephone calls for people who have hearing problems. I'm a _____ relay operator.

9. I design and set up communication systems. I'm a voice communication _____.

10. I fix problems with telecommunication systems. I'm a telecommunications _____.

11. I repair telephone lines on utility poles. I'm a telecommunications _____.

12. I can provide you with all the information you need. I'm a telecommunications sales _____.

WORKPLACE LOCATIONS

B WHAT'S THE LOCATION?

1. You can contact me at the central relay (office   line).

2. If you're having problems, you should contact someone in the 611 (install   call) center.

3. If you're interested in setting up a new system, contact the telecommunications (repair   sales) center.

4. One of the operators in the (611   711) call center can help you place a TTY call.

EQUIPMENT, TOOLS, & OBJECTS

C WHAT'S THE ITEM?

_d_	1. door	a. truck	___	9. staple	i. meter	___	17. phone	q. control
___	2. wall	b. mount	___	10. lay-up	j. tester	___	18. coaxial	r. detector
___	3. satellite	c. tower	___	11. frequency	k. trunk	___	19. remote	s. pole
___	4. roof	d. sensor	___	12. mounting	l. gun	___	20. motion	t. outlet
___	5. dial	e. reel	___	13. PBX	m. strap	___	21. indoor	u. features
___	6. cell	f. plate	___	14. PIM	n. bracket	___	22. utility	v. siren
___	7. bucket	g. tone	___	15. cable	o. wheel	___	23. wall	w. interface
___	8. cable	h. dish	___	16. pole	p. stripper	___	24. network	x. cable

WORKPLACE ACTIONS

D TELECOMMUNICATIONS *IN ACTION!*

1. We need to attach _____.
   a. the trench
   b. the cable *(circled)*
   c. the dial tone
   d. the passcode

2. I'm going to connect _____.
   a. the staple gun
   b. the hardhat
   c. the phone
   d. the upgrade

3. Did you type in _____?
   a. a message
   b. a wheel
   c. the test lines
   d. a pole

4. I'm trying to drill _____.
   a. a cable
   b. a wire
   c. an alarm
   d. a hole

5. I'm now going to wire in _____.
   a. the conduit
   b. the smoke detector
   c. the drill
   d. the case number

6. Are you going to hook up _____?
   a. the mounting bracket
   b. the lineperson belt
   c. the cable stripper
   d. the alarm control box

7. It's time to backfill this _____.
   a. keypad
   b. dial tone
   c. trench
   d. roof mount

8. Did you program _____?
   a. the wall
   b. the cable remote
   c. the safety gloves
   d. the shovel

9. We're pleased to offer _____.
   a. this wall outlet
   b. a signal
   c. a case number
   d. an upgrade

10. It's time to lay down _____.
    a. conduit
    b. a dial tone
    c. a satellite dish
    d. the cell tower

11. I need to create _____.
    a. fiber optic cable
    b. a case number
    c. a satellite
    d. a handset

12. It's time to screw on _____.
    a. the spool
    b. the siren
    c. the PBX trunk
    d. the message

13. Did you code in _____?
    a. the digital compass
    b. the boot pole climber
    c. the coaxial cable
    d. the phone features

14. Who is going to reply to _____?
    a. the telephone socket
    b. this customer's question
    c. the coaxial connector
    d. the cable reel

15. Can you customize _____?
    a. the PBX software
    b. the trench
    c. the cell tower
    d. the wall outlet

WORKPLACE COMMUNICATION

E WHAT ARE THEY SAYING?

_d_ 1. coordinate on a task

____ 2. ask about completion of a task

____ 3. ask about the scope of work

____ 4. troubleshoot a problem

____ 5. gather information

____ 6. report on progress of a task

____ 7. offer to help a customer

____ 8. assist a TTY device user

____ 9. reprimand a co-worker

____ 10. deal with a customer complaint

____ 11. remind a co-worker about a task

____ 12. compliment an employee

a. "Another five minutes and I'll be finished up here."

b. "You'd better call the central office and see if the line is activated."

c. "You did a good job."

d. "I'll need you to feed me about 50 feet of cable."

e. "Good morning. Relay operator 1328."

f. "Did you remember to program the privacy feature on the extension?"

g. "The homeowner's mad. We have to go back in."

h. "Is the trench finished yet?"

i. "How can I help you?"

j. "How many voicemail boxes will you need?"

k. "What rooms are we hooking up for cable?"

l. "Your safety is frayed! Don't you check your equipment?"

1 computer/network administrator
2 network engineer
3 computer service technician
4 computer installer
5 technical support specialist
6 information systems security specialist
7 data entry keyer
8 information processing worker

a computer network administrator's office
b LAN* schematic
c server rack cabinet
d wiring/network closet
e CAT6* cable batch
f data floor box
g antivirus software
h data entry input
i OCR* program

* LAN = local area network
  CAT6 = category 6
  OCR = optical character recognition

What occupations do you see?
What objects do you see?

9 customer support specialist

10 help desk technician

11 computer repair technician

12 data recovery specialist

13 systems analyst

14 computer programmer

*UI = user interface

15 game producer

16 game designer

17 UI* artist

18 game tester

19 video game music composer

20 mobile app developer

21 mobile app designer

j computer repair & support center

k help desk

l computer repair lab

m workbench

n data recovery room

o laminar flow cabinet

p programming department

q program flowchart

r source code

s debugging software

t digital design/ development studio

u framework software

v game storyboard

What kinds of computers and other technology devices do you use?
How and when do you use them?

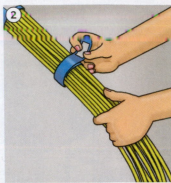

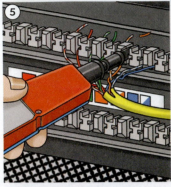
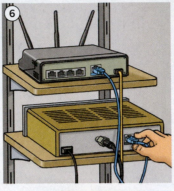

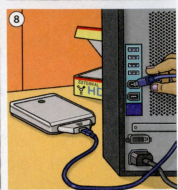
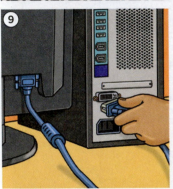
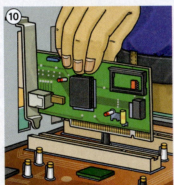

1 review a LAN schematic
2 bundle and band CAT6 cables
3 fish CAT6 cables through walls
4 add a hard drive to a RAID*

5 punch down a patch panel
6 attach a wireless router to a modem
7 connect a computer to a data floor box
8 connect an external drive to a computer

9 attach a monitor with a DVI* cable
10 install an internal network adapter
11 load software
12 install virus detection and network security software

13 train an employee on new software
14 enter data
15 scan a document
16 capture text in an OCR program

*RAID = redundant array of independent disks
DVI = digital visual interface

Look at pages 272 and 273. What are the people doing? Describe their actions.

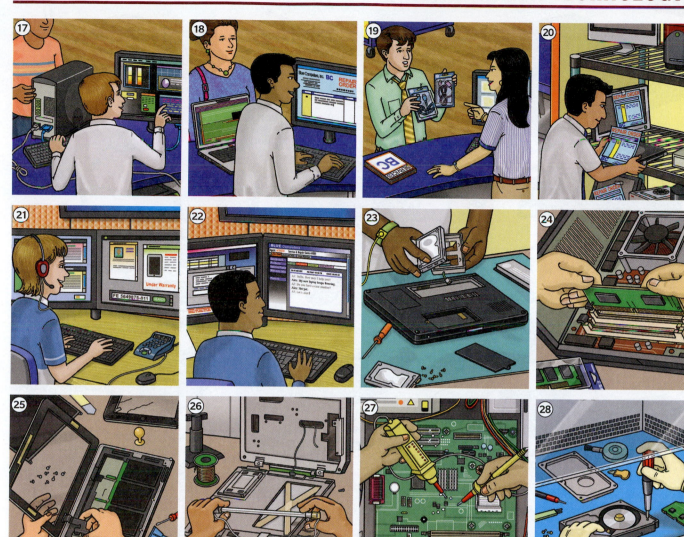

17 run a diagnostic test
18 write up a repair order
19 recommend the proper cable to a customer
20 store an item to be repaired

21 answer technical support questions
22 have a live chat session with a customer
23 change a hard disk
24 add RAM*

25 replace the touch screen digitizer on a tablet
26 replace a monitor backlight
27 measure voltage on a motherboard
28 repair a hard disk drive

29 write programming source code
30 test a mobile app on different devices
31 design a video game
32 test a game and write a defect report

* RAM = random access memory

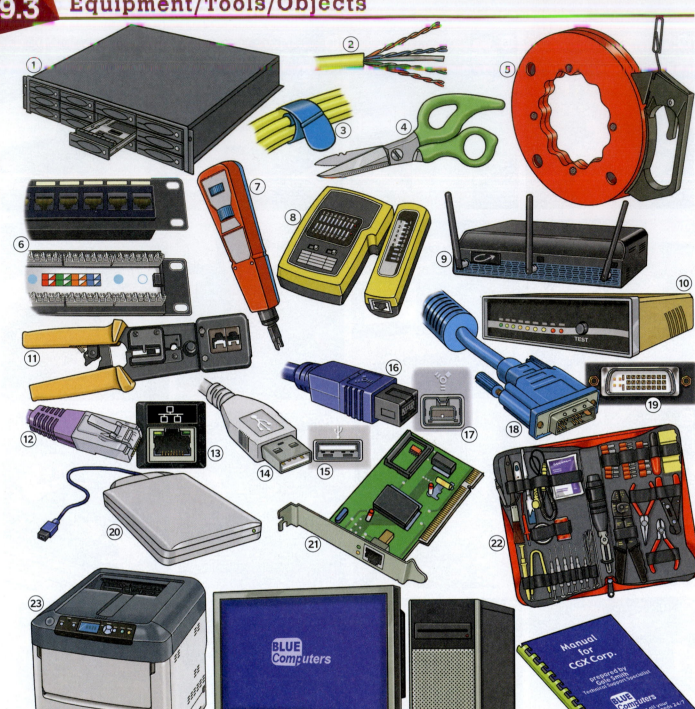

1 RAID
2 CAT6 cable
3 cable wrap
4 cable scissors
5 fish tape
6 patch panel
7 punch-down tool

8 patch panel/cable tester
9 enterprise router
10 industrial modem
11 CAT6 crimp tool
12 Ethernet cable connector
13 Ethernet input port
14 USB* cable connector

15 USB input port
16 FireWire cable connector
17 FireWire input port
18 DVI monitor cable connector
19 DVI monitor input port
20 external hard drive

21 internal network adapter
22 computer tool kit
23 workgroup/network printer
24 monitor
25 mini desktop tower
26 software training manual

* USB = universal serial bus

Look at pages 272–275. What equipment, tools, and objects do you see?

27 laptop	**32** voltage tester	**37** internal hard drives	**42** code editing software
28 tablet	**33** butane soldering	**38** support center live chat	**43** mobile devices
29 micro tools	iron and blower	**39** hard disk cloner	**44** mobile apps
30 antistatic/	**34** motherboard	**40** blowing brush	**45** artist's interactive tablet
ESD* mat	**35** antistatic bag	**41** compressed air sprayer	**46** artist's stylus
31 RAM*	**36** hard drive sled		

* ESD = electrostatic discharge
RAM = random access memory

1 Two Computer Service Technicians

One computer service technician is offering to help the other.

A. Do you need any help running the cables?
B. No. I just have to run them to the rear workstation.
A. Do you have enough CAT6 left?
B. Probably not. Could you get another box from the truck?
A. Sure.

2 A Computer Service Technician & a Computer Installer

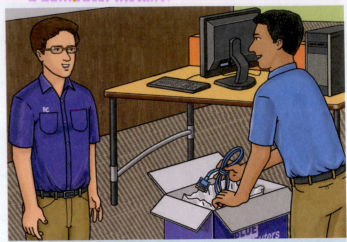

A computer service technician is checking on the progress of an installation.

A. Are you almost done hooking up that workstation?
B. Yes. I just have to connect the monitor.
A. Did you install the network adapter?
B. Yes. I installed it in slot 3.

3 Two Computer Service Technicians

Two computer service technicians are working on an installation.

A. Here are the last three hard drives for the RAID.
B. Thanks. I'll install them and then we can roll the cabinet into the network closet.
A. Take your time. They're still bundling the cables in there.
B. Okay. I'll let you know when I'm done.

4 A Network Administrator & an Information Systems Security Specialist

A network administrator is checking on the completion of a specialist's work.

A. Have you installed the security software at all the computer workstations?
B. Yes. I also installed it on all your laptops.
A. So we're all set with antivirus protection and network security?
B. You're good to go!

1–3 You're a computer service technician working on an installation. Coordinate tasks with a co-worker and offer to help.
4 You're a network administrator for a company. Check on the completion of an installer's or specialist's work.

5 A Customer & a Help Desk Technician

A customer is explaining a problem to a help desk technician.

A. My laptop is running slow when I try to use more than one graphics program at a time.

B. Let's take a look. I see you have only 2 gigabytes of RAM. That isn't enough for the graphics programs you're running.

A. What do you recommend?

B. You can add up to 6 more gigabytes for $129.99. That includes installation.

6 A Customer Support Specialist & a Customer

A customer support specialist is helping a customer with a problem.

A. Do you have the serial number for your tablet?

B. Yes. It's FE 5649875-011.

A. Thank you. Your tablet is still under warranty. What seems to be the problem?

B. The battery isn't charging any more.

7 A Systems Analyst & a Computer Programmer

A systems analyst is checking on the progress of a computer programmer's work.

A. How are you coming along with that section of code?

B. I've already done 50 lines. I'm almost finished.

A. After you complete it and run it, let me know the results.

B. Okay. Will do.

8 A Mobile App Designer & a Mobile App Developer

A mobile app designer is checking on the progress of a project.

A. How's the app coming along?

B. We're not there yet. It's working on the phone, but not on the tablet.

A. Is it a design problem?

B. I don't think so. I think it's a bug* in the resource layout file. I'll let you know.

* bug = defect

5 Describe a problem you have had with technology. What was the problem? How did you solve it?

6 You're a customer support specialist for a technology company. Help a customer with a problem.

7 Coding has become an important skill that is now taught in many elementary and secondary schools. Why do you think it's important? Where and how do people learn these skills in your area?

8 Do you use apps? If so, which apps do you use most often? Why?

A HOW TO PUNCH A PATCH PANEL

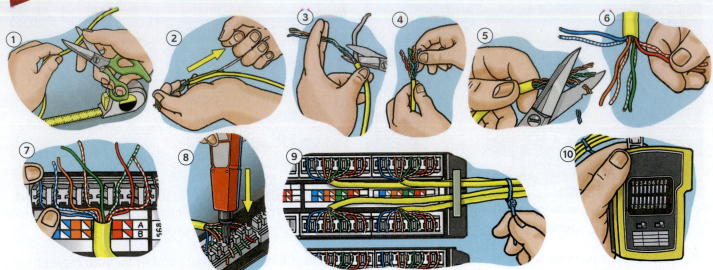

1 Measure and cut cable to the length needed using cable scissors.
2 Remove cable insulation using zipper string.
3 Cut off insulation at about 1.5 inches down.
4 Straighten the cable pairs and place them next to each other in the correct order.

5 Hold the cable pairs tightly together and cut them as straight as possible.
6 Recheck the sequence of the wires.
7 Insert the wires into the punch-down plugs, starting with the blue wires to the left.

8 Use a punch-down tool to punch down and cut off excess wire.
9 After all the cables are punched down, tie them together.
10 Test the cable connections.

B HOW TO SET UP A COMPUTER WORKSTATION

1 Review the work order for the workstation.
2 Unpack the monitor and tower.
3 Plug the monitor into the monitor input in the back of the tower.
4 Unpack and connect the keyboard to the first USB port.

5 Connect the mouse to a USB port on the keyboard or on the back of the tower.
6 Connect to the LAN with an Ethernet cable from the back of the tower to the CAT6 floor box outlet.

7 Plug the monitor and tower into a surge protector.
8 Power on the monitor and tower.
9 Connect peripherals.

C HOW TO REPLACE AN INTERNAL HARD DRIVE

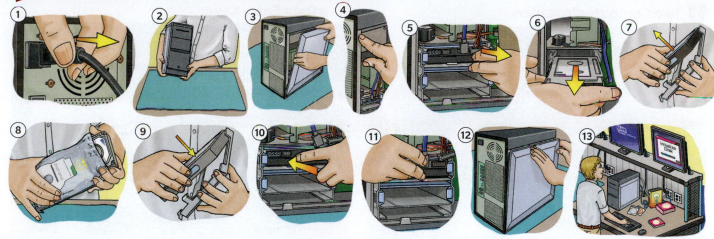

1 Disconnect the power.
2 Put the computer on an antistatic mat.
3 Open the case.
4 Touch the metal casing of the computer to discharge any static electricity.
5 On the hard drive, disconnect the power supply and interface cables.

6 Remove the mounting sled from the drive bay.
7 Remove the old hard drive from the mounting sled.
8 Carefully remove the new hard disk from the static shielding bag.
9 Snap the new hard disk into the mounting sled.

10 Slide the mounting sled back into the drive bay.
11 Attach the interface cable and the power supply cable, making sure all connections are snug.
12 Secure the cover onto the computer.
13 Reinstall the operating system, software, and drivers.

D HOW TO DEVELOP A VIDEO GAME

1 Write a game script.
2 Create storyboards.
3 Create a production schedule.
4 Create sketches of game environments.
5 Create sketches of game characters.

6 Program the game engine.
7 Finish designing the game environments.
8 Finish creating game characters.
9 Record voices, sound effects, and music.

10 Port digital art, audio files, and video files to the game engine.
11 Test the game on different platforms.
12 Identify bugs and fix them.

1 Two Computer Installers

A computer installer is asking for feedback.

A. I finished banding and bundling the cables. How do they look?
B. Okay. Except for one thing: you didn't label the bands.
A. Oh. My mistake. I'll do that now.
B. Let me know when you're finished and I'll check again.

2 A Technical Support Specialist & a Data Entry Keyer

A technical support specialist is giving positive feedback.

A. So do you remember how to get into the data entry screen?
B. I press the shift key and F5 key. Right?
A. That's right. You're a fast learner. It usually takes longer to train people on this program.
B. Thanks.

3 Two Computer Repair Technicians

One computer repair technician is correcting another.

A. You goofed on this repair!
B. Oh. What did I do wrong?
A. The hard drive on this computer was supposed to be replaced, not repaired.
B. Let me see the repair order. Oh. You're right. Sorry about that. I'll work on it right away.

4 A Game Designer & a Game Developer

A game designer is asking for feedback.

A. How do you like the underground environment I designed for the video game?
B. Honestly, I don't think the game should take place underground. It's too dark.
A. Okay. I can ask the artist to create something outdoors that's brighter and more colorful.
B. Good. That'll be better.

1 You're a computer installer. Ask a co-worker for feedback (about something you did incorrectly).
2 You're a technical support specialist giving training to someone. Give the person positive feedback.
3 You're a computer repair technician. Correct a co-worker who did something wrong.
4 You're a video game designer. Ask a co-worker for feedback.

OCCUPATIONS

computer installer
computer programmer
computer repair technician
computer service technician
computer/network administrator
customer support specialist
data entry keyer
data recovery specialist

game designer
game developer
game producer
game tester
help desk technician
information processing worker
information systems security specialist

mobile app designer
mobile app developer
network engineer
systems analyst
technical support specialist
UI (user interface) artist
video game music composer

EQUIPMENT, TOOLS, & OBJECTS

antistatic bag
antistatic mat
antivirus protection
antivirus software
app
artist's interactive
   tablet
artist's stylus
audio file
backlight
battery
blowing brush
bug
butane soldering iron
   and blower
cable connections
cable connector
cable insulation
cable scissors
cable tester
cable wire
cable wrap
CAT6 cable
CAT6 cable batch
CAT6 crimp tool
CAT6 floor box outlet
chat session
code
code editing software
compressed air sprayer
computer
computer tool kit
data
data entry input
data entry screen
data floor box
debugging software
defect report

device
diagnostic test
digital art
document
drive bay
driver
DVI cable
DVI monitor cable
   connector
DVI monitor input port
enterprise router
ESD mat
Ethernet cable
Ethernet cable connector
Ethernet input port
external drive
external hard drive
F5 key
FireWire cable connector
FireWire input port
fish tape
framework software
game characters
game engine
game environment
game script
game storyboard
gigabytes
graphics program
hard disk
hard disk cloner
hard disk drive/hard
   drive
hard drive sled
industrial modem
interface cable
internal hard drives
internal network adapter

laminar flow cabinet
LAN schematic
laptop
metal casing
micro tools
mini desktop tower
mobile apps
mobile devices
modem
monitor
motherboard
mounting sled
mouse
network adapter
network security
   software
OCR (optical character
   recognition) program
operating system
operating system
   software
patch panel
patch panel/cable tester
peripherals
platform
power supply cable
production schedule
program flowchart
programming source
   code
punch-down plugs
punch-down tool
RAID
RAM
repair order
resource layout file
security software
serial number

server rack cabinet
shift key
software
software training manual
sound effects
source code
static electricity
static shielding bag
storyboard
support center live chat
surge protector
tablet
technical support
   question
text
touch screen digitizer
tower
training manual
underground
   environment
USB cable connector
USB input port
USB port
video file
video game
virus detection software
voltage
voltage tester
warranty
wireless router
work order
workbench
workgroup/network
   printer
workstation
zipper string

INFORMATION TECHNOLOGY

WORKPLACE LOCATIONS

computer network administrator's office

computer repair & support center

computer repair lab

data recovery room

digital design/development studio

help desk

programming department

wiring/network closet

WORKPLACE ACTIONS

add a hard drive to a RAID

add RAM

answer technical support questions

attach a monitor with a DVI cable

attach a wireless router to a modem

bundle and band CAT6 cables

capture text in an OCR program

change a hard disk

connect a computer to a data floor box

connect an external drive to a computer

design a video game

enter data

fish CAT6 cables through walls

have a live chat session with a customer

install an internal network adapter

install virus detection and network security software

load software

measure voltage on a motherboard

punch down a patch panel

recommend the proper cable to a customer

repair a hard disk drive

replace a monitor backlight

replace a touch screen digitizer on a tablet

review a LAN schematic

run a diagnostic test

scan a document

store an item to be repaired

test a game and write a defect report

test a mobile app on different devices

train an employee on new software

write programming source code

write up a repair order

WORKPLACE COMMUNICATION

ask a co-worker for feedback

check on the completion of a task

check on the progress of an installation

check on the progress of someone's work

check on the status of a project

correct a co-worker

give positive feedback

help a customer with a problem

offer to help a co-worker

work with a colleague on an installation

OCCUPATIONS

A WHAT ARE THEIR JOBS?

administrator	composer	help desk	mobile app	recovery	technician
analyst	designer	installer	produce	security	tester
artist	engineer	keyer	programmer	specialist	worker

1. Sharon is a computer _____installer_____. She installs computer systems.
2. Jason creates games for mobile devices. He's a _____ developer.
3. I provide service and product information to customers. I'm a customer support _____.
4. Ramon creates the content and environment of video games. He's a game _____.
5. Alicia manages computer networks. She's an _____.
6. I work with programmers, designers, and artists to develop games. I'm a game _____.
7. My sister creates music for video games. She's a video game music _____.
8. I enter lists of items, numbers, and other data into computers. I'm a data entry _____.
9. Kevin repairs and maintains computer equipment. He's a computer repair _____.
10. Jennifer designs and monitors computer networks. She's a network _____.
11. I respond to requests from computer users. I'm a _____ technician.
12. Juan creates interfaces for software programs and websites. He's a UI _____.
13. I restore information that is lost from a computer system. I'm a data _____ specialist.
14. Alexander writes computer software. He's a computer _____.
15. I protect the information on computer systems. I'm an information systems _____ specialist.
16. Jonathan tests video games before they are released to the public. He's a game _____.
17. Greta designs and implements information systems. She's a systems _____.
18. I keep records and provide information to customers. I'm an information processing _____.

WORKPLACE LOCATIONS

B WHAT'S THE LOCATION?

_d_ 1. I work in a computer repair _____.
___ 2. Someone is here from the programming _____.
___ 3. Meet me in the computer network administrator's _____.
___ 4. There's a problem in the data recovery _____.
___ 5. I'm looking for a job at a digital design _____.
___ 6. I think I need to call the help _____.
___ 7. We need to contact the computer repair and support _____.

a. office
b. center
c. room
d. lab
e. desk
f. studio
g. department

EQUIPMENT, TOOLS, & OBJECTS

C HOW ARE THEY THE SAME?

| antistatic | cable | data entry | Ethernet | internal | punch-down |
| antivirus | CAT6 | DVI | hard disk | mobile | video |

1. _____ video _____
file & game

2. _____
input & screen

3. _____
apps & devices

4. _____
bag & mat

5. _____
tool & plugs

6. _____
cable connector & input port

7. _____
protection & software

8. _____
connections & insulation

9. _____
cloner & drive

10. _____
cable & monitor

11. _____
hard drives & network adapter

12. _____
crimp tool & cable batch

D WHAT'S THE ITEM?

_d_	1. micro	**a.** order
___	2. patch	**b.** effects
___	3. shift	**c.** mat
___	4. sound	**d.** tools
___	5. repair	**e.** string
___	6. zipper	**f.** key
___	7. drive	**g.** panel
___	8. ESD	**h.** bay

___	9. serial	**i.** file
___	10. tool	**j.** session
___	11. audio	**k.** number
___	12. source	**l.** adapter
___	13. artist's	**m.** tape
___	14. chat	**n.** code
___	15. fish	**o.** stylus
___	16. network	**p.** kit

___	17. defect	**q.** sled
___	18. soldering	**r.** wrap
___	19. cable	**s.** manual
___	20. graphics	**t.** report
___	21. hard drive	**u.** brush
___	22. flow	**v.** program
___	23. blowing	**w.** iron
___	24. training	**x.** cabinet

WORKPLACE ACTIONS

E ACTIONS IN COMMON

1. *Mobile apps & games* are things you (scan   test).

2. *External drives & computers* are things you (connect   enter).

3. *Virus detection* and *internal network adapters* are things you (write   install).

4. *Monitors* and *wireless routers* are things you (bundle   attach).

5. *Monitor backlights* and *touch screen digitizers* are things you (replace   punch down).

F INFORMATION TECHNOLOGY *IN ACTION!*

add	bundle	design	fish	install	punch down	review	train	write up
answer	capture	enter	have	measure	replace	run	write	

1. I need to _____write up_____ a repair order for you.

2. We'll need to _____ all of your company's data.

3. We'll _____ all of your employees on the new software.

4. Let's _____ a hard drive to this RAID.

5. I can teach you how to _____ text in an OCR program.

6. We'll definitely _____ network security software on your system.

7. I'd like to be able to _____ programming source code

8. We need to _____ the voltage on the motherboard.

9. I'm attempting to _____ and band these CAT6 cables.

10. We'll be happy to _____ any of your technical support questions.

11. We'll need to _____ the CAT6 cables through the walls.

12. I have no idea what the problem is. We'll need to _____ a diagnostic test.

13. It looks like we're going to have to _____ the touch screen digitizer on this tablet.

14. Our goal is to _____ an exciting video game that millions of people will download.

15. I'll definitely need to _____ the LAN schematic.

16. Is it possible for us to _____ a live chat session to discuss that?

17. I just started working here. I'm still learning how to _____ a patch panel.

WORKPLACE COMMUNICATION

G WHAT ARE THEY SAYING?

_d_ 1. check on a co-worker's progress

___ 2. offer to help

___ 3. ask about completion of a task

___ 4. help a customer with a problem

___ 5. report on the progress of your work

___ 6. ask for feedback

___ 7. give positive feedback

___ 8. correct a co-worker

___ 9. give negative feedback

___ 10. respond to feedback

a. "What seems to be the problem?"

b. "It's too dark."

c. "How do the cables look?"

d. "Are you almost done hooking up that workstation?"

e. "Oh. My mistake."

f. "You goofed on this repair!"

g. "Do you need any help running the cables?"

h. "I'm almost finished."

i. "You're a fast learner."

j. "Have you installed the security software at all the workstations?"

Wind Energy
1 wind turbine technician
2 tractor-trailer truck driver
3 boom crane operator
4 residential wind energy installer

Solar Energy
5 solar photovoltaic assembler
6 quality control specialist
7 solar installation technician
8 electrician

Geothermal Energy
9 geothermal installer
10 pump technician
11 geothermal technician

Conversion Energy
12 waste oil reclamation truck operator
13 restaurant worker
14 conversion technician
15 chemical technician

a wind turbine
b wind turbine base
c wind turbine section
d substation
e nacelle
f backsheet
g rail system
h piling truck
i drill pipe
j borehole
k grout mixer and pump
l geothermal heat pump
m waste oil reclamation truck
n filtering machine

What green energy sectors do you see?
What occupations do you see in each sector?

What objects do you see?
What types of green energy exist in your area?

Energy Efficiency

16 energy auditor
17 homeowner
18 insulation specialist
19 handyman
20 electrician
21 window installer

22 appliance installer
23 traffic signal installer
24 urban forester
25 conservation technician
26 door installer
27 foam insulation installer
28 construction worker

o attic
p blower door test unit
q loose insulation blower equipment
r energy-efficient window
s recycling dumpster
t foam insulation mixing system

What occupations do you see?
What objects do you see?

What are some ways people can make their homes more energy efficient?

Recycling

1 recyclable collections driver
2 MRF worker
3 MRF sorter
4 MRF technician

Forest/Land/Agriculture

5 forester
6 conservation technician
7 farm worker/laborer
8 farm manager
9 CSA* organizer
10 CSA member

* CSA = community supported agriculture

Environmental Remediation

11 environmental technician

Air Pollution

12 air pollution specialist
13 environmental installation technician
14 dust collection specialist

a materials recovery facility (MRF)
b recycling collection truck
c vertical baler
d tree farm
e packing area
f test location
g air quality monitoring site
h cyclone particle collector
i baghouse

What occupations do you see?
What objects do you see?

Is there recycling where you live? What do you recycle?
Is air pollution a problem in your area? Tell about it.

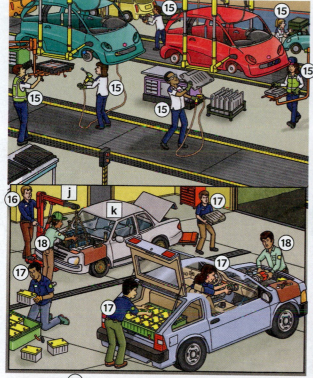

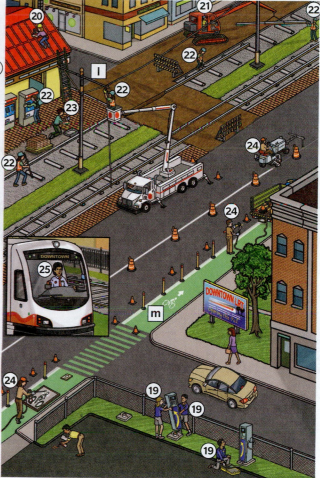

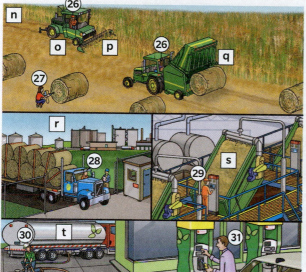

Electric Vehicle Production & Conversion

15 assembly line worker
16 assembly line hoist operator
17 EV* technician
18 EV mechanic
19 charging station installer

* EV = electric vehicle

Light Rail Transportation

20 construction worker
21 crane operator
22 light rail worker
23 bricklayer
24 road construction worker
25 light rail operator

Biofuel Production

26 agricultural equipment operator

27 farm manager
28 flatbed truck driver
29 biorefinery production operator
30 ethanol transport driver
31 customer

Brainstorming Session

32 industrial designer
33 design assistant
34 engineer
35 assistant engineer

j hoist
k donor car
l light rail power pole
m bike path
n switchgrass farm
o tractor
p mower
q baler
r biorefinery
s process vessel
t ethanol delivery truck

What occupations do you see? What objects do you see? | Do you think electric vehicles will replace vehicles that use gasoline? Why or why not? How can public transportation be improved to help the environment?

1 tighten a tower bolt
2 attach a cable to a tower section
3 guide the rotor blade assembly into the nacelle
4 place a photovoltaic cell on a backsheet
5 inspect cells
6 screw in roof mounts
7 wire an inverter
8 put down surface casings and rings
9 add powder grout to the mixer
10 push a pipe down the drill hole
11 dig a header trench
12 hook up a geothermal heat pump
13 suction out used oil
14 hook up a hose to the rendering tank
15 remove debris from the filtration system
16 test feedstock

Look at page 288. What are the people doing? Describe their actions.

17 take an image with a thermal imaging infrared camera
18 do a smoke stick test
19 set up a blower door test unit
20 review an energy audit with a homeowner

21 blow in loose fill insulation
22 change incandescent light bulbs to CFL* light bulbs
23 replace an old refrigerator with an energy-efficient one
24 install an energy-efficient window

25 install weather stripping on an exterior door
26 hang a new door
27 dispose of old materials in a recycling dumpster
28 drill a hole through brick grout

29 cover holes with aluminum foil tape
30 fill a wall with insulation through a drilled hole
31 convert a traffic light to solar LED*
32 plant a tree

* CFL = compact fluorescent light bulb, LED = light-emitting diode

Look at page 289. What are the people doing? Describe their actions.

1 dump recyclables at an MRF
2 push recyclables onto a belt
3 sort through recyclables
4 bale cardboard

5 plant saplings
6 fill crates with produce
7 load crates for delivery
8 sign up a CSA member

9 lay out a boom
10 collect water samples
11 retrieve habitat samples
12 tag a bird

13 take an air quality reading
14 check particle output
15 inspect a baghouse for leaks
16 change a filter

Look at page 290. What are the people doing? Describe their actions.

17 position an underbody battery on a chassis
18 install a charging system inlet
19 hoist an engine from a donor car
20 install gauges

21 wire batteries together
22 connect a DC* controller to an electric motor
23 bolt a rail to a concrete tie/sleeper
24 attach catenary wire to a power pole

    * DC = direct current

25 paint road lines
26 install a bollard on the street
27 operate a light rail vehicle
28 stencil a logo on a bike path

29 run a charging station test
30 bale switchgrass
31 regulate temperature flow
32 brainstorm ideas

Look at page 291. What are the people doing? Describe their actions.

1	torque wrench	7	residential upwind turbine	13	biodiesel tester	18	attic air chute
2	photovoltaic cell	8	galvanized conduit	14	thermal imaging infrared camera	19	smart thermostat
3	magnifying glass	9	geothermal furnace			20	EE* light
4	solar pathfinder	10	drill pipe section	15	smoke stick	21	solar traffic light
5	solar panel	11	spooler	16	blower door	22	foam dispensing gun
6	inverter	12	grease disposal container	17	loose fill insulation	23	insect trap

* EE = energy-efficient

Look at pages 288–289 and 292–293. What equipment, tools, and objects do you see?

24 push broom	**30** CSA share board	**37** leg gauge	**44** concrete tie/sleeper
25 recycled bale	**31** sample bottle	**38** banding pliers	**45** bolt
26 tree sapling	**32** specimen bags	**39** air particle counter	**46** transit pass machine
27 herb and vegetable seed	**33** sieve	**40** baghouse filter	**47** pavement marking stencil
28 field hoe	**34** soil step auger	**41** electric motor	**48** EV charging station
	35 water analyzer	**42** EV gauges	**49** EV test simulator
29 vegetable crate	**36** leg band	**43** rail	**50** moisture meter

Look at pages 290–291 and 294–295. What equipment, tools, and objects do you see

1 A Boom Crane Operator & a Wind Turbine Technician

A boom crane operator and a wind turbine technician are coordinating an installation.

A. Are you done bolting down the base?
B. We're almost finished.
A. Good. We're done rigging the next tower section, so we're ready whenever you are.
B. Okay. Give us about five more minutes and we'll send two techs up the base.

3 Two Geothermal Installers

Two geothermal installers are discussing the equipment needed to complete a task.

A. How far down are we?
B. About 150 feet.
A. That's halfway. So we'll need five more sections of drill pipe, right?
B. Let's see. Five sections of 30-foot pipe. Yeah. That'll do it.

2 A Quality Control Specialist & a Solar Photovoltaic Assembler

A quality control specialist is informing a solar panel assembler about a problem.

A. We need to stop production.
B. Why?
A. I'm finding a lot of small cracks in these cells. We're going to have to check the whole batch.
B. Okay.

4 A Waste Oil Reclamation Truck Operator & a Restaurant Manager

A waste oil reclamation truck operator is reporting a completed task to a restaurant manager.

A. We pumped out 190 gallons from your oil recycle container today.
B. Do you have my receipt?
A. Yes. Here you are. We'll be back next Tuesday.
B. Okay. See you next week.

1 You're working on a wind turbine installation. Coordinate tasks with a co-worker.
2 You're a quality control specialist at a solar panel assembly plant. Inform an assembler about a problem.
3 You're working on a geothermal installation. Coordinate tasks with a co-worker.
4 You're a waste oil reclamation truck operator. Report the task you've completed to a restaurant manager.

5 Two Energy Auditors

Two energy auditors are coordinating on a task.

A. The blower door is running and the house is depressurized.

B. Then we can start the smokestick testing in the conditioned space.

A. I'll go upstairs and check the windows for leakage.

B. Okay. I'll do the same down here.

6 Two Insulation Installers

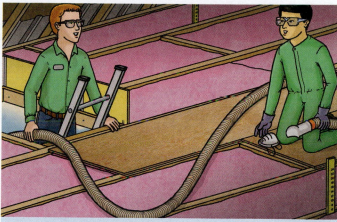

Two insulation installers are preparing to do a task.

A. Are we ready to blow in the insulation?

B. Yes. Everything's all set up here.

A. Okay. I'll head down and fill the blower. Remember to put on your mask.

B. Got it.

7 Two Window Installers

Two window installers are checking the accuracy of their work.

A. Is it level?

B. Yes. It's perfect.

A. Great! I'll go outside and caulk it.

B. All right. I'm going to continue to fill.

8 Two Foam Insulation Installers

Two foam insulation installers are solving a problem.

A. I think I have all the cracks patched, so you're good to go.

B. I'll start to pump in.

A. Looks good. Wait, there's a small leak! It's okay. I've got it!

B. All right. I'm going to start filling.

---

5 You're an energy auditor preparing to test a home. Coordinate on a task with a co-worker.
6 Why do you think the insulation installers need to use masks?
7 You're a window installer. Check the accuracy of your work with a co-worker.
8 What kind of insulation is there in the place where you live?

Workplace Communication

9 An MRF Worker & a Recyclable Collections Driver

An MRF worker and a recyclable collections driver are solving a problem.

A. That's a huge load!

B. You're telling me! There was no recyclables pickup last week because of the holiday.

A. Oh, right. Wait a minute! I need to clear more space before you can dump that load.

B. Okay.

11 Two Environmental Technicians

An environmental technician is offering to help a co-worker.

A. Have you gathered enough soil samples?

B. Not yet. I'm going to take some more samples over there.

A. Can I help with anything?

B. Yes. You could get some more specimen bags from my field case.

A. Sure thing.

10 A Farm Manager & a CSA Organizer

A farm manager is informing a CSA organizer about current and future deliveries.

A. We had a good week. I just delivered lots of lettuce, radishes, tomatoes, corn, and apples.

B. Great. You know, some members have been asking for more herbs.

A. Well, there's some parsley and basil in today's delivery, but next week we'll also have rosemary and chives.

B. Good to hear. I'll write that on the board so the members will know.

12 Two Air Pollution Specialists

Two air pollution specialists are troubleshooting a problem.

A. We aren't getting the proper CO_2 reading for this station.

B. I think I know why. Look at that monitoring wand.

A. It's bent.

B. I'll call field maintenance and have them come out to replace it.

---

9   In your community, are recyclables collected? Where are they taken?

10 Is there community supported agriculture (a CSA) in your area? Tell about it.

11 Why do you think the environmental techs are gathering soil samples?

12 What are some ways to improve air quality where you live?

13 Two EV Technicians

Two EV technicians are coordinating tasks.

A. The rear battery pack is all set.
B. Good. Now we can install the front pack.
A. I'll get the cells.
B. Okay. And I'll go and check the battery harness.

14 Two Charging Station Installers

Two charging station installers are working together on an installation.

A. Is the station lining up with the mounting bracket?
B. It looks okay on my side. How about yours?
A. It's okay here, too. I'll bolt it down.
B. And I'll get ready to do the wiring.

15 A Supervisor & a Biorefinery Production Operator

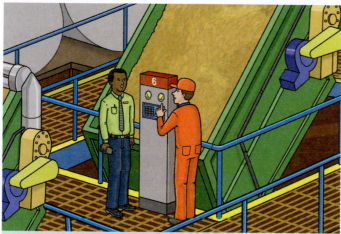

A biorefinery production operator is reporting a problem to a supervisor.

A. What's the problem?
B. This machine is running hot.
A. Have you adjusted the temperature?
B. Yes, an hour ago. But it's back up.
A. Okay. I'll call the operations manager and give her a heads up.

16 A Team of Industrial Designers & Engineers

A team of industrial designers and engineers is brainstorming a new concept.

A. I'm not sure about mounting a solar panel on the roof of the vehicle.
B. What if we redesigned it so that the solar cells are part of the roof itself?
C. Is that technically possible?
D. We'll need to evaluate that in the engineering department.

13 You're an EV technician. Coordinate tasks with a co-worker.
14 Are there charging stations for electric vehicles in your area? If so, where are they?
15 In your opinion, should biofuel production be an important source of energy? Why or why not?
16 You're an industrial designer. Brainstorm a new concept with your team.

A HOW TO INSTALL SOLAR PANELS

1 Confirm the correct position and alignment for panel installation.
2 Locate and mark the location of attic rafters.
3 Drill holes for mounts.
4 Attach mounts to the roof with bolts.

5 Apply flashing.
6 Attach rails to the mounting system.
7 Check the level of the rails.
8 Attach mounting clips to the rails.
9 Attach a solar panel to the mounting clips.

10 Wire the panels in an array together.
11 Connect array cables together.
12 Test the voltage of arrays before wiring to the inverter.

B HOW TO APPLY BLOWN-IN INSULATION TO AN ATTIC

1 Place a plywood walkway down for easy and safe access.
2 Measure space to determine coverage requirements (*length x width = square footage*).
3 Place blocking around the attic access.
4 Protect recessed lights, furnace flues, and any heat source using rigid barriers with a 3-inch clearance.
5 Install air chutes over vents.
6 Determine the depth of insulation based on its R-value.*
7 Set rulers in the attic to gauge the insulation's depth.

8 Have a helper start to fill the hopper of the blower with insulation.
9 Start at the farthest corner of the attic and work back towards the attic access.
10 Hold the hose approximately one foot above the installed insulation, maintaining an even insulation depth.
11 Blow around chutes and barriers.
12 Use enough insulation for the recommended R-value.

* R-value = resistance of heat flow through material

C HOW TO BALE RECYCLED MATERIAL

1 Apply paraffin wax to the inside chamber.
2 Place a paper sheet on the bottom of the chamber.
3 Close and latch the chamber door.
4 Fill the chamber with recycled material.

5 Close the upper loading door.
6 Turn on the baler.
7 Press the down button to engage the platen and compact the material.
8 Raise the platen.
9 Refill and compact the material until the desired bale size is reached.

10 Place a paper sheet on top of the bale.
11 Tie the bale.
12 Eject the bale.
13 Stack the bale for pickup.

D HOW TO INSTALL A PUBLIC EV CHARGING STATION

1 Make sure the underground utilities are marked before digging.
2 Dig a trench to the power source.
3 Install the electric power box.
4 Install conduit in the trench.
5 Inspect the groundwork and fill.

6 Install bracket footings.
7 Install the charging station onto a mounting bracket.
8 Wire feeder conductors to the station.

9 Install safety bollards.
10 Test the charging unit.
11 Do a final inspection.

1 Two Solar Installation Technicians

A solar installation technician is asking a co-worker to check the accuracy of his work.

A. Can you do me a favor?

B. Sure. What is it?

A. Double-check the panels on the second rail. A couple of them look askew.

B. Maybe I didn't tighten the mounting clips enough. I'll take a look right now.

2 Two Energy Auditors

An energy auditor is correcting a co-worker.

A. I'm not getting a proper reading.

B. Did you close the doors and windows on each floor?

A. I did on this floor and upstairs. I didn't check the basement windows.

B. No wonder you aren't getting a good reading! You'd better check those windows now.

3 Two Environmental Technicians

An environmental technician is asking a co-worker for feedback.

A. Can you take a look at this? Is the band on this leg too big?

B. It does look big. Did you use the gauge to measure?

A. Yes. I measured 18, which is common for a black-eyed junco.

B. Then it's probably okay.

4 Two Road Construction Workers

A road construction worker is warning a co-worker about a mistake.

A. Wait! Stop! Don't spray yet!

B. What's wrong?

A. I think you put that stencil upside down.

B. You're right. Thanks.

---

1 You're a solar installation tech. Check the accuracy of your work with a co-worker.

2 You're an energy auditor. Give correction to a co-worker.

3 You're an environmental tech. Ask a co-worker for feedback (about something you didn't do correctly).

4 You're a road construction worker. Warn a co-worker about a mistake.

OCCUPATIONS

agricultural equipment operator
air pollution specialist
appliance installer
assembly line hoist operator
assembly line worker
assistant engineer
biorefinery production operator
boom crane operator
bricklayer
charging station installer
chemical technician
conservation technician
construction worker
conversion technician
crane operator
CSA organizer
design assistant
door installer
dust collection specialist
electrician
energy auditor
engineer
environmental installation technician
environmental technician
ethanol transport driver
EV mechanic
EV technician
farm manager
farm worker/laborer

flatbed truck driver
foam insulation installer
forester
geothermal installer
geothermal technician
handyman
industrial designer
insulation installer
insulation specialist
light rail operator
light rail worker
mixing truck operator
MRF sorter
MRF technician
MRF worker
quality control specialist
recyclable collections driver
residential wind energy installer
restaurant manager
restaurant worker
road construction worker
solar installation technician
solar photovoltaic assembler
tractor-trailer truck driver
traffic signal installer
urban forester
waste oil reclamation truck operator
wind turbine technician
window installer

WORKPLACE LOCATIONS

air quality monitoring site
attic
bike path
biorefinery

materials recovery facility (MRF)
packing area
substation

switchgrass farm
test location
tree farm

EQUIPMENT, TOOLS, & OBJECTS

air particle counter
air quality reading
aluminum foil tape
array cables
attic air chute
backsheet
baghouse
baghouse filter
bale
baler
banding pliers
batteries
battery pack
biodiesel tester
blower door
blower door test unit
blown-in insulation
bollard
bolt
boom
borehole
bracket footings
brick grout
cable
cardboard
catenary wire
CFL light bulb
charging station test
charging system inlet
charging unit
chassis
chutes
CO2 reading
concrete tie/sleeper
conduit
crates
CSA share board
cyclone particle
  collector
DC controller
debris
donor car
drill hole
drill pipe

drill pipe section
EE light
electric motor
electric power box
energy-efficient refrigerator
energy-efficient window
ethanol delivery truck
EV (electric vehicle)
  charging station
EV gauges
EV test simulator
feeder conductor
feedstock
field hoe
filter
filtering machine
filtration system
flashing
fluorescent light bulb
foam dispensing gun
foam insulation mixing
  system
furnace flue
galvanized conduit
gauges
geothermal furnace
geothermal heat pump
grease disposal container
grout mixer and pump
habitat samples
header trench
herb and vegetable seed
hoist
hopper
hose
incandescent light bulb
insect trap
insulation hose
inverter
leg band
leg gauge
light rail power pole
light rail vehicle
loading door

logo
loose fill insulation
loose fill insulation blower
  equipment
magnifying glass
mask
mixer
moisture meter
monitoring wand
mounting bracket
mounting clips
mounting system
mounts
mower
nacelle
paraffin wax
particle output
pavement marking stencil
photovoltaic cell
piling truck
platen
powder grout
power pole
power source
process vessel
produce
push broom
R-value
rafters
rail system
rails
recessed lights
recyclables
recycle container
recycled bale
recycling collection truck
recycling dumpster
rendering tank
residential upwind turbine
rigid barriers
road lines
roof mounts
rotor blade assembly
safety bollard

sample bottle
saplings
sieve
smart thermostat
smoke stick
soil sample
soil step auger
solar cells
solar LED
solar panel
solar pathfinder
solar traffic light
specimen bags
spooler
stencil
surface casings
switchgrass
temperature flow
thermal imaging
  infrared camera
torque wrench
tower bolt
tower section
tractor
traffic light
transit pass machine
tree sapling
trench
underbody battery
used oil
vegetable crate
vents
vertical baler
voltage
walkway
waste oil reclamation
  truck
water analyzer
water samples
weather stripping
wind turbine
wind turbine base
wind turbine section

WORKPLACE ACTIONS

add powder grout to a mixer

attach a cable to a tower section

attach catenary wire to a power pole

bale cardboard

bale switchgrass

brainstorm ideas

blow in loose fill insulation

bolt a rail to a concrete tie/sleeper

change a filter

change incandescent light bulbs to CFL light bulbs

check particle output

collect water samples

connect a DC controller to an electric motor

convert a traffic light to solar LED

cover holes with aluminum foil tape

dig a header trench

dispose of old materials in a recycling dumpster

do a smoke stick test

drill a hole through brick grout

dump recyclables at an MRF

fill a wall with insulation through a drilled hole

fill crates with produce

guide a rotor blade assembly into a nacelle

hang a new door

hoist an engine from a donor car

hook up a geothermal heat pump

hook up a hose to a rendering tank

inspect a baghouse for leaks

inspect cells

install a bollard on a street

install a charging system inlet

install an energy-efficient window

install gauges

install weather stripping on an exterior door

lay out a boom

load crates for delivery

operate a light rail vehicle

paint road lines

place a photovoltaic cell on a backsheet

plant a tree

plant saplings

position an underbody battery on a chassis

push a pipe down a drillhole

push recyclables onto a belt

put down surface casings and rings

regulate temperature flow

remove debris from a filtration system

replace an old refrigerator with an energy-efficient one

retrieve habitat samples

review an energy audit with a homeowner

run a charging station test

screw in roof mounts

set up a blower door test unit

sign up a CSA member

sort through recyclables

stencil a logo on a bike path

suction out used oil

tag a bird

take an air quality reading

take an image with a thermal imaging camera

test feedstock

tighten a tower bolt

wire batteries together

wire an inverter

WORKPLACE COMMUNICATION

ask a co-worker for feedback

ask a co-worker to check the accuracy of his or her work

brainstorm a new concept with colleagues

check the accuracy of your work

coordinate tasks with a co-worker

correct a co-worker

discuss equipment needed to complete a task

inform a client about current and future deliveries

inform a co-worker about a problem

offer help to a co-worker

prepare with a co-worker to do a task

report a completed task

report a problem to a supervisor

troubleshoot a problem with a co-worker

warn a co-worker about a mistake

work with a co-worker to complete a task

work with a co-worker to solve a problem

OCCUPATIONS

A WHAT'S THE CATEGORY?

air pollution	charging station	dust collection	flatbed truck	light rail	quality control
appliance	construction	ethanol transport	foam insulation	mixing truck	recyclable collections
assembly line	crane	farm	geothermal	MRF	solar installation

workers

assembly line

_____

_____

operators

_____

_____

_____

specialists

_____

_____

_____

installers

_____

_____

_____

drivers

_____

_____

_____

technicians

_____

_____

_____

B WHAT KIND OF ENERGY?

Air Pollution (AIR)	Forest/Land/Agriculture (FLA)
Biofuel Production (BIO)	Geothermal Energy (GEO)
Conversion Energy (CON)	Recycling (REC)
Electric Vehicles (EV)	Solar (SOL)
Energy Efficiency (EE)	Wind Energy (WND)

SOL **1.** solar installation technician

_____ **2.** turbine tech

_____ **3.** window installer

_____ **4.** MRF technician

_____ **5.** photovoltaic assembler

_____ **6.** geothermal technician

_____ **7.** waste oil reclamation truck operator

_____ **8.** charging station installer

_____ **9.** energy auditor

_____ **10.** environmental installation tech

_____ **11.** conversion technician

_____ **12.** door installer

_____ **13.** residential wind energy installer

_____ **14.** chemical technician

_____ **15.** ethanol transport driver

_____ **16.** foam insulation installer

_____ **17.** CSA organizer

_____ **18.** dust collection specialist

_____ **19.** electric vehicle mechanic

_____ **20.** appliance installer

_____ **21.** recyclable collections driver

_____ **22.** conservation technician

WORKPLACE LOCATIONS

C WHAT'S THE LOCATION?

| attic | biorefinery | farm | location | monitoring | packing | path | substation | switchgrass |

1. This _____ **substation** _____ collects energy generated by the wind turbines.
2. We're trying to make our house more energy efficient, so we're adding foam insulation in our _____.
3. It's important to maintain healthy vegetation on every tree _____ in this country.
4. Many people are trying to save fuel. As a result, we see more and more people these days on the bike _____ in the downtown area of our city.
5. It's important to fertilize regularly on a _____ farm.
6. The _____ in our community produces a great deal of power and heat.
7. We continually check the air at this air quality _____ site.
8. We use this test _____ to conduct air pollution tests.
9. Vegetables from the farm are put into containers in this _____ area.

EQUIPMENT, TOOLS, & OBJECTS

D HOW ARE THEY THE SAME?

| electric | EV | power | solar | water |
| energy efficient | geothermal | recycling | tower | wind turbine |

1. _____ **recycling** _____
   collection truck & dumpster
2. _____
   window & refrigerator
3. _____
   cells & pathfinder
4. _____
   base & section
5. _____
   pole & source
6. _____
   motor & power box
7. _____
   charging station & test simulator
8. _____
   analyzer & samples
9. _____
   furnace & heat pump
10. _____
   bolt & section

E WHAT'S THE ITEM?

c 1. piling	a. pliers	___ 6. bracket	f. samples	___ 11. insect	k. stick
___ 2. leg	b. meter	___ 7. habitat	g. car	___ 12. rendering	l. trap
___ 3. moisture	c. truck	___ 8. specimen	h. trench	___ 13. safety	m. filter
___ 4. banding	d. sample	___ 9. header	i. footings	___ 14. baghouse	n. bollard
___ 5. soil	e. band	___ 10. donor	j. bags	___ 15. smoke	o. tank

GREEN JOBS

WORKPLACE ACTIONS

F "GREEN" ACTIONS!

1. hook up _____
   a. road lines
   b. a heat pump
   c. water samples
   d. grout

2. install _____
   a. recyclables
   b. crates
   c. a bollard
   d. particle output

3. operate _____
   a. a light rail vehicle
   b. roof mounts
   c. a bird
   d. feedstock

4. plant _____
   a. cells
   b. a filter
   c. samples
   d. saplings

5. tag _____
   a. ideas
   b. cardboard
   c. the temperature
   d. a bird

6. fill _____
   a. gauges
   b. crates
   c. switchgrass
   d. a traffic light

7. wire _____
   a. water samples
   b. road lines
   c. batteries
   d. insulation

8. stencil _____
   a. a trench
   b. CSA members
   c. insulation
   d. a logo

9. tighten _____
   a. a bolt
   b. a turbine
   c. a sapling
   d. a soil sample

10. run _____
    a. a door
    b. a test
    c. oil
    d. leaks

11. convert _____
    a. water
    b. samples
    c. a traffic light
    d. a filter

12. attach _____
    a. oil
    b. a cable
    c. recyclables
    d. feedstock

13. drill _____
    a. a hole
    b. cells
    c. a bollard
    d. a smoke stick test

14. hang _____
    a. a tree
    b. insulation
    c. a tower
    d. a door

15. dig _____
    a. a vent
    b. a trench
    c. a pump
    d. water

16. brainstorm _____
    a. mounts
    b. energy
    c. ideas
    d. roads

17. regulate _____
    a. windows
    b. temperature
    c. power poles
    d. walls

18. paint _____
    a. insulation
    b. leaks
    c. cells
    d. road lines

19. sort through _____
    a. recyclables
    b. a traffic light
    c. a door
    d. a power pole

20. suction out _____
    a. rails
    b. temperature flow
    c. a window
    d. oil

WORKPLACE COMMUNICATION

G WHAT ARE THEY SAYING?

__d__ 1. discuss equipment needed for a task

_____ 2. report a completed task

_____ 3. coordinate on a task

_____ 4. give a safety warning

_____ 5. check on the accuracy of work

_____ 6. solve a problem

_____ 7. offer to help a co-worker

_____ 8. inform a co-worker about a problem

_____ 9. brainstorm a new concept

_____ 10. ask a co-worker for feedback

_____ 11. warn a co-worker about a mistake

a. "Remember to put on your mask."

b. "This machine is running hot."

c. "I think I have all the cracks patched, so you're good to go."

d. "So we'll need five more sections of drill pipe, right?"

e. "Stop! You put that stencil upside down."

f. "If you go upstairs and check for leakage, I'll do the same down here."

g. "Is the band on this leg too big?"

h. "Is it level?"

i. "We pumped out 190 gallons from your oil recycle container today."

j. "Can I help with anything?"

k. "What if we redesigned the solar cells?"

Appendix

The **CareerView** technology goal is to prepare you to use and produce digital content—to be able to find, evaluate, organize, create, and present information in a way that gets you ready for the world of work and continuing education. Through Tech Tasks in each unit, you and your classmates will bring your interests, your research, your skills, and your creativity to the class as you prepare and present information to each other. Try to do these tasks for every unit you study in **CareerView**. These tasks are an important part of your learning process, and you are in charge. (It will be easier to do these tasks using a computer, but you should also be able to do many of them using a smartphone.)

TECH TASK 1:

(After you complete a unit's Lessons 1, 2, and 3)

Use the O*Net Career Exploration Tools at the mynextmove.org website (or use your state's similar website) to research information about an occupation in the unit. Prepare to answer these questions:

- Where does a person with this job work?
- What does a person do in this job?
- What tools and equipment does a person use in this job?
- What skills and abilities are important to do this job well?
- What technology might a person use in this job?
- What kind of person will be interested in this work?
- What level of education is required?
- What kind of job training and experience is required?
- What is the job outlook? (Will this be a good job with good opportunities in the future?)
- What is the average salary? (You can find information about average national salaries, or you can find information about salaries in your area.)

The O*Net Career Exploration Tools place occupations into five *job zones* based on the amount of education, experience, and on-the-job training that jobs require.

Job Zone 1 occupations require little or no preparation.
Job Zone 2 occupations require some preparation.
Job Zone 3 occupations require medium preparation.
Job Zone 4 occupations require considerable preparation.
Job Zone 5 occupations require extensive preparation.

The **CareerView** Career & Academic Readiness Workbook has a lesson page for this activity. It includes an information chart that shows the *job zone* of each occupation in the unit. You can therefore use the chart to choose the occupation you want to research based on whether it requires a lower or higher level of education, experience, and training.

After you research the information about the occupation, organize your information and prepare a short presentation. Try to use presentation software to create a slide show to present your information to the class. (You will need to do this on a computer, and your classroom will need a digital projector so you can show your presentation.) You can find many online tutorials to learn how to create your presentation. If you can, include photos and videos.

(Low-tech option: Research information about the occupation on a computer or smartphone, write a report, and give an oral presentation to the class. Or, put the information, photos, and videos on your smartphone and share your presentation with another student.)

TECH TASK 2:

(After you complete a unit's Lesson 5)

Use YouTube, WikiHow, or another online source to search for a demonstration of how to do a procedure related to the unit. The procedure might be how to operate equipment, follow safety instructions, or do a task on the job that requires a series of steps. (The workbook suggests search terms you can use to find interesting procedures, but you can also find your own.) Write out the instructions and, if you can, prepare a slide show presentation for the class. Use a computer or smartphone to make screenshots of steps in the procedure and include them in your presentation. You can also use the smartphone camera to take photos of the steps.

(Low-tech option: Do a demonstration for the class to model the steps of the procedure. Or, use your smartphone camera to display the steps and share your presentation with another student.)

TECH TASK 3:

(Any time)

Visit a workplace related to the unit, interview a worker there about the person's job, and report back to the class. If you have permission from the workplace and the worker, use a smartphone camera's video function to record some or all of the interview and share it with the class.

Smartphone video tips:
- Stand close to the interviewee for better video and audio quality.
- Hold the smartphone horizontally instead of vertically in order to fill the screen.
- Hold it steady to avoid shaking or distortion.
- Record the video so you can keep it or transfer it to a computer. (Don't use a Stories app in which videos disappear after 24 hours.)
- If you have video editing skills, use one of the simple video-editing apps available for smartphones or computers to create a video presentation of your interview.

TECH TASK 4:

(While you work on a unit's Lesson 8 Skills Check)

Browse the web to find an interesting news story about an occupation or workplace in the unit. For example, look for an article about an unusual occupation or workplace, a safety issue, working conditions, employee rights, or job outlooks. Prepare a summary of the news story, and present it to the class.

TECH TASK 5:

(Along the way, and at the end of the course)

A final workbook lesson gives information about the importance of managing your social media reputation—the photos and comments by you and about you that appear on popular social media platforms. As you prepare for future employment and continuing education, begin to review your social media presence and think about what you might want to delete and how you might improve what appears about you on these platforms.

As a final workbook activity, you will create your own LinkedIn profile on this popular employment networking platform. In your profile you can describe your education, your work experience, your interests, and other information about yourself that will be helpful as you prepare to apply for a job or continue your education.

UNIT 1   (Pages 14–15)

A. WHAT ARE THEIR JOBS?

1. cashier
2. trucker
3. store manager
4. stock clerk
5. security person
6. warehouse manager
7. sales associate
8. customer service

B. WHAT'S THE LOCATION?

1. e
2. h
3. g
4. f
5. a
6. d
7. c
8. b

C. WHAT'S THE ITEM?

1. c
2. f
3. h
4. g
5. i
6. j
7. b
8. a
9. e
10. d
11. q
12. k
13. o
14. t
15. p
16. s
17. r
18. n
19. m
20. l

D. WHAT'S THE ACTION?

1. swipe
2. unpack
3. change
4. operate
5. use
6. check
7. redeem
8. sign
9. arrange
10. assist
11. lift
12. confirm
13. take
14. make
15. recycle
16. give

E. WHAT ARE THEY SAYING?

1. g
2. d
3. j
4. a
5. h
6. b
7. i
8. f
9. k
10. e
11. c

UNIT 2   (Pages 28–29)

A. WHAT ARE THEIR JOBS?

1. server
2. busperson
3. chef
4. food prep supervisor
5. short-order cook
6. cashier
7. pastry chef
8. hostess
9. cafeteria attendant
10. hospital dietitian
11. dishwasher
12. kitchen manager

B. WHICH ONE DOESN'T BELONG?

1. cafeteria (The others are different kinds of cooks.)
2. receiving (The others are areas where food is prepared.)
3. dietitian (The others take people's orders.)
4. busperson (The others prepare food.)
5. kitchen manager (The others work in the public part of the restaurant.)

C. WHAT'S THE LOCATION?

1. d
2. g
3. a
4. c
5. f
6. b
7. e

D. WHAT'S THE ITEM?

1. d
2. a
3. e
4. c
5. b
6. i
7. f
8. j
9. h
10. g

E. WHAT'S THE ACTION?

1. greet
2. load
3. replenish
4. supervise
5. boil, broil
6. weigh
7. check
8. decorate
9. resolve

F. WHAT ARE THEY SAYING?

1. f
2. d
3. i
4. b
5. h
6. a
7. c
8. e
9. g

UNIT 3   (Pages 42–43)

A. WHAT ARE THEIR JOBS?

1. landscape supervisor
2. tree trimmer
3. custodian
4. grounds maintenance worker
5. pesticide handler
6. window washer
7. security person
8. HVAC mechanic
9. cleaning supervisor

B. WHAT'S THE LOCATION?

1. e
2. a
3. b
4. f
5. d
6. c

C. WHAT'S THE ITEM?

1. f
2. c
3. h
4. a
5. g
6. e
7. d
8. i
9. b
10. l
11. q
12. o
13. j
14. r
15. m
16. k
17. p
18. n

D. WHAT'S THE ACTION?

1. f
2. c
3. g
4. a
5. d
6. b
7. h
8. e
9. k
10. n
11. i
12. o
13. p
14. j
15. m
16. l

E. WHICH ACTION DOESN'T BELONG?

1. change (The others are "lawn" actions.)
2. do repairs (The others are "removing" actions.)
3. mow (The others are "floor" actions.)
4. fertilize (The others are "cleaning" actions.)
5. maintain HVAC equipment (The other are "cutting" actions.)
6. shampoo carpets (The others are "outdoor" actions.)
7. plant shrubbery (The others are "indoor" actions.)
8. pick up litter (The others are "liquid" actions.)

F. WHAT ARE THEY SAYING?

1. l	5. c	9. g
2. f	6. k	10. e
3. a	7. b	11. i
4. h	8. j	12. d

UNIT 4 (Pages 56–57)

A. WHAT ARE THEIR JOBS?

1. esthetician
2. salon manager
3. hair stylist
4. shampooist
5. receptionist
6. manicurist
7. colorist
8. makeup artist
9. massage therapist

B. WHAT'S THE LOCATION?

1. c	3. f	5. b
2. e	4. a	6. d

C. WHAT'S THE CATEGORY?

1. cutting	4. plug in	6. hair
2. brushes	5. feet	7. makeup
3. combs		

D. COSMETOLOGY IN ACTION!

1. b	6. a	11. b
2. a	7. b	12. c
3. d	8. a	13. a
4. c	9. c	14. b
5. b	10. a	15. c

E. WHAT ARE THEY SAYING?

1. f	4. c	7. a
2. d	5. b	8. g
3. h	6. i	9. e

UNIT 5 (Pages 70–71)

A. WHAT ARE THEIR JOBS?

1. welder
2. fabricator
3. packing clerk
4. factory line supervisor
5. assembler
6. pinstripe artist
7. paint robot operator
8. receiving clerk
9. factory helper
10. shipping clerk
11. quality control tester
12. distribution clerk
13. hand packer
14. technical engineer

B. WHAT'S THE LOCATION?

1. e	4. i	7. d
2. g	5. b	8. f
3. a	6. h	9. c

C. WHAT'S THE ITEM?

1. d	6. h	11. o
2. c	7. f	12. k
3. e	8. i	13. n
4. b	9. j	14. m
5. a	10. g	15. l

D. MANUFACTURING IN ACTION!

1. seal	4. attach	7. weld
2. unload	5. solder	8. bend
3. tighten	6. snap	9. put

E. WHAT ARE THEY SAYING?

1. e	5. i	9. g
2. k	6. c	10. h
3. b	7. f	11. j
4. a	8. d	

UNIT 6 (Pages 86–87)

A. WHAT'S THE OCCUPATION?

1. brickmason
2. carpet installer
3. electrician
4. paperhanger
5. carpenter
6. drywall installer
7. glazier
8. plumber
9. roofer
10. carpenter's helper
11. insulation contractor
12. blockmason apprentice
13. drywall taper
14. electrician's assistant
15. flooring installer
16. skylight installer
17. tile installer
18. HVAC tech

B. WHAT'S THE ASSOCIATION?

1. d	4. c	7. e
2. a	5. b	
3. f	6. g	

C. WHAT DO CONSTRUCTION WORKERS DO?

1. b	7. b	13. c
2. a	8. d	14. b
3. c	9. b	15. d
4. b	10. c	16. a
5. c	11. d	
6. a	12. a	

D. WHAT ARE THEY SAYING?

1. g	5. k	9. e
2. d	6. b	10. c
3. f	7. l	11. h
4. a	8. i	12. j

UNIT 7   (Pages 105–107)

A. WHAT'S THE OCCUPATION?

1. bulldozer operator
2. ceiling tile installer
3. brickmason
4. glazier
5. electrician
6. blockmason
7. plumber
8. steelworker
9. carpenter
10. stonemason
11. HVAC technician
12. plasterer
13. surveyor
14. pipefitter
15. flagger
16. roofer
17. construction foreman
18. construction laborer
19. cement mason
20. construction safety officer

B. WHAT'S THE ITEM?

1. d
2. f
3. a
4. h
5. c
6. e
7. b
8. g
9. l
10. o
11. i
12. k
13. p
14. j
15. n
16. m
17. t
18. v
19. q
20. x
21. s
22. u
23. r
24. w

C. WHAT DO THEY HAVE IN COMMON?

1. concrete
2. trucks
3. foundation
4. glass
5. safety
6. surveyor
7. metal
8. rebar
9. brick
10. wood

D. WHAT'S THE ACTION?

1. f
2. d
3. g
4. a
5. b
6. c
7. e

E. WHAT DO CONSTRUCTON WORKERS DO?

1. b
2. c
3. a
4. c
5. d
6. b
7. a
8. c
9. b
10. c
11. a
12. d
13. c
14. b
15. a
16. d

F. WHAT ARE THEY SAYING?

1. f
2. c
3. h
4. j
5. a
6. g
7. k
8. b
9. d
10. e
11. i

UNIT 8   (Pages 120–121)

A. FIND THE RIGHT PERSON!

1. d
2. e
3. h
4. a
5. n
6. f
7. g
8. c
9. b
10. m
11. i
12. p
13. q
14. o
15. j
16. l
17. k

B. WHERE ARE THEY?

1. bay
2. department
3. pit
4. room
5. station

C. WHAT'S THE ITEM?

1. e
2. g
3. a
4. f
5. c
6. h
7. d
8. b
9. m
10. o
11. i
12. p
13. k
14. l
15. n
16. j
17. s
18. u
19. w
20. q
21. x
22. t
23. v
24. r

D. DANILO'S AUTO REPAIR

1. prepared
2. checked
3. charged
4. inspected
5. drained
6. changed
7. exchanged
8. examined
9. installed
10. replaced
11. changed
12. rotated

E. WHAT ARE THEY SAYING?

1. g
2. d
3. j
4. i
5. b
6. f
7. a
8. h
9. e
10. c

UNIT 9   (Pages 134–135)

A. FIND THE MEDICAL CARE SPECIALIST!

1. RN
2. EMT
3. dietetic aide
4. anesthesiologist
5. patient transport attendant
6. physical therapist
7. respiratory therapist
8. surgeon
9. physical therapist assistant
10. orderly
11. visiting nurse
12. surgical technician
13. home health aide
14. CNA
15. emergency room technician

B. WHERE ARE THEY?
1. emergency
2. surgical suites
3. room
4. hospital
5. entrance

C. WHAT'S THE ITEM?
1. f
2. d
3. a
4. e
5. c
6. g
7. b
8. l
9. j
10. h
11. n
12. i
13. k
14. m
15. q
16. t
17. o
18. s
19. u
20. r
21. p

D. MEDICAL CARE IN ACTION!
1. b
2. c
3. a
4. d
5. b
6. a
7. c
8. d

E. WHAT ARE THEY SAYING?
1. g
2. d
3. j
4. a
5. h
6. c
7. b
8. f
9. i
10. e

UNIT 10 (Pages 148–149)

A. WHO IS IT?
1. a
2. n
3. d
4. l
5. m
6. g
7. o
8. f
9. p
10. e
11. h
12. c
13. i
14. b
15. k
16. j

B. WHERE ARE THEY?
1. checkout desk
2. diagnostic lab
3. eyeglass display area
4. phlebotomy lab
5. reception
6. exam room
7. room

C. WHAT'S THE ASSOCIATION?
1. c
2. f
3. e
4. a
5. g
6. b
7. d

D. HEALTH SERVICES IN ACTION!
1. b
2. c
3. a
4. d
5. c
6. a
7. b
8. b

E. WHAT ARE THEY SAYING?
1. d
2. h
3. i
4. l
5. b
6. c
7. a
8. g
9. f
10. j
11. e
12. k

UNIT 11 (Pages 162–163)

A. WHO AM I?
1. f
2. i
3. g
4. a
5. m
6. j
7. c
8. l
9. b
10. o
11. d
12. e
13. k
14. h
15. n

B. WHAT'S THE PLACE?
1. c
2. a
3. e
4. b
5. d
6. g
7. j
8. i
9. h
10. f

C. WHAT DO THEY HAVE IN COMMON?
1. trucks
2. fire
3. security
4. wear
5. hold/carry
6. information

D. PUBLIC SAFETY IN ACTION!
1. escort
2. direct
3. apprehend
4. use
5. chase
6. search
7. collect
8. interrogate
9. review
10. confiscate
11. attach
12. frisk
13. perform
14. ticket
15. watch
16. test

E. WHAT ARE THEY SAYING?
1. e
2. g
3. j
4. l
5. h
6. b
7. i
8. a
9. d
10. c
11. f
12. k

UNIT 12 (Pages 176–177)

A. FIND THE RIGHT PERSON!
1. n
2. j
3. l
4. b
5. d
6. f
7. c
8. h
9. g
10. k
11. e
12. i
13. o
14. m
15. a

B. WHAT'S THE PLACE?
1. desk
2. station
3. department
4. area
5. center
6. window
7. service
8. agency

C. WHAT'S THE ITEM?
1. e
2. c
3. a
4. g
5. b
6. d
7. f
8. m
9. k
10. h
11. n
12. j
13. l
14. i
15. s
16. u
17. o
18. t
19. q
20. p
21. r

D. FINANCE *IN ACTION!*

1. c	4. d	7. a
2. b	5. b	8. d
3. a	6. c	

E. WHAT ARE THEY SAYING?

1. d	5. c	9. h
2. g	6. k	10. l
3. i	7. e	11. f
4. a	8. b	12. j

UNIT 13 (Pages 190–191)

A. MEET THE PEOPLE AT BLAINE ELECTRONICS!

1. office manager
2. human resource director
3. accounts payable
4. accounts receivable
5. mail clerk
6. marketing manager
7. payroll clerk
8. file clerk
9. executive secretary
10. assistant
11. sales manager
12. receptionist

B. WHAT'S THE PLACE?

1. conference
2. payroll
3. employee lounge
4. reception
5. supply room
6. human resources

C. WHAT'S THE ITEM?

1. b	7. h	13. n
2. f	8. j	14. q
3. a	9. k	15. m
4. c	10. g	16. r
5. d	11. l	17. p
6. e	12. i	18. o

D. OFFICE ADMINISTRATION *IN ACTION!*

1. b	4. a	7. c
2. c	5. b	8. a
3. d	6. c	9. c

E. WHAT ARE THEY SAYING?

1. e	5. d	9. g
2. i	6. k	10. b
3. a	7. h	11. j
4. f	8. c	

UNIT 14 (Pages 204–205)

A. WHAT'S MY OCCUPATION?

1. caregiver
2. handyman
3. delivery person
4. exterminator
5. mail carrier
6. teacher's aide
7. locksmith
8. nanny
9. carpet cleaner
10. worker
11. dog walker
12. library assistant
13. paralegal/legal assistant
14. tutor
15. coordinator
16. installer

B. WHAT'S THE PLACE?

1. c	3. b	5. d
2. a	4. f	6. e

C. WHAT'S THE ASSOCIATION?

1. c	3. a	5. d
2. e	4. f	6. b

D. WHAT'S THE ACTION?

1. lead	6. do	11. tow
2. install	7. help	12. supervise
3. check out	8. feed	13. repair
4. spray	9. sort	14. tutor
5. mount	10. deliver	15. give

E. WHAT ARE THEY SAYING?

1. f	5. e	9. h
2. j	6. k	10. d
3. a	7. c	11. g
4. i	8. b	

UNIT 15 (Pages 219–221)

A. WHAT ARE THEIR JOBS?

1. photographer
2. cobbler
3. auto glass repairer
4. barista
5. esthetician
6. interior designer
7. barber
8. tailor
9. caterer
10. baker

B. WHAT ARE THEIR JOB TITLES?

1. trainer	5. distributor	9. vendor
2. groomer	6. framer	10. specialist
3. driver	7. owner	11. proprietor
4. designer	8. assistant	12. operator

C. WE LOVE OUR JOBS!

1. jewelry
2. auto lube
3. route
4. sporting goods
5. hardware store

D. WHAT'S THE PLACE?

1. floor	4. store	7. studio
2. service	5. center	8. agency
3. shop	6. cart	

E. WHERE WILL YOU FIND THESE ITEMS?

1. k	7. a	13. e
2. j	8. p	14. l
3. h	9. f	15. r
4. b	10. c	16. n
5. m	11. q	17. i
6. d	12. o	18. g

F. BUSINESS *IN ACTION!*

1. c	7. d	13. d
2. b	8. a	14. c
3. a	9. c	15. d
4. d	10. b	16. b
5. b	11. d	
6. c	12. a	

G. WHAT ARE THEY SAYING?

1. c	5. j	9. k
2. f	6. a	10. h
3. i	7. e	11. g
4. b	8. d	

UNIT 16 (Pages 234–235)

A. WHAT'S MY OCCUPATION?

1. skycap	4. valet	7. bellhop
2. doorman	5. concierge	
3. busperson	6. housekeeper	

B. WHAT ARE THEIR JOB TITLES?

1. d	7. b	13. n
2. i	8. o	14. l
3. f	9. p	15. j
4. a	10. g	16. c
5. m	11. k	
6. h	12. e	

C. WHAT'S THE PLACE?

1. b	4. f	7. h
2. c	5. d	8. i
3. a	6. e	9. g

D. WHAT'S THE ITEM?

1. d	6. g	11. m
2. a	7. i	12. n
3. e	8. f	13. o
4. c	9. j	14. l
5. b	10. h	15. k

E. WHAT DO TRAVEL & HOSPITALITY WORKERS DO?

1. b	5. c	9. a
2. c	6. b	10. b
3. a	7. a	11. d
4. d	8. c	12. a

F. WHAT ARE THEY SAYING?

1. d	5. h	9. k
2. f	6. b	10. e
3. i	7. a	11. j
4. c	8. g	

UNIT 17 (Pages 255–257)

A. WHAT ARE THEIR JOB TITLES?

1. operator	6. manager	11. engineer
2. writer	7. editor	12. designer
3. painter	8. master	13. maker
4. model	9. reader	14. broadcaster
5. reporter	10. publisher	

B. WHAT DO THEY HAVE IN COMMON?

1. designers	5. directors	9. theater
2. editors	6. assistants	10. sound
3. technicians	7. journalism	11. fashion
4. operators	8. movies	12. television

C. WHAT'S THE PLACE?

1. e	5. l	9. d
2. i	6. c	10. j
3. a	7. h	11. g
4. k	8. b	12. f

D. WHAT'S THE ITEM?

1. c	8. k	15. q
2. f	9. n	16. u
3. a	10. h	17. s
4. g	11. m	18. o
5. d	12. j	19. t
6. e	13. l	20. r
7. b	14. i	21. p

E. THE SAME ACTION

1. d	4. g	7. e
2. f	5. c	
3. a	6. b	

F. THE ARTS *IN ACTION!*

1. b	7. a	13. d
2. c	8. b	14. b
3. a	9. a	15. c
4. d	10. c	16. a
5. c	11. d	
6. c	12. b	

G. WHAT ARE THEY SAYING?

1. h	6. i	11. e
2. k	7. c	12. n
3. f	8. l	13. j
4. a	9. b	14. d
5. m	10. g	

UNIT 18 (Pages 270–271)

A. WHAT ARE THEIR JOBS?

1. cable	5. 611	9. analyst
2. climber	6. line	10. technician
3. PBX	7. TV	11. lineperson
4. installer	8. 711	12. associate

B. WHAT'S THE LOCATION?

1. office
2. call
3. sales
4. 711

C. WHAT'S THE ITEM?

1. d
2. f
3. h
4. b
5. g
6. c
7. a
8. e
9. l
10. o
11. i
12. n
13. k
14. j
15. p
16. m
17. u
18. x
19. q
20. r
21. v
22. s
23. t
24. w

D. TELECOMMUNICATIONS *IN ACTION!*

1. b
2. c
3. a
4. d
5. b
6. d
7. c
8. b
9. d
10. a
11. b
12. c
13. d
14. b
15. a

E. WHAT ARE THEY SAYING?

1. d
2. h
3. k
4. b
5. j
6. a
7. i
8. e
9. l
10. g
11. f
12. c

D. WHAT'S THE ITEM?

1. d
2. g
3. f
4. b
5. a
6. e
7. h
8. c
9. k
10. p
11. i
12. n
13. o
14. j
15. m
16. l
17. l
18. w
19. r
20. v
21. q
22. x
23. u
24. s

E. ACTIONS IN COMMON

1. test
2. connect
3. install
4. attach
5. replace

F. INFORMATION TECHNOLOGY *IN ACTION!*

1. write up
2. enter
3. train
4. add
5. capture
6. install
7. write
8. measure
9. bundle
10. answer
11. fish
12. run
13. replace
14. design
15. review
16. have
17. punch down

G. WHAT ARE THEY SAYING?

1. d
2. g
3. j
4. a
5. h
6. c
7. i
8. f
9. b
10. e

UNIT 19 (Pages 285–287)

A. WHAT ARE THEIR JOBS?

1. installer
2. mobile app
3. specialist
4. designer
5. administrator
6. producer
7. composer
8. keyer
9. technician
10. engineer
11. help desk
12. artist
13. recovery
14. programmer
15. security
16. tester
17. analyst
18. worker

B. WHAT'S THE LOCATION?

1. d
2. g
3. a
4. c
5. f
6. e
7. b

C. HOW ARE THEY THE SAME?

1. video
2. data entry
3. mobile
4. antistatic
5. punch-down
6. Ethernet
7. antivirus
8. cable
9. hard disk
10. DVI
11. internal
12. CAT6

UNIT 20 (Pages 308–310)

A. WHAT'S THE CATEGORY?

workers
assembly line
construction
farm

installers
appliance
charging station
foam insulation

operators
crane
light rail
mixing truck

drivers
ethanol transport
flatbed truck
recyclable collections

specialists
air pollution
dust collection
quality control

technicians
geothermal
MRF
solar installation

B. WHAT KIND OF ENERGY?

1. SOL
2. WND
3. EE
4. REC
5. SOL
6. GEO
7. CON
8. EV
9. EE
10. AIR
11. CON
12. EE
13. WND
14. CON
15. BIO
16. EE
17. FLA
18. AIR
19. EV
20. EE
21. REC
22. FLA

C. WHAT'S THE LOCATION?

1. substation
2. attic
3. farm
4. path
5. switchgrass
6. biorefinery
7. monitoring
8. location
9. packing

D. HOW ARE THEY THE SAME?

1. recycling
2. energy efficient
3. solar
4. wind turbine
5. power
6. electric
7. EV
8. water
9. geothermal
10. tower

E. WHAT'S THE ITEM?

1. c
2. e
3. b
4. a
5. d
6. i
7. f
8. j
9. h
10. g
11. l
12. o
13. n
14. m
15. k

F. "GREEN" ACTIONS!

1. b
2. c
3. a
4. d
5. d
6. b
7. c
8. d
9. a
10. b
11. c
12. b
13. a
14. d
15. b
16. c
17. b
18. d
19. a
20. d

G. WHAT ARE THEY SAYING?

1. d
2. i
3. f
4. a
5. h
6. c
7. j
8. b
9. k
10. g
11. e

REGULAR VERBS

Regular verbs have four different spelling patterns for the past and past participle forms.

1. Add –ed to the end of the verb. For example: accept → accept**ed**

accept	cover	hammer	plaster	shampoo
access	credit	handcuff	play	shovel
add	curl	head back	pluck	sign
address	darken	heat	point	signal
adjust	deliver	help	polish	skim coat
administer	deposit	highlight	port	smooth
answer	design	hoist	position	soak
apprehend	direct	hook	pound	solder
ask	discard	import	pour	sort
assign	disconnect	inject	power on	spray
assist	discuss	insert	press	spray paint
attach	dish out	inspect	print	stack
attend	disinfect	install	process	start
audition	document	instruct	protect	stencil
backfill	double-check	interview	pull	stock
band	draft	label	pump	stow
blend	drain	latch	punch	straighten
boil	dress	level	push	stretch
bolt	drill	lift	radio	suction
braid	dump	listen	recheck	switch
brainstorm	dust	load	recommend	test
broil	edit	lock	record	thread
brush	eject	look	redeem	thumb through
buff	end	loosen	refill	ticket
butter	engineer	lower	register	tighten
call	enter	mail	reinstall	total
cancel	erect	maintain	repair	touch
cash	escort	mark	repeat	tow
caulk	establish	mask	replenish	train
check	explain	match	report	transport
chisel	fasten	meter	research	turn
clean	fax	mix	restack	tutor
clear	fill	monitor	restock	twist
climb	fingerprint	mount	reupholster	unload
co-sign	finish	mow	review	unpack
collect	fish	nail	roast	unroll
comb	fix	obtain	roll	upload
compact	flash	offer	rough out	vacuum
compress	fold	open	rough-sand	view
condition	follow	order	sand	visit
confirm	form	paint	saw	walk
connect	frisk	pat down	scoop up	wash
construct	gather	patrol	screw	weigh
consult	grasp	peel	sculpt	weld
contact	greet	perform	seal	wet-sand
convert	grill	pick up	search	wish
cook	groom	place	section	work
count	grout	plant	select	

2. Add –d to a verb that ends in –e. For example: activate → activated

activate	confiscate	glue	quote	shave
adhere	coordinate	grade	raise	shelve
analyze	create	guide	rake	slice
apologize	customize	handle	receive	space
appraise	deactivate	hire	reconcile	square
approve	decide	increase	recycle	squeeze
arrange	decorate	interrogate	regulate	stake
assemble	deflate	investigate	rehearse	staple
bake	demonstrate	issue	release	store
balance	determine	locate	replace	style
bale	diagnose	manage	rescue	supervise
bathe	dilate	massage	resensitize	suture
bundle	discharge	measure	reshelve	swipe
calculate	dispose	memorize	resolve	tape
capture	distribute	move	retrieve	taste
change	encode	note	revise	telescope
charge	evaluate	observe	rinse	tie
chase	examine	operate	rotate	transcribe
cleanse	excavate	organize	sanitize	tune up
close	exchange	package	save	type
code	execute	pinstripe	schedule	update
collate	explore	place	score	use
compare	fertilize	prepare	secure	welcome
compile	file	promote	serve	wipe
complete	fine-tune	provide	service	wire
compose	frame	prune	shape	

3. Double the final consonant and add –ed to the end of the verb. For example: bag → bagged

bag	drop	program	shop	tag
bus	grip	rig	snap	transfer
chop	mop	rub	squat	trim
clip	plan	scan	stop	unplug
control	plug	shim	strip	wrap
dip	prep	ship out	submit	zip

4. Drop the final –y and add –ied to the end of the verb. For example: apply → applied

apply	copy	empty	identify	specify
blow dry	deny	fry	reply	verify

IRREGULAR VERBS

The following verbs have irregular past tense and/or past participle forms.

be	was/were	been
begin	began	begun
bend	bent	bent
bind	bound	bound
blow	blew	blown
break	broke	broken
bring	brought	brought
build	built	built
catch	caught	caught
choose	chose	chosen
cut	cut	cut
deal	dealt	dealt
dig	dug	dug
do	did	done
draw	drew	drawn
drive	drove	driven
feed	fed	fed
feel	felt	felt
find	found	found
fit	fit/fitted	fit/fitted
get	got	gotten
give	gave	given
go	went	gone
grind	ground	ground
hang	hung	hung
have	had	had
hold	held	held
input	input/inputted	input/inputted
keep	kept	kept
let	let	let

lay	laid	laid
lead	led	led
make	made	made
meet	met	met
pay	paid	paid
proofread	proofread	proofread
put	put	put
read	read	read
redo	redid	redone
run	ran	run
sell	sold	sold
send	sent	sent
set	set	set
shake	shook	shaken
shoot	shot	shot
show	showed	shown/showed
shut	shut	shut
sing	sang	sung
sit	sat	sat
slide	slid	slid
spread	spread	spread
strike	struck	stricken/struck
sweep	swept	swept
swing	swung	swung
take	took	taken
tell	told	told
wear	wore	worn
wind	wound	wound
write	wrote	written

The bold number indicates the page(s) on which the word appears. The number that follows indicates the word's location in the illustration and in the word list, or if in italics, the number that follows indicates the conversation in which the word appears. For example, "architect **239**-45, *249*-15" indicates that the word *architect* appears on page 239 as item number 45, and it appears on page 249 in conversation number 15.

WORKPLACE COMMUNICATION INDEX

The bold number indicates the page(s) and the number that follows indicates the conversation where the communication skill appears. For example, "Answer a customer's question, 8-1" indicates that the communication skill appears on page 8 in conversation number 1.